Citizens of a Christian Nation

POLITICS AND CULTURE
IN MODERN AMERICA

SERIES EDITORS
Glenda Gilmore, Michael Kazin, Thomas J. Sugrue

Volumes in the series narrate and analyze political and
social change in the broadest dimensions from 1865 to
the present, including ideas about the ways people have
sought and wielded power in the public sphere and the
language and institutions of politics at all levels—local,
national, and transnational. The series is motivated by
a desire to reverse the fragmentation of modern U.S.
history and to encourage synthetic perspectives on
social movements and the state, on gender, race, and
labor, and on intellectual history and popular culture.

Citizens
of a Christian Nation

Evangelical Missions
and the Problem of Race
in the Nineteenth Century

Derek Chang

PENN

UNIVERSITY OF PENNSYLVANIA PRESS

PHILADELPHIA

Published by
University of Pennsylvania Press
Philadelphia, Pennsylvania 19104-4112

Printed in the United States of America on acid-free paper
10 9 8 7 6 5 4 3 2 1

Library of Congress Cataloging-in-Publication Data
Chang, Derek.
  Citizens of a Christian nation : Evangelical missions and the problem of race in the nine-
teenth century / Derek Chang.
    p. cm. (Politics and culture in modern America)
  Includes bibliographical references and index.
  ISBN 978-0-8122-4218-8 (alk. paper)
  1. American Baptist Home Mission Society—History—19th century. 2. Home missions—
United States—History—19th century. 3. Baptists—Missions—United States—History—
19th century. 4. Evangelistic work—United States—History—19th century. 5. African
Americans—Missions—History—19th century. 6. Chinese Americans—Missions—History—19th century. 7. Whites—United States—Attitudes—History—19th century. 8.
Missionaries—United States—Attitudes—History—19th century. 9. Racism—Religious
aspects—Baptists—History—19th century. 10. United States—Race relations—Religious
aspects—History—19th century. I. Title.
  BV2766.B5C47 2010
  266'.6131—dc22
                                  2009029499

For my family
With special love and gratitude for Lauren, Max, and Isabel

CONTENTS

Introduction

Evangelical Christianity and the Problem of Difference

Behold, they are one people, and they have all one language; and
this is what they begin to do: and now nothing will be withholden
from them, which they purpose to do.
Go to, let us go down, and there confound their language, that they
may not understand one another's speech.
So the Lord scattered them abroad from thence upon the face of all
the earth: and they left off to build the city.
> Genesis 11:6 (ASV)

The vail shall separate unto you between the holy place and the
most holy.
> Exodus 26:33 (ASV)

IN THE SPRING of 1882, Fung Chak, a missionary of the American Baptist
Home Mission Society (ABHMS), penned a letter to the organization's Executive Board in New York City from his post in Portland, Oregon. Fung
supervised the city's Chinese Mission School and wrote ostensibly to galvanize
support for Baptist efforts among the over eighty thousand Chinese residing in the United States. But he also offered a criticism of the treatment his
countrymen faced in America. A decade of virulent anti-Chinese protest had

just culminated in the passage of the Chinese Exclusion Act, a federal law that barred the entry of laborers from China. It was the nation's first immigration restriction targeted at a specific national group. Fung pointedly observed that Chinese "meet with all the vices but very few of [America's] virtues. They see the worst side of all classes and very little of the better."[1]

While Fung Chak voiced his concerns about anti-Chinese actions, Henry Martin Tupper, a white northern ABHMS missionary in Raleigh, North Carolina, was assembling his annual report to the same executive board. By any standard Tupper was a veteran missionary. In 1882, he had been proselytizing among black southerners for seventeen years, and in collaboration with other teachers, ministers, and students, could boast of having established Shaw University, the first black college in the South and a centerpiece of the northern missionary effort among former slaves. Yet even with this impressive institutional foundation, Tupper, in writing his annual report, had to choose his words carefully. Shaw had begun as a religious branch of the post–Civil War Reconstruction project, and Tupper and the mission continued even after the withdrawal of federal troops in 1877 marked the official end of Reconstruction. Tupper's annual report, like other dispatches from mission fields, would highlight success and downplay conflict. While emphasizing the accomplishments of the mission's African American participants, Tupper nonetheless intimated that his black brethren were working against mounting odds. "They seem to have developed *will power*, and have learned to push ahead," reported the missionary.[2]

Fung's letter and Tupper's report indicate home missionaries' growing concern as the storm clouds of white supremacy seemed poised to eclipse the hope of Emancipation and open immigration. Although legalized segregation in North Carolina was still decades away, the formal end of Reconstruction cleared the way throughout the South for white "redemption" led by the Democratic Party. As Tupper wrote his report, Democrat and former Confederate officer T. J. Jarvis occupied the governor's mansion. Meanwhile, as Fung was composing his letter, the U.S. Congress was debating the Chinese Exclusion Act. The law's passage in early May meant that Fung and others from China had to endure more than even the local threats of violence; they would now have to contend with state-sponsored surveillance and the threat of deportation.[3]

Yet even as Fung and Tupper signaled their anxieties, Chinese and black Baptists, affiliated with but separate from the ABHMS missions in Portland and Raleigh, demonstrated their resolve by shoring up their own institutions.

Fung's mission had just collected money for the construction of a Baptist chapel in southern China run by Dong Gong, his predecessor in Portland. Dong's work in Guangdong (Canton) was more than a continuation of the evangelical labors he had undertaken in Oregon. There he had established prayer meetings, Sabbath schools, and congregations throughout the state. Dong's chapel in Guangdong was an extension of a network of Baptist institutions that linked Chinese brethren along America's Pacific Coast and across the ocean, providing transnational migrants and U.S. immigrants alike with support and refuge. The loosely connected complex of churches, schools, missions, meetings, and individuals provided Chinese traversing the Pacific and residing in the United States with spiritual and material succor. It was also a form of social organization that depended not on the increasingly hostile American nation as the arbiter of belonging but on Christian belief and fellowship.

And in Raleigh, Nicholas Franklin Roberts, who had entered Shaw just six years after the Civil War ended and who was a professor of mathematics there, was called to the pulpit at the city's Second Baptist Church.[4] This seemingly mundane occurrence was emblematic of similar events that replayed throughout the state and the region. In that uneasy time between the end of Reconstruction and the dawning of de jure segregation, black Baptists established autonomous churches, schools, and associations, and men and women educated at mission schools like Shaw preached, taught, and proselytized. In North Carolina alone, Roberts, who was one of the founders of the state's black Baptist association and who would temporarily assume leadership of Shaw after Tupper's death, joined an array of mission-educated African Americans who pastored congregations and taught at every level of education. These religious and educational leaders, along with their congregants, students, and supporters, formed crucial institutions as the betrayal of the promise of Emancipation grew more evident. In these churches, religious classes, and schools, black Baptists sustained their souls and their communities, in the process crafting a language of citizenship independent of the South's political and legal arbiters.

Fung and Tupper, Dong and Roberts, Oregon and North Carolina, Chinese and blacks. Two different missions among two disparate populations. The ABHMS even formed different committees to supervise its work among the two groups. But while the evangelical organization devoted far greater resources to the South than to any other mission field, its missionaries, theorists, officials, and supporters, like much of the popular press and literature of the time, had become preoccupied with both the "Negro Problem" and the

"Chinese Question." In fact, the separate evangelical tracks converged, though not for the first time, in the words of the Reverend E. G. Robinson. Just a few months after Fung presented his grievance, Dong collected funds, and Roberts took over the pastorate of Second Baptist, and as Tupper was writing his report, Robinson linked the mission fields in his analysis of "Race and Religion on the American Continent," an address presented before the Baptist Autumnal Conference in Brooklyn, New York.[5]

Robinson's speech struck at the heart of late nineteenth-century white American racial anxieties. The Baptist educator and theologian spoke frankly of his concern about the present condition and future role of the "despoiled" and "half Christianized African of the South" and the "despised" and heathen "Mongol" settling on the Pacific Coast. Yet rather than joining the growing chorus of voices urging segregation, disfranchisement, and exclusion, Robinson argued for a broader imagining of the nation. As he boldly asserted that blacks were "entitled to be treated in all legislation . . . as every other American citizen," he proclaimed that there was "no reason for not giving [the Chinese] a hearty welcome" and chastised his fellow Americans for a "narrow minded political economy and a narrow-eyed statesmanship" that resulted in "a decidedly hostile policy."[6]

Even with this more expansive sense of who might be included in the nation, Robinson did not depart from what had become the dominant racial discourse of the period; the assumptions inherent in the Negro Problem and the Chinese Question are evident throughout his address. Robinson and other officials and white missionaries of the ABHMS shared with advocates of segregation and exclusion a fear that Emancipation and immigration might result in the irreparable depredation of American society. Although they had been resolutely antislavery and pro-Union and they had lauded the flow of immigration from China as a boon to proselytizing, American Baptists also worried that blacks emerging from the bleakness of slavery and Chinese coming from the stagnant, heathen "Orient" might weaken the nation's social fabric.[7] North and South had been reunited after a ferocious and deadly civil war, and East and West had been linked by rail. But amid the conviction that America was realizing its continental dream lay the fear of disorder brought by scale and by scope. American Baptists worried that unconverted blacks and heathen Chinese threatened their monument to God.

Increasingly, white Americans—especially politicians and policymakers—reacted to these worries by advocating violent, restrictive, and, ultimately, exclusionary remedies. In the South, whites responded to the promise of

Emancipation and Reconstruction with Judge Lynch and Jim Crow. In the American West, race riots punctuated the steady beat of discriminatory legislation and everyday intimidation that led to but did not end with the Exclusion Act.

But Robinson offered a solution to the perceived "problems" of black freedom and Chinese immigration. His solution offered the possibility not of reinforcing America's traditional equation of whiteness and national belonging but of disrupting it. His solution rested on his faith in America as a Christian nation. Robinson believed that white evangelicals—particularly his denomination's ABHMS—had an obligation to minister to black southerners and Chinese immigrants if the United States had any hope of fulfilling its destiny as the divinely chosen vehicle for bringing about the reign of God's kingdom. Invoking Mark's version of the Great Commission (Christ's commandment to "Go ye into all the world, and preach the Gospel to the every creature" [Mark 16:15]) and Paul's sermon at Thessalonica ("He has made from one blood every nation of men to dwell on the face of the earth" [Acts 17:26]), Robinson reminded his audience of the fundamental evangelical commitment to the propagation of Christianity to all: "Christianity," he intoned, "knows no distinction among the races."[8]

Rather than imposing limits on the growing migration from China and the rights of freedpeople and their descendents, evangelicals like Robinson found a solution to the problem of difference in the religious conversion of all non-Christians—white, black, and Chinese alike. Spiritual conversion would be accomplished through education, and converts would experience not just a religious rebirth but a broad-based social and material change as well. From providing basic literacy to teaching skilled trades and professional training, the evangelical enterprise aimed at combining worldly "uplift" with its sacred mission. This combination of secular and sacred transformations, not skin color, would endow men and women with the qualities worthy of American belonging.

His was a compelling vision. But it ultimately succumbed to the specter of racial difference. Even as they declared the possibility of blacks and Chinese belonging to the nation, a principle premised on the equality of souls, American Baptist evangelicals underscored the cultural and historical roots of difference that made such inclusions unlikely. Any possibility of inclusion that their religious belief may have enabled was tempered—indeed frustrated—by assumptions of cultural and religious difference that fed racist stereotypes. By the 1880s, Robinson and other evangelicals were growing less and less confident that Chinese and blacks could fully join the American polity.[9]

Robinson, in fact, went to great pains to emphasize the difference—and separateness—of the Chinese and blacks in America. He alleged that the character of "the industrious, the quiet and unobtrusive Mongol" enables him to work "better and cheaper" than white Americans and pointed out that "there is little or no better prospect, that the Mongol will ever be permitted to contribute to the general fusion of bloods." For blacks, the defining difference could be found in historical experience, for "the victim of prejudice and a thousand indignities from the mean and vulgar" had resulted in "two races" so separated that "no man thoroughly in his sense can expect that the African will lose his identity by mingling with other races." In sum, Robinson asserted, blacks and Chinese "will never contribute their share to make up the typical American."[10]

In this book, I map the religious and racial world that E. G. Robinson, Fung Chak, Dong Gong, H. M. Tupper, and N. F. Roberts inhabited and helped to create. At the most fundamental level, I chronicle the efforts of native-born, European American evangelicals of the American Baptist Home Mission Society to proselytize among African Americans and Chinese during the last third of the nineteenth century. The Baptist denomination's primary organization for domestic evangelizing, the ABHMS was established in 1832 as an institutional manifestation of the broader home mission movement growing out of the Second Great Awakening and the Great Revival. By the late nineteenth century, not only would the organization have direct and indirect links to the Republican Party (such as the ABHMS president and New York Supreme Court Justice and U.S. Senator Ira Harris) but it would assert itself as one of the nation's most active evangelical groups, particularly in its ministries to African Americans in the South and Chinese on the Pacific Coast. By 1900 it had helped establish a vast array of important and lasting institutions for black southerners, including Shaw University in Raleigh, North Carolina, and Morehouse and Spelman Colleges in Atlanta, as well as a considerable network of mission schools and churches for Chinese immigrants, including the still-active Chinese Baptist Church in Portland, Oregon, and the First Chinese Baptist Church in Fresno, California.

But what would seem, at first glance, to be a single, straightforward institutional history in fact consists of three interrelated stories. There is the story of the Baptist missionary society's ambitions—of the organization's desire to transform America into a Christian republic and to stave off the disorder and uncertainty wrought by rapid demographic, social, and economic change during the late nineteenth century. American Baptists held a deep faith in what I call "evangelical nationalism"—the overlapping civic and religious belief in the exceptional, providential destiny of America as a Christian nation. This belief was fueled by the mandate to convert more souls and supported by geographic and demographic expansion. However, few other social and political changes challenged the evangelical belief in a Christian nation so much as the arrival of tens of thousands of "heathen" Chinese in the United States and the release from bondage of millions of blacks. Although many former slaves called themselves Christian, ABHMS missionaries saw in their Afro-Christianity more in common with heathen practice than Sunday school orthodoxy. But even as these phenomena disquieted them, they also recognized opportunities for proselytizing. For evangelical nationalists, Christianity could, as one minister noted, "unify all those discordant elements."[11]

There is also the story of black-missionary interactions in the South set against the broader dramas of Emancipation, Reconstruction, and Jim Crow. In the South, former slaves made Baptist missions—especially churches and schools—an integral part of how they envisioned their post-Emancipation lives. In those hopeful years following the Civil War, black southerners engaged northern mission projects with a faith not just in Christianity but in the goodwill of the missionaries and in the opportunities to shape their own lives. Even as the hope of Reconstruction faded, ex-slaves and their children vigorously built and defended their temples of worship and learning. For these Baptists, institutional autonomy and educational attainment remained at the center of their understanding of freedom.[12]

Last, there is the story of Chinese-missionary contact. Chinese who migrated to America's Pacific Coast quickly discovered that their hopes and desires clashed with movements for exclusion. Those who participated in Baptist missions in Oregon and elsewhere engaged evangelical projects variously—with faith in their conversion, with optimism about the opportunities provided by a mission education, with hope that missionaries might be able to shield them from the growing anti-Chinese movement. Yet even while they sought the services provided by mission projects and made demands on the local elite and national mission board to accommodate them, they also helped to create institutions that joined a dense web of associations, businesses, and less formal formations that enabled them to establish lives and communities in the United States.[13]

Each of these tales is connected to the others. As the ABHMS attempted to maintain its vision of converting the nation into an orderly, moral community, the group directed an increasing amount of time, resources, and attention toward ministering to blacks and Chinese, the populations that symbolized—or were, in their analysis, most responsible for—the threat of moral and social disorder. In turn, black and Chinese proselyte populations responded—especially through local, "on-the-ground" interactions—by variously accommodating, adapting, refusing, and resisting dominant definitions of religious, national, racial, and cultural difference. Meanwhile, seemingly disparate mission fields in the South and on the Pacific Coast developed at roughly the same time, were buffeted by similar social and political currents, and, perhaps most interestingly, held comparable—even related—consequences for meanings of national belonging and identity for black and Chinese participants.

I follow the interweaving threads of these three stories, moving between national discussions of the evangelical project and the implementation of—and responses to—local missionary efforts in Raleigh and Portland. The American Baptist mission in Raleigh began in 1865, a few months after the end of the Civil War, and grew into a Baptist church and Shaw University. Local Baptists in Portland established the Chinese Mission School in that city nine years later. Although San Francisco's Chinese population was larger, the Portland school became the longest continuously running mission to the Chinese on the Pacific Coast. Both of these institutions were embedded within broader local, regional, and national systems of racial, social, and political hierarchy, and each was part of the national evangelical movement to transform America and the world. *Citizens of a Christian Nation* thus links national, regional, and local aspects of citizenship, race, and religion in America, providing insights into both the construction of race and racial knowledge and the lived experience of those who were racially marked.[14]

Within these intersecting stories, I frame three arguments that explore the mutually constitutive nature of race, religion, and the nation. First, I argue that American Baptists' evangelical nationalism was a central component of a religiously and culturally derived discourse of race. Second, I contend that home missions, in addition to being vehicles through which missionaries' ideas about race were created and deployed, were also sites where African Americans and Chinese immigrants contested and rearticulated notions of racial difference. Finally, I make the case for the necessity of understanding racial formation and race relations in comparative perspective.[15]

My first argument hinges on an analysis of home mission ideology and practice. Even as they expressed a prescriptive understanding of the nation based on Christianity—one that might undercut other types of exclusions—American Baptists articulated ideas of difference based on race. In fact, the very foundation of the missionary project rested on the elaboration of difference between Christian missionaries and yet-to-be converted blacks and Chinese. This hierarchy was reinforced through an ethnographic literature, written by evangelicals, that produced and disseminated racial stereotypes. Thus, even as E. G. Robinson echoed Paul's sentiments about the equality of souls, he could also assert, based on missionaries' observations, the fundamental differences between the "pious" Chinese, who may have learned the forms of Christianity but whose faith remained suspect, and the "spiritual" Negroes, whose faith was unquestioned but who had little knowledge of theology, and between those two groups and the unexamined normative white Christian.[16]

Citizenship and national belonging figured centrally in this hierarchy of difference. In particular, by linking their domestic and foreign mission efforts Baptist evangelicals effectively marked black and Chinese populations that resided within the territorial borders of the United States as outsiders.[17] Robinson, for instance, expressed his belief that the best future for blacks rested not in the United States in "the shadow of the white man" but, ultimately, in Africa.[18] And the notion of Chinese "foreignness"—their alien culture as well as their (perceived) sojourning status in the United States—was reinforced by missionary rhetoric and programs that not only emphasized Chinese return migration but also made domestic proselytizing the key to converting all of China.[19] In essence, the mission project, through a language of religion, culture, nation, and transformation, made race.[20]

My assertions that this process occurred in the late nineteenth century and that home missionaries were crucial participants in it represent significant revisions in the historical literature. For many scholars, definitions of race that pivoted not solely on biology but on the interplay of cultural and physical difference and national identity constituted the "new racism" or "cultural racism" of the post–World War II (and post-Nazi) world.[21] But American evangelicals anticipated this form of difference making during the last third of the nineteenth century. Moreover, this perspective on the home mission project differs considerably from historian Peggy Pascoe's contention that domestic evangelicals were "antiracists who anticipated the distinction between biologically determined race and socially constructed culture" and who challenged "biological determinism as it applied to ethnic minority women."[22] Despite their articulation of national citizenship based on shared Christianity, domestic missionaries, in fact, were complicit, although perhaps inadvertently so, as they grounded their evangelical efforts in notions of racial difference.[23]

My second argument focuses on the ways that black and Chinese Baptists understood home mission proselytizing efforts. Emboldened by Emancipation, former slaves sought ABHMS missions to help them realize their dreams of freedom. Crossing the ocean in search of better lives for themselves and for their families, Chinese also looked to ABHMS projects to help them accomplish their aims. Over the years, this faith in the promise of conversion would be tested as the hierarchical relationships engendered by evangelical uplift frustrated black and Chinese hopes more often than it facilitated them, and as local, regional, and national movements toward segregation and exclusion grew in intensity.

Nevertheless, black and Chinese mission participants used white-sponsored evangelical projects as starting points from which to branch outward and establish autonomous and semiautonomous associations and organizations. Barred from citizenship, Chinese created a transnational network of Christian institutions that traversed the Pacific Ocean and offered the possibility of fellowship, belonging, and dignity through a kind of cosmopolitan Christianity.[24] In the meantime, blacks, though relegated to second-class citizenship, focused on a spectrum of religious and educational institutions that, as historian Raymond Gavins has observed, fostered "an attitude of protest against Jim Crow" that later would serve as the staging ground for a more concerted assault on de jure segregation.[25]

Finally, I argue that the processes of racial formation evident in the home mission project are best understood *comparatively*. In a sense, I take my cues from W. E. B. Du Bois's *The Souls of Black Folk*. In this seminal work published in 1903, Du Bois asked, "How does it feel to be a problem?" and asserted, perhaps even more famously, that "the problem of the Twentieth Century is the problem of the color-line."[26] Following Du Bois's insight, I displace the late nineteenth-century problems of racial difference in America—the Chinese Question and the Negro Problem—with a different problem, that of white supremacy.

But to observe that legalized segregation and immigration exclusion evolved from the same white supremacist impulse has little explanatory power.[27] I therefore document the ways that white supremacy took different local and regional forms during the late nineteenth century in an effort to demonstrate how racializing discourses—in the South, in the West, among Baptist missionaries—produced similar but distinctive notions of difference.

By the end of the nineteenth century, white supremacy would successfully mark both blacks and Chinese as "outsiders" to the national polity. But the path to exclusion was neither certain nor direct. Such a comparative analysis of local and regional racial systems yields crucial insights into the various forms, not always visible, that white supremacy took during the late nineteenth century.

An exploration of variations on the theme of white supremacy—from the increasingly common and ultimately dominant form exemplified by Jim Crow and Chinese exclusion to the subtle form articulated by Baptist missionaries—only accomplishes part of the work. The way that each group attempted to claim citizenship or stake their place in a particular locale or within the national polity also took different forms and was rooted in specific historical contexts. In part, each group's different relationship to Christianity and Christianity's different position within black and Chinese communities remained crucial distinctions. Pursuing individual or group advancement thus worked differently for blacks and Chinese who emerged from mission institutions as community leaders. But the broader experiences, traditions, and legacies of each group and from which they could draw to combat white supremacy also made a difference. Although relegated to second-class citizenship status during the Jim Crow era, African Americans nevertheless could claim belonging to the nation in ways that Chinese could not. Political rights as well as religion and cultural traditions functioned as a crucial variable as blacks and Chinese attempted to create communities and mediate race relations.

Late nineteenth-century domestic missionary work is an especially promising subject for the study of racial formation. Home missions were multileveled projects that addressed everyday behavior, material conditions, academic and religious education, national citizenship, and spiritual salvation. For those portions of the book that deal with missionary intent, rhetoric, and practice, I am able to rely on a relatively rich collection of documents—institutional records, published missionary writings, and a handful of extant personal papers in manuscript collections. I have tried to capture the depth of the home mission project by hewing closely to those sources.

But mission records are often frustratingly silent when it comes to the thoughts, desires, and beliefs of those whom evangelicals hoped to convert. They can also be distorted by the missionaries' self-interested and culturally narrow perspectives. Institutional sources generally reveal more about their authors than about those to whom evangelicals minister.[28] In part, my approach to the subject makes a virtue of this particular vice, for the cultural judgments of missionaries form a crucial part of my story. At the same time, I have treated missionary-generated documents as "points of departure" for understanding the lives of mission proselytes.[29] A close reading of Baptist home mission records and an acknowledgment that black and Chinese activities neither began nor ended in formal mission institutions provides a foundation from which to reflect on how these two groups received the evangelical overture—and how they countered the cultural racist discourses deployed by home missionaries.

The documents produced by ordinary African Americans living in the Jim Crow South or Chinese immigrants on the Pacific Coast—those to whom Baptist home missionaries ministered—only on rare occasion have been saved. Recovering their "voices"—their intentions, their goals, their thoughts, their beliefs—remains an exercise in informed guesswork. Nonetheless, there are strategies. In addition to the interpretive tactic of reading missionary records "against the grain" for what the characterizations of blacks and Chinese might reveal, a handful of scholars of both African American history and Asian American history point to other empirical and conceptual possibilities, shifting the focus from narrow explorations of missionary-proselyte relations to broader realms. These scholars show the way toward understanding the agency of proselytes—and the constraints they experienced—through a wider array of sources and a more panoramic angle of vision.[30]

This is a crucial methodological point, and I build upon it. A broader perspective provides a way into understanding how blacks and Chinese received mission programs not only by tracking their actions through institutional records but also by examining their interactions and connecting them to communities and social formations beyond the formal purview of home missions.[31] In this sense, I have used the traditional sources of social historical inquiry to move beyond limited institutional conceptions of congregation to explore a more expansive definition suggested by historian Earl Lewis's study of segregation-era Norfolk, Virginia. Lewis argues that black residents of Norfolk transformed the language of segregation by emphasizing black congregation over white power.[32] *Citizens of a Christian Nation* thus offers a sustained examination of the missionary enterprise, from evangelical discourse to experiences of black and Chinese congregation.

My approach, then, is to provide in each chapter a different view of the missionary-proselyte relationship. I have proceeded from the premise that the different and often differing perspectives each group of historical actors—white mission-

aries, African Americans, Chinese—brought to the home mission project illuminate the fears and hopes, frustrations and ambitions, coercion and resistance,
accommodation and rearticulation that formed the essence of the evangelical
enterprise. In some chapters, the anxieties and desires of white evangelicals take
center stage, and the African Americans and Chinese to whom they minister
recede to the background. In other chapters, black and Chinese communities
and their collective aspirations assume the starring roles while white missionaries fade to the margins as supporting characters. In still others, an ensemble cast
plays out the story of missionary-proselyte encounters.

Yet while these thematic examinations of American Baptist home missions allow me to "zoom in" on specific cases to portray the rich and complex
dynamic of the evangelical enterprise, I have not completely eschewed a sense
of change over time. Each of the chapters, taken in sequence, traces the trajectory of race relations in the American South and on the Pacific Coast. The
book begins in the mid-1860s on the cusp of what American evangelicals,
African Americans, and Chinese all hoped would be a new era, an era characterized by a faith in freedom and immigration and stalked by the fear of disorder. It concludes as the nineteenth century draws to an end with the nation
transformed by white supremacy.

Finally, a note on my specific denominational focus is necessary. Baptists
represent a particularly illuminating case. The vigor with which denominational organizations like the ABHMS pursued institution-building among
freedpeople in the American South was rivaled only by the Congregationalists'
American Missionary Association, and the Baptist commitment to missions to
Chinese on the Pacific Coast (as well as in China) had few equals in scope and
scale. More compellingly, Baptists, more than any other evangelical denomination, emphasized local autonomy and congregational authority and eschewed
ecclesiastical hierarchy. Basic to Baptists' view of their denomination as the
most fundamentally democratic, this core belief accentuated the tensions at
the heart of home mission ideology and practice. At the forefront of dilemmas
facing missionaries was the question of when proselyte communities would be
deemed self-sufficient enough (spiritually, as well as financially) to be independent of missionary supervision and guidance. This question underscored the
uneven power relations between missionaries and proselytes and confounded
straightforward notions of congregational authority and democratic practice.

In fact, missionaries and mission theorists often asserted that the ultimate
goal of their evangelizing was the creation of autonomous black and Chinese

churches and schools. It was a goal whose timetable for "success" remained the matter of fundamental dispute. And yet even as the mission schools and congregations that are the focus of my study remained under white evangelical control throughout the late nineteenth century, the broader field of black and Chinese Baptist activity indicates local, regional, and even transnational modes of congregation. Historian Glenda Gilmore has elegantly and persuasively argued that the social and spatial relations of the Jim Crow order are best imagined as a kind of "stiff-sided box where southern whites expected African Americans to dwell."[33] The architects of the Exclusion Era regime designed a similarly rigid container that Chinese immigrants were expected to occupy. Each box may have been constructed of different materials, but the functions were similar. This book, in part, is an exploration of the constitution of those constrained spaces.

But the desires of the white supremacist nation make up only part of the story. The aspirations of African Americans and Chinese propelled them to expand and attempt to destroy the limits that constrained them. Indeed, the activities of blacks and Chinese who came into contact with Baptist home missions provide ample testimony to their desire and willingness to transgress their respective places in a white supremacist society. As they engaged with evangelical projects, negotiated boundaries, and lived lives outside of those projects, they created and nurtured models of belonging. Inspired by their hope and faith in Emancipation and immigration, African Americans and Chinese established communities that sustained their bodies and souls, their humanity and dignity, as the twin veils of segregation and exclusion divided the nation.

CHAPTER I

"A Grand and Awful Time"

We are living, we are dwelling, in a grand and awful time,
In an age on ages telling; to be living is sublime.
Hark! the waking up of nations, hosts advancing to the fray;
Hark! what soundeth is creation's groaning for the latter day.
"We Are Living, We Are Dwelling"
Arthur C. Coxe (1840)

WHEN DELEGATES AND officials of the American Baptist Home Mission Society (ABHMS) convened in Cleveland, Ohio, for their thirty-first annual meeting, a somber mood pervaded the proceedings. It was May 21, 1863, and there seemed to be precious little to celebrate for the members of the denomination's principal organization for domestic proselytizing. Indeed, the prospects for evangelizing must have seemed dismal, for the very nation they had pledged to convert was imperiled by a ferocious and protracted civil war. It was a war rooted in slavery and precipitated by secession—a calamity foreshadowed by the 1845 schism of Baptists in America. Ever since northern officials refused to commission slave-holding missionaries and southerners walked out of the ABHMS, northerners had dominated the Society, and, to the Yankee Baptists who gathered in Cleveland, recent events undoubtedly appeared ominous. In December 1862, Union forces had been routed at Fredericksburg, and, just two weeks before the annual meeting, northern troops suffered another demoralizing defeat at Chancellorsville. To make matters worse, the winds of war that seemed to be blowing against the North's military efforts sent public opinion sailing against the Union government, a trend exemplified by the necessity for and outrage against the 1863 Enrollment Act that had been passed by Congress earlier that spring. The nation's situation, if anything, had worsened since the last annual meeting when the ABHMS Executive Board had lamented the "appalling disturbance of our once happy National Union."[1]

The Society's motto declared, "North America for Christ"; yet the group's continental ambitions were being thwarted by the war. Resources for home missions had diminished considerably since the outbreak of hostilities, and Baptist labors declined precipitously. Between 1860 and 1863, contributions to the Society decreased by more than 40 percent.[2] The ABHMS had ceded missionary duties in the South to the Southern Baptist Convention (SBC) after the 1845 split, and Baptist evangelical activity among the growing Chinese population on the West Coast had reverted completely to local support and control with the start of the war. In May 1863, the ABHMS could hardly make the claim that it was fulfilling its continental mandate.

Yet when the Society's recording secretary, E. T. Hiscox, compiled the annual report in which the meeting's proceedings were published, he chose to sound a note of hope. The goal of the ABHMS was conversion—spiritual and social transformation in its broadest sense—and few conditions provided greater prospects for comprehensive change than turmoil. Quoting a hymn to preface his discussion, Hiscox declared, "We are living, we are dwelling, in a grand and awful time."[3] While acknowledging the daunting challenges that lay ahead, Hiscox nonetheless emphasized the opportunities created during this turbulent period. He insisted that "the opportunities for successful [missionary] labor were never before as great."[4]

To be sure, the recording secretary's optimism was born of a deep faith in the righteousness of his evangelical cause and was intended, at least in part, to revitalize flagging support for the Society. Nevertheless, Hiscox could point to encouraging signs for the evangelical enterprise despite the recent battlefield reversals. On January 1 President Abraham Lincoln's Emancipation Proclamation had taken effect, emboldening an organization that, almost twenty years earlier, had disavowed slavery. Soon after the war had begun, as slaves flocked to Union lines, the ABHMS had appointed Rev. Howard Osgood to investigate the condition of African Americans at Fortress Monroe, South Carolina, and to report on the potential for home missions. Lincoln's decree further encouraged the missionary organization, and one of the group's managers had recently been sent to Washington, D.C., on another fact-finding mission.[5]

The Civil War had drawn national evangelical attention away from the growing Chinese population in America. Before the war, Southern Baptists had supported a small but active mission in northern California, but limited resources and energy made it impossible to sustain national sponsorship of the mission. Still, in 1862 Congress had passed and Lincoln had signed the first Pacific Railway Act, paving the way for the construction of a transcontinental railroad. Hiscox could not know that, within three years, thousands of Chinese would be employed by the Central Pacific Railroad. Nevertheless, the prospect of a railroad that would connect America's coasts signaled the possibility of the nation fulfilling its continental destiny, provided an argument for evangelicals interested in safeguarding the morality of the increased western settlement that would result from the railroad, and brought home missionaries to the edge of their territory, poised to support foreign endeavors in "heathen" lands like China.[6]

But Hiscox's enthusiasm and sense of hope reflected more than an interpretation of recent events. It also revealed the comprehensive ambitions of the Baptist home mission project. In his report, he surveyed the possibilities wrought both by "the breaking down of the middle walls of partition between the North and the South" and by the "Pacific slope . . . a field where the reapers may follow the plowmen, and gather a harvest at once." Hiscox acknowledged that the challenges and opportunities that confronted the nation—the "grand and awful time"—rested upon what twenty-first-century observers might refer to as America's multiracial character. Indeed, he provided home mission officials and advocates with an astonishing vision of the nation's future: "It is Europe, it is Asia, it is Africa, it is all of these brought together upon our own continent."[7]

Over the next decade Baptist evangelicals labored prodigiously to make Hiscox's vision of a racially inclusive Christian nation a reality. By the end of the 1860s, in addition to the dozens of missions sponsored by local and regional Baptist associations, the ABHMS directed religious workers in thirty-three states and territories, stretching from the eastern seaboard to the Pacific Coast, from the upper Midwest to the deep South. Its laborers toiled among ex-slaves in ten of the eleven former Confederate states, as well as in Kentucky and Washington, D.C., and it had recently appointed three missionaries to work exclusively among Chinese in California. By 1873, the Society was sponsoring seven theological schools for African Americans in the South, and the first of several Chinese mission schools in California had been operating for three years. Within two years, the ABHMS would be called on by local Baptists to expand its network of Chinese mission schools by helping to sponsor the endeavor in Portland. Between 1863 and 1873, contributions to the ABHMS increased more than 82 percent, and its operating budget had grown to almost a quarter of a million dollars.[8]

This decade of Baptist home mission growth occurred against a backdrop of dynamic social and political change. Within months of the 1863 annual meeting, northern troops delivered decisive victories at Vicksburg and Gettysburg, shifting the momentum of the Civil War toward eventual Union victory, and, earlier that year, the Emancipation Proclamation had moved the abolition of slavery to the center of northern war aims. Victory thus meant that various plans for reunion and reconstruction would have to address the new status of black southerners. At the same time, reunion reinvigorated efforts for developing the Far West, attracting emigrants from all over the world to populate and work the region. Many of the Chinese laborers hired by the Central Pacific Railroad beginning in 1865 had originally been attracted to the United States by the discovery of gold in California. As the economy of the Pacific Coast expanded (due, in large part, to the extension of rail lines), so too did employment and agricultural opportunities. Between 1860 and 1870, the Chinese population in the United States increased almost 81 percent. It would grow another 67 percent during the 1870s.[9]

For Baptist home missionaries, the post–Civil War reunion of North and South and the linking of Atlantic and Pacific Coasts by rail signaled a new era in their evangelical efforts. Bolstered by what appeared to them to be the realization of America's continental "manifest destiny," home mission advocates rededicated themselves to claiming "North America for Christ." Yet in this new era, the movement to fulfill the promise of America's Christian destiny turned specifically on the conversion of racialized populations.[10]

Martin Brewer Anderson's May 1865 presidential address at the ABHMS annual meeting in St. Louis placed missions to blacks and Chinese squarely at the center of the larger mission to transform America. The influential head of the Baptist-sponsored University of Rochester presided over a gathering still grieving over the assassination of Abraham Lincoln. Anderson's remarks tried to make sense of the "awful deed" that had occurred only a few weeks earlier, and he concluded that no matter who actually had conspired to kill Lincoln (he suspected former Confederate leaders), slavery, the Civil War, and the South were ultimately to blame. "We do know that a system which sought to carry us back to the darkness of the tenth century—human slavery—has fitly culminated in a foul and unnatural murder," intoned Anderson. Lincoln's death, he declared, would be forever "associated, in history, with slavery and the instigators of the cruel and murderous war just closed."[11]

Yet Anderson appealed to his fellow evangelicals to see beyond their anguish and to make certain that this tragedy would "lead us on to more exertions in behalf of the cause of Christ." For Anderson, opportunity arrived in the guise of disquietude over the status of freedpeople and the loyalty of white southerners. The ABHMS president recognized that the combination of revolutionary freedom and retrograde defiance was explosive. Positioning Baptist home missionaries between newly emancipated African Americans and recently defeated whites, Anderson decried what he perceived to be both the ignorance and religious defects with which blacks emerged from slavery and the truculence of the "many civilians" who "do not appreciate that the Rebellion is crushed."[12]

He next shifted his gaze from the South to the West, and here, too, fear played the handmaiden to evangelical opportunity. In part, the prospect of the transcontinental railroad intensified attention to the westward migration that had been the raison d'être of the antebellum home mission movement. "The Pacific Railroad . . . will soon be completed to San Francisco—a great *iron river*, that will roll by villages and settlements which must spring up along its margin," predicted Anderson. "We must go and carry the gospel to those who people the territory through which it passes." The disorder of mass migration could be averted by sending missionaries west "to look after [settlers'] spiritual welfare and keep alive the holy fire of religion and morality."[13]

But even as the ABHMS president imagined a railroad connecting the two coastal boundaries of the continent, he identified an even more foreboding threat lurking to the west. The transcontinental railroad, asserted Anderson, "will when completed bring us, as it were, three thousand miles nearer the great missionary fields of Asia. . . . Thus, we shall soon have 'flanked' heathenism and be able to attack it in the rear."[14] Although he did not elaborate, Anderson almost certainly saw the conversion of the thousands of Chinese residing in the United States as the opening volley in his flanking maneuver. Baptist domestic missionaries had been active among the Chinese in California before the outbreak of the Civil War, and, as the ABHMS made preparations to appoint an evangelist dedicated to this population in 1869 and 1870, it echoed Anderson's assessment that economic development of the West Coast, accelerated by the railroad, had made the Chinese one of the most pressing demands of the Society.[15] In an analog of the organization's understanding of the challenges presented by the reunification of North and South, Baptist home missionaries positioned themselves between the "heathen" Chinese who posed a grave danger to American Christian civilization and the social and moral disorder of white settlers that found its articulation in what one mission official would later call "un-Christian race prejudice."[16]

As he first faced south and then west from St. Louis, Martin Brewer Anderson articulated the postbellum charge to Baptist evangelicals. In part, he reiterated the decades-old goal of the home mission movement "to organize communities into congregations" and "give them pastors."[17] The desire for social stability and moral order reflected a long-standing commitment to the formation Christian communities that would serve as the basis for the creation of a Christian nation and, through foreign mission work, the extension of a Christian empire. As in the antebellum home mission movement, evangelicals blurred the line between the sacred and secular, the religious and civic. Yet in the post-Emancipation South and in the rapidly developing West, evangelicals cast the threat to Christian community and, thus, the Christian nation in racial terms. Although Baptist missionaries often believed that vituperative white reactions to black Emancipation and Chinese immigration were as much a danger to their project as unconverted freedpeople or Chinese, the challenge to establish and maintain national and religious order remained rooted in notions of racial difference and determinations of who could or could not belong to the nation.

In the early 1830s, the home mission movement had been sparked by the fires of evangelicalism's Second Great Awakening and Great Revival and fueled by western migration. Antebellum home missionary associations developed as mechanisms to disseminate the religious, cultural, and social ideas of evangelical revivals over time and space, thus institutionalizing the era's spiritual passion and vision for society. Focusing particularly on the creation of moral and religious communities across the expanding nation, home missionaries and officials turned their attention toward the establishment and maintenance of religious orthodoxy and social order. They hoped to fashion western communities along northeastern social and moral norms.[18]

Among Baptists, the 1832 establishment of a national body to provide organizational support for and supervision of domestic missions indicated the seriousness with which they took this evangelical enterprise. Baptists, more than any other Protestant denomination, prized local and congregational independence and decentralization, but those who organized the American Baptist Home Mission Society believed that only a national association could address the grave dangers posed by the western extension of the nation.[19] In the words of the institution's first historian, the Society was to be "the providential agency for the concentration of the efforts of the denomination, in the contesting with irreligion and error the possession of this land, in supplying destitute regions with Gospel privileges, and in laying religious foundations for the populous future of the continent."[20]

The language of one of its founders, Massachusetts minister Jonathan Going, illustrates the urgency with which home mission advocates viewed their cause. Basing his assessment on an 1831 tour of the Mississippi Valley and on his correspondence with cofounder and domestic missionary John Mason Peck, he believed that "a mighty effort must be made, and by the body of evangelical Christians in the United States, and made soon, or ignorance and heresy and infidelity will entrench themselves too strongly to be repulsed." Should ignorance, heresy, and infidelity prevail, warned Going, "our republic will be overturned and our institutions, civil and religious, will be demolished." For Going and other home mission advocates, there was little difference between America's spiritual welfare and its civic well-being. The fate of the growing republic depended on the equally rapid dissemination of the gospel.[21]

It is important to note that Baptists were not alone in this belief. The ABHMS was part of a broader, multidenominational movement that, despite some denominational variation, was remarkably ecumenical. In general terms, evangelical ideology was strikingly similar among Congregationalists, Presbyterians, Methodists, and Baptists. Across denominations, missionaries shared what religious historian Laurie F. Maffly-Kipp has identified as a "belief in the innate superiority of American character" and a faith in America's particularly evangelical character.[22]

These overlapping secular and sacred concerns formed the essence of the evangelical nationalism at the heart of the home mission project. Evangelical nationalism provided a comprehensive vision of America's exceptional and providential destiny as a Christian nation. The Society's first annual report made this clear when it summoned "men to the support of this work, by every principle of enlightened patriotism and of Christian salvation."[23] Rooted in the evangelical conviction that all souls were capable of coming to Christ through conversion and spurred both by Christ's Great Commission to "go ye into all the world, and preach the Gospel to every creature" (Mark 16:15) and by the territorial and demographic expansion of the United States, this ideology framed the home mission project. Founding ABHMS manager Steven Chapin, in fact, placed the American nation at the center of his interpretation of humanity's salvation, for "she is destined to be the chief instrument in bringing every anti-christian nation under the power of the cross."[24]

This vision of what religious historian Martin E. Marty has called the "righteous empire" survived the Civil War.[25] In 1883, for instance, Indiana minister and home mission advocate Lemuel Moss echoed the Society's first annual report and sounded the twin themes of evangelical nationalism by declaring, "Every missionary of this Society has been an apostle of freedom; every preacher of this Society has been a spiritual agent of our great Government, carrying everywhere thoughts of civil freedom."[26] American Baptists believed home missions to be the primary instrument of evangelical Christianity, and, thus, the key to safeguarding American civilization and society.

Yet while the ABHMS remained committed to evangelical nationalism, slave Emancipation and the increased immigration of the Chinese tested the limits of the Society's definition of the nation. The Society never questioned its ministry to either group, but African Americans and Chinese immigrants—considered culturally alien, religiously heathen or unorthodox, physically identifiable, and, increasingly, biologically distinctive—symbolized the new challenge to the orderly fulfillment of America's evangelical destiny. The dual engines of national and spiritual expansion that drove evangelical nationalism toward a single goal—the creation of a Christian America—could also propel the home mission project in conflicting directions.

On one hand, the impulse to form stable Christian communities (the building blocks of the nation) placed a premium on social order. The desire for a unified nation, premised on a shared religious vision, required the implementation of a moral and social norm, modeled and regulated by a chosen class. Evangelicals hoped to shape the communities in which they ministered to fit this vision of a society led by educated stewards and premised upon a web of mutual obligation, not personal rights and liberties, that linked elite, middle, and common classes. The first generation of home mission advocates, by insisting that missionaries take a lead role in territorial expansion, emphasized their resolve that religious and moral education—the "civilizing process"—be at the heart of the development of new communities in the trans-Mississippi West. It was a marked departure from more aggressive (and often more violent) forms of expansion.[27]

On the other hand, there lay within evangelicalism what British historian Susan Thorne has called the "egalitarian promise of inclusion."[28] This strain of evangelical thought placed individual agency above predestination and held the possibility that all were equal in sin and salvation. The idea that God had endowed all people with the ability to achieve salvation held vast democratic possibilities, and the emphasis on the experience of personal conversion, the so-called voluntary principle at the core of the Second Great Awakening and the Great Revival, complemented the Baptist denomination's devotion to congregational autonomy and its democratic implications.[29] Although this belief in the equality of souls all too rarely found its expression in worldly matters, it did provide a basis for actions that indicated an egalitarian ethos, such as when several prominent northern Baptists established the American Baptist Antislavery Convention in 1840. Arguing that slavery undermined the evangelical belief in all people as "free moral agents," this group's deep-seated objections to slavery helped precipitate the schism between northern and southern Baptists and was part of the larger antislavery and abolitionist movements.[30]

In the abstract, at least, evangelicals could hold these competing ideas in tension with one another. Particularly for Baptists, the belief in an organically and orderly religious community led by God's word and under the stewardship of a moral elite was a necessary counterweight to the threat of disorder brought by the value placed on democracy. In practice, home missionaries resolved this fundamental contradiction by integrating both ideas as parts of a comprehensive process of transformation. Using conversion as the pivot, evangelicals did, indeed, at least theoretically, open the spectrum of those who might be included in the new Christian community to a broader array of people. However, making this diversity of souls "homogenous" became a crucial goal (as well as the primary method) of evangelization.[31]

Conversion, in this sense, was assimilative. The transformation of the soul that would take place with the acceptance of Christ would not only allow converts entrance into the Christian community; it would also render them fit (i.e., trustworthy enough) to participate in civil society by tempering their innate sinfulness and by providing a common bond to others. Baptist minister Lemuel Moss described the transformative effect of evangelical Christianity when he explained that "a free people will never be constituted or held together by an iron band. They must be held together by something that is powerful enough to assimilate and purify and elevate and unify all those discordant elements that may come within its range."[32]

It is significant that Moss's discussion occurred in the late nineteenth century. During the antebellum era, the idea of broadening who might be included in this Christian nation, while theoretically encompassing, meant practically that Europeans beyond those considered "Anglo Saxon" might be worthy of evangelizing and belonging. The actual racial-cultural spectrum of difference that evangelicals imagined they would be engaging was relatively narrow. The evangelical nationalism espoused during this earlier period was formed by the nexus of early to mid-nineteenth-century emerging notions of Anglo-Saxonism and evangelical Protestantism.[33] Yet after the Civil War, as Baptist missionaries turned their attention toward African Americans and Chinese, there lay within their enterprise the potential to disrupt the equation between national identity and whiteness. Evangelicals granted that the boundary between Christian and non-Christian—as well as American and non-American—was porous. For groups that had been marked racially, this standard of belonging—seemingly premised not on race, but on religion—held radical possibilities, and, for home missionaries, this was precisely why their project was so important.

Indeed, evangelicals who were concerned about the potential for disorder had to look no further than Emancipation and Chinese immigration. Ominous signs seemed endemic in the South. The assassination of President Abraham Lincoln—a shock in and of itself—awakened suspicions among northern Baptist evangelicals already sensitive to southern obstinacy. In the wake of Lincoln's murder, the ABHMS Committee on the State of the Country blamed "the fiendish spirit of slavery and secession" and warned of the necessity of "extinguishing . . . [the] dying embers" of the Confederacy and "utterly exterminating from every foot of our territory the last remnants of slavery."[34]

The following year, a fire in Petersburg, Virginia, confirmed the feeling of northern skeptics. On May 1, 1866, arsonists burned down two black churches, including the African Baptist Church, and attempted to set two others afire. At the ABHMS annual meeting later that month in Boston, missionary Edgar Smith reported on the conflagration's effect on the black Baptist congregation. Smith's account focused primarily on a recitation of the damage done and the faith and determination of the African American members of the church. Other reports, however, made much of the fact that the intent of the arsonists was to intimidate and discipline black residents of the city. *Harper's Weekly* led its story by noting that "there is enough left of the old barbarism of slavery to incite to the wanton destruction of churches for no other reason than that they are frequented by colored people."[35]

But maintaining order among vanquished southerners was only half the battle. According to the 1865 Committee on the State of the Country, an "indispensable condition of an assured peace" was safeguarding the rights of former slaves, and this was no mean feat.[36] American Baptists believed that generations of enslavement had so stunted the spiritual and material lives of black southerners that it was absolutely necessary for Baptist evangelicals to provide the social, moral, and religious foundation for the practice of these rights.

Indeed, only two years earlier, the ABHMS Executive Board had dispatched the chair of the committee, Hamilton C. Fish, to Washington, D.C., to investigate the condition of ex-slaves in the area. Fish provided what would become a benchmark for the evangelical analysis of the condition of African Americans (still referred to as war "contraband"), describing in great detail their religious state in the District of Columbia and nearby Alexandria, Virginia. He informed the Executive Board that "these contrabands are very religious people . . . and there is, no doubt, much real piety among them. But it often has with it a strange inter-mixture of ignorance and superstition and downright immorality." For Fish, freedpeople's spiritual deficiencies bore a direct relationship to their temporal circumstances. Scenes of "half-clad" men, women, and children "lodging in shanties, sheds, old slave pens, tents and barracks, seven to fifteen persons" to a room seemed to confirm Fish's Calvinist sense of election. If slavery had not so diminished their religious and moral capacity, then surely they would be more materially prosperous. Instead, slavery had almost eradicated "the distinguishing traits of humanity." In this sense, it became clear early on that, for northern Baptist evangelicals, the post–Civil War mission to ensure peace and stability would focus on the condition of former slaves.[37]

On the Pacific Coast, the idea that Chinese immigration might be a cause for special evangelical attention had occurred even earlier. Baptist evangelicals had been alleging the spiritual, moral, and social deficits of Chinese for decades. Adoniram and Ann Judson had become the first Baptist missionaries to Asia in 1813, and, from their post in Burma, they treated mission supporters and readers of the religious press to exhortative dispatches that described the decadence of Asian people, society, and religion.[38] Advocates of overseas evangelical work applied the Judsons' characterizations of the "heathen" Burmese and their "savage" culture to the Chinese, magnifying and multiplying the need for missions based on China's much larger population. Thus, in 1834, the *American Baptist Missionary Magazine* could publish an editorial asserting that China was a country "hardly penetrated with a single ray of light. . . . Nowhere has Satan a seat on earth to be compared in extent with that which he holds in seeming triumph . . . in the . . . so-called 'celestial empire.'"[39]

And even before large-scale movement to the United States began, Baptist evangelicals believed that the Pacific—which they had been crossing for decades to proselytize in Asia—could easily form a "channel of emigration."[40] When migration did begin in the late 1840s and 1850s, it did not take long for home missionaries to lay claim to this population. In October 1852, the Southern Baptist Convention's Home Mission Board reported that it had appointed two new missionaries to California, one of whom would labor exclusively among the Chinese.[41] However, it is unclear whom the board appointed or if the missionary ever began work. Two months later, the San Francisco Baptist Association was still hoping that someone would be sent to minister to the city's Chinese population, declaring it one of the area's most pressing needs. The San Francisco body scolded its national brethren, using italics to emphasize the situation's urgency: "*Two years ago a good Chinese missionary should have been stationed at this point.*"[42]

The Southern Baptist Convention would soon appoint J. L. Shuck as its missionary to Chinese in California, and, in April 1854, he would set sail from New Orleans to San Francisco to take up his commission.[43] Shuck ministered in California until his retirement in 1861, and nationally sponsored missions to the Chinese ceased until after the Civil War. By 1869, the ABHMS, in a stronger fiscal position than its southern counterpart, would reenter the field, supporting two evangelists to work among the Chinese in California.[44]

In this second, post–Civil War effort, Baptists argued that Chinese immigrants deserved the same evangelical "boldness and zeal" as freedpeople, for the Chinese were, "as surely as God's purposes are moved on to perfection, bound to become a great national problem."[45] For these home missionaries, the problem, in fact, was much like the one they faced in the South. In both regions, they saw themselves caught between a religiously destitute and racially different population that threatened the foundations of American civilization and a resentful and vituperative white population that jeopardized social order through un-Christian, often violent, means.

For these evangelicals, the dangers to Christian American society were both numerous and manifest. In part, the experience of scholars and missionaries in Asia informed the discourse about the effect of Chinese on America. When immigration from China began, a Baptist publication warned, "There is something in the Chinese character and constitution which renders them more inaccessible to the influences of the gospel than the large majority of other heathen nations."[46] By the late 1860s, as immigration increased, the threat became more palpable. In 1868 and 1869, Presbyterian missionary Augustus Ward Loomis published a series of articles in the *Overland Monthly* that chronicled various aspects of Chinese life in San Francisco, ranging from business and employment data to social relations and religious practices.[47] He emphasized the ways in which Chinese immigrants had stubbornly retained cultural practices and altered the American city. Even the cityscape seemed changed. Just as the erection of Christian churches transformed and "sacralized" the landscape of England's North American colonies in the late seventeenth and early eighteenth century, the building of Buddhist temples struck Loomis and others as part of the *de*sacralization, or heathenization, of American cities and towns.[48] For Loomis, the temple "for the worship of heathen deities" on the corner of Mason Street and Post Street, just a block or so from the cluster of Christian churches on Union Square, was a tangible reminder of the non-Christian nature—the foreignness—of the Chinese population in the United States and an affront to the Christina roots of American culture.[49] "We read of 'the dark places of the earth,'" warned Loomis. "But here are spots which are dark enough, under the droppings of our own sanctuaries."[50]

While the most obvious threat to evangelical nationalism emanated from the Chinese themselves, missionaries identified a second hazard in the guise of the white reaction to immigrants. Just as evangelicals decried the recalcitrance of southern whites when it came to African American freedom, they were quick to condemn the un-Christian treatment of immigrants on the West Coast. "The cruelty and abuse with which the Chinaman has been received on the Pacific coast cannot be supported by a Christian sentiment," asserted one Baptist publication.[51] "Cruelty and abuse" could take many forms, and, although missionaries often referred to extralegal acts, they also commented on other types of violence directed toward the Chinese, including structural arrangements—legal, economic, and political—that resulted in physical and nonphysical injury.[52] As early as 1852, the leading Baptist missionary publication condemned the "mass of ignorance" exemplified by California Governor John Bigler's anti-Chinese diatribe to the state legislature, and, seven years later, when California's supreme court invalidated a measure prohibiting Chinese immigration into the state, the same periodical expressed its relief under the headline, "Glad to Hear It."[53] Baptist evangelicals would continue to denounce the growing movement against the Chinese. When the 1882 Chinese Exclusion Act became law, the ABHMS, after "animated" discussion, passed a "deprecatory" resolution, arguing that the new legislation ran counter to the tenets of evangelical nationalism: The law was "contrary to the fundamental principles of our free government, and opposed to the spirit of the Christian religion."[54] The Society's corresponding secretary, Henry Lyman Morehouse, acerbically referred to the law as the act of an only "nominally Christian nation."[55] Morehouse's comment foreshadowed a more comprehensive campaign he would spearhead ten years later as the offending legislation came up for renewal.

Baptist missionaries found themselves caught between the Scylla of black and Chinese heathenism and the Charybdis of antiblack and anti-Chinese movements. The course they charted both anticipated more fervent predictions about the perils of unrestricted black freedom and Chinese immigration and offered an alternate solution. By the end of the nineteenth century, the "Negro Problem" and the "Chinese Question" would become commonplace topics in American discussions of race, and, in a general sense, the evangelical concern during the 1860s and 1870s foretold these discussions.

As historian David W. Blight has observed, by the century's end, for many white Americans, the Negro Problem "referred to blacks as the obstacle to national progress, as a people to be reformed or eliminated, as a social crisis demanding solutions."[56] This formulation pushed black southerners out of the polity, either because slavery had impeded their progress or because some inherent quality had made progress impossible. In fact, in this version of the Negro Problem, African Americans were deemed a kind of foreign population within the nation's borders. For Charles Francis Adams II, speaking to a southern white audience in 1908, "the portentous Race Question" turned on the fact that "this awful and mysterious Afro-American Sphinx" was a "distinct alien."[57]

Immigration from China introduced another alien population to the United States, and the formulation of this phenomenon as a "question" and a "problem" also left little doubt that the Chinese were not organic to most understandings of the American polity. In part, the cultural foundation for this position had been laid even before the first large-scale migration of Asians to the United States, and the mid-century and post–Civil War representations made by politicians and national publications of Chinese workers as "coolies"—or unfree or contract laborers—linked them to a system of labor many considered to be both immoral and incompatible with American ideas of freedom and free labor. The threat of so-called coolies to America's hard-won free labor system only increased as more and more Chinese entered the United States, providing a more visible symbol of an alien, exotic menace.[58] *Harper's Weekly* concluded in 1879 that encouragement of "unrestricted immigration" should cease because "the European easily blends with the American, but the Asiatic remains an absolute alien."[59]

Yet if the shadow of alien others lay to one side of the evangelical nationalist route to national redemption, then the whirlpool of antiblack and anti-Chinese agitation swirled on the other. To a remarkable degree—particularly as the nation edged toward Jim Crow and immigration exclusion—Baptist home mission officials maintained that part of both these great late nineteenth-century race problems resided not just with blacks and Chinese but with white Americans and their lack of Christian acceptance. In 1883, *Baptist Home Mission Monthly* made its view of those who harassed blacks clear when it derided the unidentified "hater of schools for the colored people" who had shot at the ABHMS school in Live Oak, Florida, characterizing the perpetrator as "a 'cracker' from the pine woods—who probably cannot read or write and hates to have the colored people above him!"[60] Baptist officials were no less vehement when condemning "the barbarous treatment by nominally Christian people" of Chinese on the West Coast.[61]

Perhaps the most concise articulation of the precarious route Baptist evangelicals hoped to follow was offered by the ABHMS Executive Board in 1871. Insisting that it worked "with an even vigorous hand for the good of all classes and races of the human family," the board proclaimed that its "missionaries are peace-makers. . . . Wherever man hates his fellow, or race is hostile to race," continued the board, "[missionaries] remind the people that God is the just and loving Father of us all, and that his searching eye is upon us. They preach to men that Jesus died for all alike, that all the race are brethren, and that the finally redeemed are to be gathered from the earth out of every nation, kindred, and tribe under heaven."[62]

Here, then, was a reiteration of E. T. Hiscox's 1863 vision of a racially inclusive Christian nation and a possible "solution" to both the Negro Problem and the Chinese Question: assimilation through conversion. Indeed, for these postwar evangelicals, Christianity stood as the fundamental measure of inclusion. Remaking black and Chinese populations through Christian education and evangelical conversion not only would tame the threat of heathenism, it would also calm the swirling eddies of white opposition. This belief would lead Baptist home mission organizations to become advocates for black citizenship rights and to decry immigration restriction from China. But it would also reinforce missionaries' hierarchical notions of Christian supremacy—ideas bound inextricably to their understandings of nation, culture, and even race. As Baptist home missionaries entered the field to minister to African Americans and Chinese, this was the fundamental tension with which they would have to contend.

CHAPTER 2

Faith and Hope

And he dreamed. And behold, a ladder set up on the earth, and
the top of it reached to heaven. And behold, the angels of God
ascending and descending on it.
    Genesis 28:12 (ASV)

We are climbing Jacob's ladder
We are climbing Jacob's ladder
We are climbing Jacob's ladder
Brothers, sisters, all
Every rung goes higher and higher
Every rung goes higher and higher
Every rung goes higher and higher
Brothers, sisters, all
    "Jacob's Ladder" (traditional)

THE WHITE MISSIONARY and black churchmen who met on December 1,
1865, in the basement of the Guion Hotel on Edenton Street in Raleigh had all
traveled a long way. Henry Martin Tupper, a thirty-four-year-old Union Army
veteran and seminary-trained missionary, had arrived in the southern city less
than eight weeks earlier from his native Massachusetts. The six African American ministers and deacons, whose names are lost to the historical record, had
also come from distant points—some quite literally and all metaphorically. At

least one, a former "plantation preacher," was one of the hundreds of ex-slaves who had migrated from the countryside to Raleigh in the months after the Civil War. And in the aftermath of the final surrender of Confederate troops outside of nearby Durham that spring, all six had joined four million other black southerners in the sweet journey from bondage to freedom.[1]

Tupper and the black ministers and deacons had come to Raleigh by rail, by carriage, and by foot, but those conveyances only describe their mode of transportation. Faith and hope carried them there. Each participant was exploring the possibilities brought by the dawning of a new era of Emancipation. For Tupper, Union victory meant the end of a slave regime that he had risked life and limb to defeat. It also meant an obligation and commitment to minister to the poverty-stricken, uneducated, and "heathen" former bondmen—a duty animated by his faith in evangelical Christianity. For the black churchmen, the meeting was as simple and as immense as freedom. It was one of a number of activities—extraordinary and everyday—that constituted their hard-won status as freedpeople. As slaves, they had been barred by law and by custom from formal education and, in many cases, from unsupervised religious activity. That they were now attending a meeting as students, that the meeting was a theological class to begin their formal training as ministers and congregational leaders, that they were meeting in a public building—these were all signs of a faith not just in Christianity but in the promise of Emancipation.

Nine years later and almost three thousand miles away, Baptist missionaries and students gathered in Portland, Oregon, to inaugurate another evangelical venture. They, too, had come from afar. As in Raleigh, individual names have been lost, but records indicate that on November 13, 1874, "seventy-five Chinamen" met with Baptist missionaries in Portland's Good Templar's Building, just down the street from the city's First Baptist Church. Most of the Chinese, if not all, hailed originally from southern China. Some arrived in Portland via San Francisco, others from coastal fishing hamlets and mining settlements. The two missionaries also came by way of San Francisco and southern China. Dong Gong had migrated to northern California from his native Canton (Guangdong) some years earlier, and he was accompanied by a white evangelist named E. Z. Simmons, whose mission work had taken him from his native Mississippi to China. He had recently returned to the United States to assume a post in San Francisco.[2]

Like their counterparts in North Carolina, the men who assembled in the Good Templar's Building arrived from distant points, propelled by faith and hope to America's Pacific Coast. Twenty-six-year-old E. Z. Simmons traveled to Portland to introduce Dong Gong to local Baptists; he would return to California within days. But the establishment of an Oregon Chinese mission was an extension of his commitment to evangelical work and was yet another adventure to add to his journeys in China and California—voyages that he could only have dreamed about as a sickly young man in Kossuth, Mississippi. Dreams of another sort brought Chinese to Portland. For almost a generation, the West Coast of the United States had been luring migrants from economically devastated southern China with tales of Gam Saak, or Gold Mountain. For those who attended that inaugural class, the mission may have engendered any number of possibilities—something new for the curious, a place to learn for the ambitious, somewhere to worship for the faithful, a path to inclusion for the prospective settlers, a protected space for the harassed and scared. For Dong Gong, it was an unprecedented opportunity both to make a living and to remain true to his beliefs. As the missionary hired to establish this project, he would enjoy a status that must have seemed unfathomable when he first arrived in the United States years earlier as a laborer, and his faith to be both Chinese and Christian would be severely tested over the next few years.

In Raleigh in 1865 and in Portland nine years later, diverse currents converged to form critical religious, social, and interracial institutions. In the rented basement room in Raleigh's Guion Hotel, the dreams and ambitions of the northern missionary and the freedmen came together to form what would become Shaw University. Although the confluence of these streams did not always flow smoothly, Shaw would nonetheless become one of the most important African American educational institutions in the late nineteenth-century American South. Similarly, those who gathered in Portland's Good Templar's Hall could claim to be present at the founding of a lasting institution—the city's Chinese Mission School. At least nominally and by sponsorship, the Chinese Mission School was a project of the First Baptist Church, and later it was partially supported by the national ABHMS, but in reality it was more of a collective, if not always completely cooperative, endeavor among Chinese participants, commissioned missionaries and teachers, and local city leaders.

The two Baptist missions were established a continent apart, and, at first glance, the projects in Raleigh and Portland appear to be very different indeed. Located in sections of the United States that have been treated as both distinctive and exceptional, the missions also ministered to populations whose histories, with a few notable exceptions, have remained separate.[3] And, in fact, the cities that hosted the missions developed from particular local experiences and contexts.

Baptist missionaries and advocates, however, understood the evangelical labors in Raleigh and Portland to be both similar and parts of a larger project, and these two perspectives provide the basis for some important insights. They suggest, first of all, that the two missions and, especially, the regions and social systems in which they developed are comparable. Baptist home missionaries believed they were bringing to each proselyte population a universal belief in evangelical Christianity, and the particularities they observed, experienced, or ignored as they attempted to put those ideas into action calls attention to the specific local conditions, as well as the common characteristics, that shaped black-white relations in the South and Chinese-white relations in the West. Moreover, evangelicals believed the home mission efforts in the South and the West to be parts of a broader, transformative endeavor to create a Christian nation. Each regional project thus demonstrates the ways in which national discourses of belonging were alternately expanded and confounded by assessments of racial and cultural difference. The missions to African Americans and Chinese emanated, in part, from the same general faith in late nineteenth-century evangelical Christianity and were animated by similar senses of hope in what a future bound to that faith might hold. Yet missionaries' efforts also stemmed from a desire for social and moral order, and their attempts to convert the nation—to make Christianity the national norm—expose a whole history of possibilities and limits, contestation and conflict. And as this history comes to light, so too does the history of blacks and Chinese who received this evangelical message in the midst of their own quests. For black southerners, the end of slavery promised the opportunity to fashion a broadly conceived freedom. For Chinese immigrants, the journey across the Pacific represented a chance to fulfill, in the words of one folk song, ambitions "as big as the ocean and as high as the sky."[4] Exploring the different ways that African Americans and immigrants received the evangelical overture and the various methods they devised for coping with the developing onslaught of race-based exclusion during the late nineteenth century gestures toward a comparative study not just of regional white supremacies but also of racial formation.[5]

Those who attended the initial meeting in Raleigh in 1865 found a very different city than those who would assemble in Portland nine years later would find. Each city's history, recent fortunes, and prospects for the future made these locales, in fundamental ways, distinctly dissimilar. The North Carolina meeting took place in a state capital still in shock from the South's defeat. Raleigh's prominence had always stemmed not from commerce but from government, and the city situated on the Carolina piedmont is perhaps most noteworthy as the first state capital in the nation to be planned and as President Andrew Johnson's birthplace.[6] Before the Civil War, Raleigh ranked as only the fourth largest city in the state—about half the size of Wilmington—with fewer than 5,000 residents.[7] During the war, early Union victories on the coast resulted in blockades and an influx of refugees. Although Raleigh had been spared destruction by northern forces during the spring of 1865, the war seemed to swirl around the city. In March, Union troops under the command of General William T. Sherman had fought the last major battle of the Civil War south of Raleigh at Bentonville. In the battle's aftermath, Sherman made Raleigh his headquarters and accepted General James E. Johnston's surrender on April 26 in nearby Durham. After the war, when the piedmont region became home to tobacco and textile manufacturing, Raleigh, lacking both a major river and a major railroad, would remain most significant as the locus of the state's political and administrative power.[8]

By contrast, the founding meeting of the Chinese Mission School in Portland took place in a city made prosperous by geography and commerce. Portland's location near the confluence of the Columbia and Willamette Rivers made it a vital link between San Francisco's booming commercial center to the south and the farmlands of the Willamette Valley. As the city grew up in the imposing shadow of Mt. Hood, it also became a major trading nexus for the gold camps of the upper Columbia region. The growth of railroads would enhance San Francisco's stature as the pre-eminent city on the Pacific Coast and would help Seattle to overtake Portland as the Northwest's most important urban center by 1900, but Oregon's largest city, throughout the late nineteenth century, continued to grow and thrive. In 1874, while Raleigh was still recovering from the Civil War, Portland stood as the dominant city in the Northwest.[9]

The immediate social and political landscape of Raleigh and Portland differed as well. In 1865, Raleigh was in turmoil, reeling from defeat and adjusting with some difficulty to Emancipation. The relatively lax federal supervision of presidential Reconstruction allowed the state's white elites to attempt to impose severe limits on black freedom, but, with the ascendancy of congressional Reconstruction, the stalwarts of "white men's republicanism" found themselves losing ground to a new political coalition of Unionists, northern Republicans, and African Americans.[10] In Portland, the city's elite had been busy consolidating power in the years preceding the mission's founding in 1874. The city had been incorporated twenty-three years earlier, and its founding families and commercial pioneers asserted control quickly, creating a formidable local aristocracy with roots in commercial trade and transportation and with a firm grip on benevolent associations, churches, and other social institutions.

But for Baptist evangelicals, many of the same dangers that made Raleigh appear to be such a perilous place also threatened Portland's seeming stability. For officials of the ABHMS, Raleigh and Portland both were situated on the nation's periphery, dangerously far from Northeastern influence. The Yankees who dominated the ABHMS believed that the post–Civil War South and the mid- to late nineteenth-century Far West required religious and social guidance to accompany political and economic development.[11] Baptist mission officials were deeply suspicious of treasonous and recalcitrant former Confederates who had used the Bible to justify slavery, and, although local elites in Portland seemed to be very much in control of their city, northeastern evangelicals maintained a healthy skepticism toward the moral rectitude of westerners. These fears of regional disorder were only compounded by the end of slavery and increased Chinese immigration.

In fact, it was a demographic quality as much as geography that suggested to home mission advocates similarities between the two fields. The nonwhite populations of Raleigh and Portland both had increased at stunning rates in the years preceding the establishment of Baptist home missions in each locale. Although the total populations of both cities had grown, the increase in the number of African Americans in Raleigh and the number of Chinese in Portland far outpaced anything experienced by each respective white population. Between 1860 and 1870, Raleigh's white population increased by almost 36 percent while the black population almost doubled. Between 1870 and 1880, the number of whites in Portland more than doubled, but the Chinese population grew by a stunning 265 percent.[12]

The demographic shifts in both cities reflected broader social transformations, and the uncertainty wrought by these changes signaled an opportunity for Baptist evangelicals. The antebellum home mission movement had been driven by geographic expansion and the desire to quell social and moral chaos too, so the attention paid to the post–Civil War South and the developing Far West is not surprising. What distinguished these postbellum projects from their predecessors, however, was their explicitly racial context. The fall of the slave-holding regime in the South and the Emancipation of some four million slaves was perhaps more dramatic than the relatively rapid influx of Chinese immigrants on the West Coast, but in both regions what had seemed to be settled racialized social systems underwent unprecedented challenges. African Americans and Chinese became unmistakable symbols of disorder.

What appeared most dangerous to Baptist evangelicals was both deeper and more specific than the grim prospect of a truncated peace in the South or an undisciplined settlement of the West. African American freedom and Chinese immigration (as well as both groups' claims to equality) directly challenged American traditions of white supremacy, disrupting the historic link between national identity and whiteness. After centuries of bonded African American labor, "black"—or "colored" or "Negro"—had become equated with "slave." In a society envisioned by its European American citizens as free, blacks embodied the very opposite of republican freedom and sat at the nadir of the social and racial hierarchy.[13] The white supremacist tradition that defined the American polity similarly affected Chinese in the United States. In particular, the Naturalization Law of 1790 had established the principle that only "free white persons" held the right to become citizens, and, while an 1870 amendment to the law granted the right to naturalization to people of African descent, the barrier to other nonwhites remained.[14] Moreover, allegations that immigrants were "cheap labor" or "coolies" invited comparisons to slavery—comparisons that fueled fears of a Chinese threat to the free labor system and, thus, to American freedom and citizenship.[15]

Historian George M. Fredrickson has characterized white supremacy as "the attitudes, ideologies, and policies associated with the rise of blatant forms of white or European dominance over 'nonwhite' populations."[16] Black Emancipation and Chinese settlement threatened to undo the historic dominance of white Americans. Baptist home missions occurred both in response to these new challenges and within local contexts where the specific struggles over race and belonging played out. In the South, a racial system rooted in slavery appeared to follow the Confederacy to the dustbin of history, and contests over what would take its place assumed center stage. On the Pacific Coast, European American settlers had dreamed of establishing new territories free not just from the complications of racial and slavery politics but from blacks in general. The arrival of Chinese, necessitated in part by the desire to develop the economy of the region, was a rude awakening, and what, then, to do with this alien and nonwhite population became central to late nineteenth-century evaluations of the Far West's social order.

*   *   *

As Henry Martin Tupper and the black churchmen assembled in the rented basement room to convene their first class, North Carolina wrestled with its slave-holding past. Historian Larry E. Tise contends that the state "clearly originated as a slaveholding colony," and, although it established its slave code "long after" neighboring Virginia and South Carolina, the Old North State had codified racial slavery by the mid-1700s. During the antebellum decades of the nineteenth century, the state legislature passed increasingly restrictive laws to control both slave and free black populations. In 1830, for example, the General Assembly made it illegal to teach slaves to read or write while making manumission more difficult. In 1835, free blacks in North Carolina lost the hallmark of citizenship when the state's constitutional convention adopted a provision that stripped them of the vote. These laws—and others like them— helped to create and protect a political, economic, and social hierarchy that circumscribed black political participation, expropriated the fruits of black labor, and relegated black residents to second-class status.[17]

When the Civil War ended, white North Carolinians moved almost immediately to try to limit the rights of freedpeople through a series of "Black Codes."[18] Most notably, the legislation sought to ensure a stable labor supply for white planters through statutes that restricted contract rights, made it easier for black children and apprentices to be bound out, and established labor penalties for vagrancy.[19] However, the significance of the Black Codes extended far beyond labor, attacking the foundations of black freedom. The laws, according to historian Raymond Gavins, "began to legalize the customary distance between blacks and whites."[20] An official with the Federal Bureau of Freedmen, Refugees, and Abandoned Lands (the Freedmen's Bureau) went so far as to claim, in congressional testimony, that white North Carolinians were trying to "re-establish slavery just as it was before." Colonel Eliphalet Whittlesey feared that "they would enact laws which would make the blacks virtually slaves."[21]

As Gavins has so persuasively argued, the white supremacist assumptions of the Black Codes were "grounded in everyday practice, including brute force" more than they were enshrined in law. White vigilantism and violence between white employers and black laborers sought to impose and maintain a racialized social and economic order. In just seventeen months, from August 1, 1865, to the end of 1866, the Freedmen's Bureau in North Carolina reported the murders of fifteen freedpeople. Whites also attempted to sustain the traditions of slavery with the lash. One Freedmen's Bureau report, for example, listed in bureaucratically stark fashion a litany of accusations made against whites: "Morrison Miller charged with whipping girl Hannah (colored). . . . Wm. Wallace charged with whipping Martha (colored)."[22]

But physical violence was only the most dramatic manifestation of white desires to reimpose a white supremacist social order. Acts of brutality went hand-in-glove with other types of coercive behavior. Most notably, reports of the expropriation of black labor appear even more ubiquitously than cases of violence. One weekly Freedmen's Bureau report from the late summer of 1865 read, "Henry, (colored) complains that his former master has driven him off without paying him anything whatever. . . . Sarah, (colored) complains that she has been working for a gentleman and that he has driven her off and will not pay her. . . . Emma, (colored) complains that the gentleman for whom she has been at work has driven her off and will not pay her."[23]

If, in 1865, the Baptist home mission in Raleigh evolved in a city grappling with its slavery past and the meaning of black freedom, then the mission in Portland, in 1874, developed in a state confronting a racial landscape made new not by a change in the status of a population already present but by the introduction of a racialized immigrant group. During Oregon's early history, first as a territory and then as a state, residents had made white supremacy a central feature of its statutory law. Unlike the South where the large black population made a policy of subordination and hierarchy the most practical strategy, Oregon's founders focused on excluding nonwhites from their territory. At the first meeting of white settlers to organize a provisional government in 1843, participants voted to prohibit slavery. The following year, the provisional government reiterated the prohibition and required slaveholders to emancipate their chattel. Lest the exclusionary intent of the law be confused with an egalitarian one, the new government added a measure compelling all blacks to leave the territory within three years. Those who failed to leave could be punished by whipping.[24]

Thirteen years later, in the late summer and early fall of 1857, delegates convened in the territorial capital of Salem to draft a constitution in preparation for statehood, and pursuing Oregon's whites-only status was among the highest priorities. Some of the most significant discussions sought to maintain the exclusionary precedent of the territory. Delegates, for example, agreed to include a ballot measure, to be voted on at the same time as the proposed constitution, which would exclude slavery *and* African Americans from the new state.[25]

Yet even in the mid- to late 1850s, Oregon's leading residents could not fail to recognize the emergence of another nonwhite group. The 1850 federal census had neglected to count Chinese in the territory, but the manuscript schedules of the 1860 census recorded a small but significant presence in the state.[26] Enumerators listed 22 Chinese residing in Portland and 113 in the southern county of Josephine. In the meantime, counties in northern California provided a glimpse of what Oregonians might expect in the future. In Sacramento County, for instance, between the 1852 state census and the 1860 federal census, the total population increased some 94 percent while the Chinese population alone grew over 115 percent.[27]

Although Portland and Oregon would experience a much more abrupt increase in Chinese immigration in the 1860s and 1870s, the constitutional representatives in Salem took note of this regional trend by weaving the Chinese into their discussions of race and rights. In some cases, the deliberations only implicitly referred to this population. In a debate over a section of the constitution that purported to provide equal property rights to "foreigners" who became residents, delegates offered two telling amendments. In the first, Matthew Deady, president of the convention and a justice on the territory's Supreme Court, urged that "white" be inserted before "foreigners," an unmistakable, if implicit, reference to immigrants from China. In the second, W. W. Bristow suggested an addition that would empower the legislature to regulate the entrance of people ineligible for U.S. citizenship. In light of the *Dred Scott* decision which had denied U.S. *and* state citizenship rights to all blacks when it was issued just a few months earlier and given the precedent of the 1790 Naturalization Act, which restricted citizenship to "free whites," this second measure was almost certainly directed at African Americans and non-European immigrants, specifically the Chinese. Both amendments passed.[28]

But perhaps most revealing was the debate over voting rights in which Chinese and blacks were explicitly discussed. The original draft of the constitution was based, in part, on the antiblack restrictions of the territorial charter and declared, "No negro or mulatto shall have the right [of] suffrage." At least two delegates had concerns. L. F. Grover, who chaired the convention's committee on a bill of rights and would later serve as the state's representative in Congress, proposed that the restriction be expanded and the word "Chinaman" be added. Judge Deady hoped to amend the section with even more sweeping language: "No persons, other than those of the pure white race, shall have the right of suffrage." Grover's simpler formulation won the day.[29]

Deady's unabashedly white supremacist amendment may have been offered in response to an earlier exchange with Delazon Smith, a Democratic journalist who soon would represent Oregon in the U.S. Senate. This debate had pivoted on a section of the constitution to provide for "free and equal elections." Deady revealed his obsession with keeping Oregon exclusively white by demanding a clarification: He wanted to know explicitly what "free" meant. Smith, in a pointed (and somewhat grumpy) reply that revealed conventional wisdom, remarked that "it did not mean Chinese or niggers. He thought the term sufficiently explicit."[30]

Local laws added to exclusionary constitutional provisions. City of Portland ordinances singled out Chinese washhouses for additional taxes and restricted the use of buildings as Chinese residences.[31] Women who engaged in prostitution—along with their male exploiters/employers—also became common targets for legal sanction.[32] By the time First Baptist Church began deliberations on the merits of a mission school, recently incorporated East Portland, just across the Willamette River, had passed a statute prohibiting the employment of Chinese laborers on its public works projects.[33] A few weeks later, Portland followed suit with a similar law. The city also added an ordinance that required 550 cubic feet of air per inhabitant in a dwelling. Although unstated in the legislation itself, the local newspaper made no mystery of who the target was. It bragged that the cubic air ordinance had "temporarily freed the city of several hundred of our superfluous Chinese population."[34]

Even with these state controls—legislative fiat and police enforcement—white supremacy in Oregon, as in North Carolina, was rooted in everyday practice and violence. Portland's newspaper, *The Oregonian*, recorded periodic assaults on Chinese businesses and individuals by whites beginning in the early 1860s. In the first such case reported, white youths vandalized a Chinese business in late summer 1861. By the mid-1860s, reports included a "brutal assault" of a Chinese man. These seemingly individual attacks take on broader significance when understood within a context of increasing anti-Chinese agitation and violence. Some of the first local movements began toward the end of the decade outside of Portland. To the south of the city, in Oswego, anti-Chinese agitators held a mass meeting in April 1867, and, a little farther south in Oregon City, a series of meetings and rallies occurred in early 1869. By the 1870s, groups such as the Anti-Chinese Protection Alliance and the Protectors of American Industry were appearing in Portland.[35]

Oregon's leaders were grappling with a new racial reality. To ensure white supremacy, the territorial government had found it expedient to exclude African Americans. Thirteen years later, the delegates to the state constitutional convention had to adjust to the recent influx of Chinese. Perhaps they would have preferred to emulate the exclusionary measures they had imposed on African Americans, but, with the rapid and growing influx of Chinese and the demands of regional economic development, such a prohibition seemed impossible. Instead, they moved to restrict severely the rights of this alien population. Supported by the Immigration Act of 1790, leading Oregonians made the nonwhite status of Chinese clear in their deliberations, associating these immigrants with blacks rather than European settlers. These statutes were official complements to extralegal activities and were meant to forestall any possibility of Chinese immigrant political membership in the state. In short, Oregon's leaders hoped to contain the perceived threat of the Chinese.

Significantly, even as white Oregonians moved to enact a white supremacist state that would circumscribe Chinese residents, North Carolinians faced a civil war that hinged on the role of slavery in the Union and then had to adjust to the revolutionary possibilities engendered by Emancipation. Although the restrictive Black Codes, passed during presidential Reconstruction, eventually were rolled back, they revealed the desires of the state's white elite to maintain tight controls over the newly freed black population. The presence of an interested federal government during Reconstruction might protect black North Carolinians from the most extreme forms of this white supremacist vision of the state, but proponents of "white men's republicanism," in the first years after the war, served notice that they, like white Oregonians, would seek to institute a social order premised on the containment of black rights.

It is important to remember, however, that the desires to reaffirm the white supremacist social and political order and to contain the threat of nonwhites in Oregon and North Carolina did not occur in a vacuum. Those who sought to reinstitute the rough contours of racial slavery in the South or who hoped to limit Chinese rights and prospects in the West also were responding to the actions of freedpeople and immigrants, respectively, who laid claim to a sense of civic belonging that would have been unimaginable just a few years earlier. The movements to restore white supremacy in the wake of Emancipation and in the face of increasing Chinese immigration occurred not only in response to general demographic and political changes but also in reaction to blacks and Chinese who acted on their own ideas about who might be included in the nation. As much as white Americans seemed to view Emancipation and immigration with trepidation, blacks and Chinese enthusiastically seized the opportunities they had helped to make.

In fact, black freedom was not so easily undone, and the immediate post-Emancipation years saw unprecedented assertions of black power that sought to bury the state's white supremacist tradition once and for all. A week before Tupper's arrival in North Carolina, black delegates from throughout the state concluded a five-day meeting at the city's African Methodist Church. From September 29, 1865, to October 3, the North Carolina Freedmen's Convention, in the words of the gathering's president, "met to deliberate in a Christian spirit upon the best interests of our people,—holding up before God and men as our motto, 'Equal rights before the law.'"[36] The statewide assembly emanated from numerous local mass meetings and was called in advance of the state's Constitutional Convention.[37] The appeal for local meetings had made it clear that the goal was to ensure the rights of black North Carolinians. It declared, "The time has arrived when we can strike one blow to secure those rights of Freedmen that have been so long withheld from us. . . . Let the entire colored population of North Carolina, assemble in their respective town-ships, and speak their views."[38]

The business discussed and resolutions settled upon during the Freedmen's Convention illuminated a spectrum of activities by which black North Carolinians hoped to define their freedom. Rev. John W. Hood, the gathering's presiding officer, emphasized political rights and equal protection under the law. "I think the best way to prepare a people for the exercise of their rights is to put them in practice of those rights. . . . We want three things,—first, the right to give evidence in the courts; second, the right to be represented in the jury-box; and third, the right to put votes in the ballot-box. These rights we want, these rights we contend for, and these rights, under God, we must ultimately have." Delegates also took up the issue of labor rights, imploring the Constitutional Convention to protect free-laboring blacks from unscrupulous employers who "withheld a just compensation, or have awarded such pay as would not support the laborer or his family." In fact, this was their "first and engrossing concern": "how we may provide shelter and an honorable subsistence for ourselves and families." Delegates also focused on education, debating at length the wisdom of calling for the establishment of black schools. In the end, a simple sentence encapsulated freedpeople's sense of aspiration and the central role education would play: "We desire education for our children, that they may be made useful in all relations of life." [39]

The formal political, social, and economic rights that delegates advocated during the Raleigh convention expressed an encompassing and radical vision of a new, post-Emancipation society. In Hood's demand for the vote and for the right to testify in court and to serve on juries, he signaled that freed-people maintained an understanding of Emancipation that necessitated full and equal citizenship years before the Fourteenth and Fifteenth Amendments enshrined that definition in the Constitution. In their desire to make the standard for labor rights hinge not just on protection from employers but on the ability to support a family with a living wage, freedpeople offered a vision of the new economic relations brought by Emancipation that differed from the liberal free labor ideology espoused by white northern Republicans.[40] In the simple but unyielding appeal for schooling, ex-slaves demonstrated their belief that education—especially public education—could be a key factor in permanently undoing the slave system and transforming the social and racial hierarchies that had supported it.[41]

But this cluster of rights constituted only part of a larger structure of freedom that black North Carolinians (and their counterparts throughout the South) conveyed in a myriad of ways. With a sense of hope rooted in what Robin D. G. Kelley has called "freedom dreams," black southerners emerged from slavery determined to strengthen and secure their families and communities.[42] They elaborated on institutions and practices created and fostered in bondage and conceived of new ones all pivoting on a desire for individual and community autonomy and independence.[43] From symbolic and behavioral acts, like adopting new names or assuming new modes of dress or refusing to yield the sidewalk to whites, to material practices and institution building, such as the claiming of plantation lands for subsistence cultivation or pooling resources in a mutual aid society or creating a community school, ex-slaves asserted a broad definition of freedom.[44]

Black participation in Raleigh's Baptist mission signified this expansive sense of freedom. Many of those who helped to establish the mission or who would become the mission's main constituency followed the broader demographic pattern of rural to urban migration evident throughout the post-Emancipation South. The precipitous increase in the city's black population that occurred as the Civil War came to a close—the very demographic trend that northern missionaries and white southerners viewed with such trepidation—was, indeed, symbolic of the age of Emancipation. In the fall of 1867, the editor of a local white newspaper could raise the specter of "the great mass of unbleached Americans" that had flocked to Raleigh for "nearly three years," but, for freedpeople, migration to the city was a crucial part of exercising their newly won freedom. Perhaps this is what the editor meant when he claimed that Raleigh was to blacks in the region as "Mecca is to followers of

Mohemet [*sic*]." Not only did mobility itself signify freedom, but migration specifically to a city also meant greater access to already established African American institutions, more economic opportunities, and the protection of the federal government.[45]

In Raleigh, ex-slaves found all of these things, and, in Henry Martin Tupper, a sympathetic northern missionary. These were essential resources as they attempted to establish autonomous institutions through which to craft their post-Emancipation lives. In particular, the creation of their own churches—what historian Daniel W. Stowell has called black religious reconstruction—signified a fundamental social and ideological break from the slave regime, and, in this endeavor, Raleigh's freedpeople must have welcomed the opportunity presented by Tupper's evangelical overture.[46] Before the war, the city's First Baptist Church had been one of many biracial congregations throughout the South where black Christians worshipped under the watchful eye of white ministers and white coreligionists. With the defeat of the Confederacy, however, a mass departure from these white-controlled institutions began in earnest, and First Baptist Church was no different. Even before Tupper's arrival, First Baptist's black members took the first steps toward founding their own institution by creating a Sunday school that met in the church's basement.[47]

The significance of this movement can hardly be overstated. Most obviously, the establishment of separate, autonomous churches enabled black southerners to practice a form of Christianity they had cultivated during slavery. Slaves of African descent had been exposed to Christianity since at least the eighteenth century, and attempts to proselytize them increased during the nineteenth century. Yet while white masters and their clergy hoped to inculcate blacks with a gospel of subservience, many slaves heard a message not of deference and subordination but of dignity, equality, and liberation.[48] Albert J. Raboteau perhaps best describes the role of Afro-Christianity in the slave quarters. "In the context of divine authority, the limited authority of any human was placed in perspective," writes Raboteau. "By obeying the commands of God, even when they contradicted the commands of men, slaves developed and treasured a sense of moral superiority and actual moral authority over their masters."[49]

Many of the discrepancies between the message preached by masters and the religion practiced by slaves can be attributed to the resonance between the emancipatory theology and egalitarian possibility bondmen and women found within, for instance, the Book of Exodus and their own social position and aspirations. However, it is equally significant that slave religion held a second, perhaps even stronger, current that also tempered or muted the creed of deference espoused by white southerners. As Raboteau and others have acknowledged, though perhaps to varying degrees, enslaved Christians adapted the religion of their masters not only to their social circumstances but to the traditions and beliefs transmitted through time and generations from Africa. As Sterling Stuckey has so passionately argued, "slaves brought intuitive, aesthetic, and other values to black Christianity, distinguishing it from white Christianity. . . . Religion was for many slaves . . . an African version of Christianity marked by an awareness of the limits of the religion of whites."[50]

The creation of separate houses of worship thus represented something more than an institutional break from the arrangements they had experienced under slavery. It signified a new era in which blacks could fulfill the prophecy of the scripture. To be sure, the institutional aspects of this black exodus from biracial congregations were important, too, for sanctified space could also be used for social gatherings and political meetings. Nevertheless, in those first years of freedom especially, the establishment of black churches created crucial spaces in which freedpeople could experience fellowship and congregation with each other and with God. Through this form of worship and community building, they reminded each other not only of the distance they had traveled in the short time since slavery but also of their determination—and the scriptural forecast—not to return. Establishing black churches provided autonomous physical spaces for ex-slaves' political, social, and religious lives and also a crucial way to exercise their post-Emancipation independence. Indeed, leaving white-controlled churches symbolized God's deliverance of his chosen people.[51]

Yet financial hardship often proved to be a formidable obstacle to fully realizing this sacred and secular freedom. That Raleigh's embryonic black Baptist church's Sunday school met in the basement of white-run First Baptist Church was not at all unusual. Historian William Montgomery notes that "for most black congregations . . . obtaining a place to conduct their church services was a struggle. Before they could obtain suitable buildings, many of them were forced to work out borrowing or sharing arrangements with other congregations."[52] In locales like Raleigh, where the federal government had established a presence or where northern evangelicals had sent missionaries, freedpeople who, to paraphrase Eric Foner, left bondage with little more than their freedom, could find allies and aid from northern whites—an important alternative to obtaining help from former masters.[53] Indeed, in Raleigh, not only did Tupper's offer to lead a religious education class and establish a mission indicate the promise of a church, but he demonstrated his ability to gain access to federal aid by prevailing upon the Freedmen's Bureau to help him lease the space for his class.[54]

Tupper's mission had a broader aim than providing religious training to ex-slaves. From the beginning, the Baptist missionary, with the support from the ABHMS Executive Board, had believed education to be a central component of his project in Raleigh. In February 1866, for example, the Executive Board's corresponding secretary, J. S. Backus, endorsed Tupper's desire to "teach the colored brethren self-reliance" and intimated that the missionary's work would entail worldly matters as well as spiritual ones.[55] The response of black North Carolinians to this educational mission was swift and enthusiastic, echoing broader trends throughout the South.[56] Within three months of the first class meeting in December 1865, a Freedmen's Bureau official reported, "There is also a night-school for grown colored people who are compelled to work during the day. It is held three evenings each week, and is always crowded. It is astonishing how eager these negroes are to learn to read and write. . . . The building in which the freedmen's school is held is open every evening, excepting school nights for prayer meetings. I strolled on to one of these meetings the other evening and went in. The room was well crowded with men and women."[57]

In time, the divergent goals of black autonomy and missionary tutelage would cause overt discord in the mission, but, at the outset of Emancipation at least, the tensions between African American desires for a particular kind of freedom and white evangelical uplift took a backseat to a temporary accord in which missionaries provided necessary resources and encouragement and ex-slaves brought a keen interest and a hopeful trust. Historian Daniel Stowell sums up freedpeople's understanding of their Reconstruction-era relationship with missionaries succinctly: Freedpeople, writes Stowell, "offered their membership to black and white northern denominations in return for houses of worship and educational opportunities."[58]

But Stowell's concision disguises an important aspect of this relationship. To be sure, freedpeople met the evangelical overture cautiously; they accepted neither naively nor uncritically all that northern missionaries taught or proclaimed. But neither were all ex-slaves wholly instrumental in their choosing to accept missionary aid. To attribute black participation in projects sponsored by northern missionaries merely to a calculated decision to keep evangelical teachings at an arm's length in the quest for limited resources—a kind of quid pro quo as Stowell describes it—underestimates black optimism during this period. In the immediate wake of the Civil War, freedpeople maintained a faith in the good intentions of northern evangelicals—a faith buoyed by an assurance and resolve that had come with the triumph of Emancipation and sustained by emerging black communities.

In Raleigh, new African American neighborhoods began to appear as ex-slaves flocked to the city and its environs, and the relationship between these settlements and missions was symbiotic. Mission institutions, resources, and participants were part of the larger web of formal and informal relationships that constituted developing black communities in the post-Emancipation era. Two of the earliest neighborhoods, Oberlin and Method, evolved outside the city limits, but passages from Tupper's diary suggest that he traveled widely in his ministry, especially before the mission school began, visiting plantations and refugee encampments, including Camp Holmes, near the Seaboard Railroad Depot and not far from Oberlin. In time, community members would name a street in the neighborhood—Roberts Lane—for the Rev. N. F. Roberts, one of the early black leaders at Shaw.[59] In the city itself, East Raleigh and South Park would develop near Shaw University, influenced by their proximity to the educational institution and to the economic and governmental centers of the city.[60]

Even before these settlements solidified into recognizable neighborhoods and in the midst of the social fluidity of the immediate postwar period, nascent community organizations began to germinate in spaces where ex-slaves congregated and where they had the protection of the federal government. Union commanders designated the Guion Hotel, located just across the street from the state capitol and once a favorite lodging for state legislators and visiting entertainers, as the quarters for freedpeople who poured into the city.[61] Federal control and the proximity of potential students made it a popular spot for former slaves and missionaries to begin initiatives. The Baptist mission was only one such project to meet there; a New England Freedmen's Commission missionary named Leland established the Lincoln Day School and the Lincoln Sunday School in the same building in 1865 as well.[62] In a similar vein, just a few blocks north of the Guion, blacks congregated at the Freedmen's Bureau, looking for aid and protection, and it was near there that they established the Miles School in 1868. Rev. W. M. Warrick, who would later affiliate with the Baptist mission, soon became the school's leader.[63] Earlier that year, St. Augustine's Normal School, a mission of the Episcopal Freedman's Commission, had opened at the Union barracks at Camp Russell in the southern part of the city; later that year St. Augustine's would acquire a large tract of land near the developing black neighborhood of Hungry Neck (later two neighborhoods called "College Park" and "Idlewild").[64] Not only would the Baptist mission become an integral feature of this evolving network in black Raleigh, but the communities to which it was connected provided an immeasurable system of support to African Americans as they encountered the missionary project of uplift. Emancipation—and all of its psychological, social, and institutional manifestations—armed freedpeople with the confidence to hope for a more equitable relationship with Tupper and his ilk.

Of course, the presence of black troops in the city added an extra degree of support. Armed and battle-seasoned African Americans not only served notice to recalcitrant or uncooperative whites, they also modeled a kind of confidence that could only be expressed by people who had literally fought for their freedom. The Twenty-seventh Colored Regiment, for example, was stationed in Raleigh during the first years after the war, and soldiers from the regiment even contributed money to the Baptist mission.[65] Originally formed in Ohio, the Twenty-seventh had seen action in Virginia as part of the Army of the Potomac and took part in the assault on Fort Fisher, North Carolina, in January 1865 before becoming part of General William T. Sherman's "Campaign for the Carolinas."[66] Although consisting of free blacks from Ohio, the soldiers of the Twenty-seventh had experienced both the crucible of combat and the humiliations of unequal treatment in the Army, experiences that had made them acutely aware of the great import of postwar projects like the Baptist mission. The introduction of black troops in the Union cause, in conjunction with the Emancipation Proclamation, had irrevocably altered the character of the Civil War, making it nothing less than a crusade for liberation.[67] Determined to fight for freedom, African American soldiers demonstrated their equality through deed, and, in many cases, the decision to enlist was a straightforward claim on citizenship rights and black equality.[68] Once engaged in battle, black troops witnessed the final parity of death as they killed white men and white men killed them. At once horrific and empowering, the experience of combat proved that, in death, white "masters" and black "slaves" were equally diminished.

At the same time, African American soldiers recast themselves as liberators. The soldiers of the Twenty-seventh confronted in battle men who not only believed that blacks were inferior but, in many cases, acted upon that belief by holding slaves and supporting (indeed, fighting for) a system that would perpetuate enslavement. Combat provided black troops with the opportunity to challenge such assumptions directly, and in this challenge they galvanized a consciousness that would serve as a basis for equal citizenship rights in the postwar period.[69] Moreover, their unequal treatment in the military—lower pay, harsh and capricious treatment, the relative absence of black officers—demonstrated to African American soldiers that achieving some rights resulted not in equality but in second-class status. Having won the war to end slavery, they now made their stand in the coming struggle for equality, and for many soldiers the establishment of churches, schools, and missions must have seemed like essential weapons in the battle.

The presence of these liberators in Raleigh undoubtedly lent both moral and practical support to blacks who engaged with northern missionaries like Tupper. Believing that the Civil War and Emancipation signaled the Jubilee—the time, according to the Bible, when "ye shall return every man unto his possession, and ye shall return every man unto his family"—freedpeople met the offer of missionary aid with a confidence borne of experience and hope.[70] They acted as though true freedom—autonomy in individual, institutional, and community forms—lay within grasp. Like a rung on the ladder leading to "the house of God" and the "gate of heaven" dreamed about by Jacob in the Book of Genesis, for former slaves in and around Raleigh, the Baptist mission was one of a number of measures that would lead to (and constituted) the deliverance from slavery.[71] Although perhaps a bit wary of Henry Martin Tupper's evangelical overture, the ex-slaves who engaged with the Baptist mission in Raleigh nonetheless approached the project with faith in the emancipatory power of their religion and of education, and this faith was buttressed by the very material presence of black soldiers, a supportive federal government, and their own emerging communities.

The actions of Chinese immigrants during the late nineteenth century also threatened to disrupt the equation between national belonging and whiteness. Their entrance into the United States and, especially, their settlement challenged traditional notions of who might be considered an American, encouraging Oregon's founders to react so forcefully. In fact, legally, Chinese were clearly beyond the bounds of the nation. After all, the Naturalization Act of 1790 still applied to them, and even the question of the citizenship status of people of Chinese descent born in the United States would not be settled until the Supreme Court case *Wong Kim Ark v. United States* in 1898. But even with these federal boundaries, the measures taken by white Oregonians to restrict the Chinese suggests that they were responding to something more than the mere arrival of an alien population. Rather, white Oregonians—and white Portlanders, in particular—appear to have been reacting to a new social and racial reality in Portland that, as was the case in Raleigh, their panicky tones masked (though perhaps barely): the Chinese were establishing settlements.

Indeed, Chinese developed a dense network of institutions and relationships in the city. This evolving community provided critical support to Chinese—whether immigrants or migrants, settlers or sojourners—who worked to fulfill their hopes of economic improvement or looked for succor to assuage the pain of disappointment. As they founded social and cultural organizations and business establishments, as well as developing other less formal relationships, Chinese carved out space for themselves in an environment that was often overtly hostile. In so doing, they began the slow and uneven process of staking a claim for belonging in the rapidly growing Pacific Coast city.

The extant historical record provides little direct testimony as to the specific aspirations and motivations of those who traveled to Oregon from China during this period, but a few general deductions are possible given the evidence from other places. The 1848 discovery of gold in northern California first attracted Chinese migrants who called the region Gam Saak, or Gold Mountain. Those who left Guangdong for the United States during the nineteenth century were overwhelmingly male, and most came as laborers. The gold rush not only created opportunities in mining—either on independent claims or as laborers in bigger operations—but also produced jobs throughout the economy. As the economy in California and along the Pacific Coast expanded, so did chances for employment in agriculture, on railroads, and as industrial service workers in fish canning, laundries, and other enterprises. Generally, the Chinese were restricted to low-wage, unskilled labor. Leaving their families and villages to pursue opportunities abroad, most of these men (and a few women) intended to return home after earning enough money to help their families and purchase a return steamship ticket.

This migratory current was part of a larger stream of people from southern China. By the mid-nineteenth century, people from the region had been traveling throughout Asia for centuries, settling in places such as Thailand and the Philippines in large numbers. The outflow quickened with western imperial intervention and internal disruptions. The British Opium Wars (1839–43 and 1856–60), peasant uprisings like the Taiping Rebellion (1851–55) and the Red Turban Rebellion (1854–64), and violent civil strife between the Punti and the Hakkas over the fertile land in the Pearl River Delta all devastated Guangdong and nearby provinces. These military and political troubles took their toll on the local economy, but after the Treaty of Nanjing, which ended the first Opium War, hard times were compounded by heavy taxes levied by the Qing government to pay war indemnities. In addition, the Treaty of Nanjing and the subsequent "unequal" treaties with western powers meant a loss of government control over domestic commerce and hastened the disintegration of the traditional economy. Areas of southern China that had been engaged in commercial textile production, for example, suffered greatly after European and American textiles flooded China in the wake of the treaties. The effects of this dislocation rippled throughout the economy and were felt by warehousemen, compradors, and porters in Guandong. These economic and political circumstances created a landless and unemployed population ready to take a chance on long-distance migration.[72]

These dislocations, combined with advances in transportation technology (notably the steamship), encouraged Chinese emigrants to seek their lot at farther and farther distances. Although the point of origin was not new, the destinations were. Between 1850 and 1900 an estimated two and half million people left China for Hawaii, Canada, Australia, New Zealand, Southeast Asia, the West Indies, South America, and Africa, as well as the United States.[73] These migrants were looking for economic opportunity and hoping to better their lot and the lot of their families in China.

In this quest to improve their lives, Chinese were drawn to Oregon in increasing numbers throughout the mid- to late nineteenth century. The 1852 discovery of gold in the Rogue and Umpqua Valleys brought Chinese—and others—to the southwestern part of the territory (Oregon would be admitted to the Union in 1859). In 1870, construction in Kalama, Washington Territory, began on the Northern Pacific Railroad, bringing Chinese laborers, who were actively recruited by railroad managers, to the Pacific Northwest. In 1860, there were at least 425 Chinese in Oregon, and, within ten years, the number grew to 3,330. By 1880, there would be 9,510 Chinese living in the state.[74] Although many settled in mining, agricultural, and coastal fishing and canning regions, Chinese soon began moving to Portland to pursue employment in the service industries and as laborers. As early as December 1851, the city's newspaper contained an advertisement for a boarding house on Second Street run by "Mr. Tong Sung from China" with "first rate China cooks."[75] The earliest enumeration of Chinese in the manuscript schedules of the federal census occurred in 1860 when 22 were listed; five years later, the *Oregonian* reported a population of about 200; and by 1870, there were some 720 Chinese counted in the city.[76]

Like whites who worried about the influx of blacks into southern cities in the months and years following the Civil War and in tones that echoed the concerns of whites like A. W. Loomis in San Francisco, some observers were uneasy about the influx of Chinese in Oregon.[77] Tracking the *Oregonian* provides some insight into this persistent and pervasive angst. In March 1857, the newspaper noted that these "Children of the Sun" were beginning to come to Portland.[78] As anti-Chinese movements gained strength in other parts of the Pacific Coast, the *Oregonian* warned that the "celestials" would be looking to Oregon for refuge; by July 1864, it reported that the Chinese were arriving in the city in great numbers.[79] In 1866, the *Oregonian* declared the city to be overcrowded by Chinese, and an editorial claimed, "Portland has got the Chinaman disease, in a little worse form than most of California."[80] In the meantime, from items about brothels and "bawdy houses" to fistfights and gang wars, Chinese illegal activities became regular features of the newspaper's coverage.[81]

The cautionary tone of this reportage reveals the anxiety of white Oregonians at the new influx of immigrants into Portland; it also hints at the settlement of Chinese in the city. Indeed, throughout the 1860s, as their population rapidly grew, Chinese began establishing an institutional and community life in the city. By the early to mid-1870s, when local Baptists began planning a mission school, Portland was home to a well-established, urban Chinese quarter while a second community was evolving in a less developed part of the town.[82] In the years leading to the establishment of the mission school, white Portlanders concerned themselves mostly with the activities of those immigrants who congregated in the urban district—a flood-prone area along Front Street on the Willamette River, extending toward Third Street and bordered by C and Clay Streets.[83] The December 1866 editorial from the *Oregonian* worried that "at present the greater part of the Chinese population of Portland is located in the very heart of the city."[84] But both urban and rural enclaves attest to a spirit of settlement and community building among the Chinese population in the city.

Within the urban Chinatown, discrimination toward tenants and businesses played a large role in structuring the spatial dimensions, economic life, and social landscape of the community. Marie Rose Wong has documented a number of occasions on which white landlords were unwilling to rent to prospective Chinese tenants, but she also notes that the willingness of others to rent "undercut any hope for an ordinance restricting [Chinese] residential rights.[85] In fact, the budding Chinatown also provided a measure of insulation from the dominant white society. To be sure, interracial contact was hard to avoid. Most laborers in Portland worked for non-Chinese employers, including the Oregon Iron Company, the Oregon Central Railroad, and the city, and many Chinese-owned businesses, such as laundries and, perhaps, brothels, catered to a white clientele.[86]

Nevertheless, within this part of the city Chinese created places where they could enjoy each other's company, and vestiges of a community appeared early. In addition to Tong Sung's boardinghouse, by the end of 1865, merchants had opened tea stores and restaurants, and at least one Chinese doctor hung out his shingle.[87] And in January 1865, the *Oregonian* made reference to the first lunar new year celebration in the city—a significant public event that suggests an active and public Chinese community.[88] In 1867, residents built a temple, also referred to as a "joss house," on Alder Street to fulfill spiritual needs.[89] To cater to more worldly pursuits—and to the mostly male population—brothels were early and visible establishments in Chinatown.[90] And after November 1872, a theater became one of the most popular attractions for entertainment.[91] Grocers and merchants not only supplied familiar herbs, foods, books, and other goods, they also provided a place where men could visit with each other, tell stories, play games, and drink tea, becoming, as historian Ronald Takaki has argued, a "uniquely *Chinese-American* social institution" that was "a center of life in the Chinese community."[92] Portland boasted at least one such merchant, Tong Duck Chung and Company, before 1870; within a few years, there would be at least two more stores, the Wing On Company and the Wing Sing Company.[93]

Beyond this world of Chinese-owned and Chinese-supported businesses, migrants and settlers created a web of associations and secret societies. Although family-based groups were important forms of social organization in places like San Francisco and Sacramento, historian Hugh Clark has surmised that the "lack of homogeneity among Chinese surnames" in Portland suggests that residents relied on a broader grouping—the district association.[94] Lee Bessie Ying, in an unpublished dissertation from 1938, noted the existence of two district associations—the Hai-yen and Ning-yang Associations—but she did not indicate when these groups were established.[95] By the mid-1880s, Portland's district associations would come together under a branch of the Chinese Consolidated Benevolent Associations (CCBA) known locally as the Jung Wah Association (the CCBA in most places was also known by a modified version of its organizational antecedent's name, the Chinese Six Companies).[96]

Consisting of people who hailed from the same district in China, these, according to historian Sucheng Chan, "were the most important [social organizations] in American Chinatowns."[97] But common locality was only part of what bound members together. They also shared dialects, often settled in the same neighborhoods or towns, and tended to follow each other into the same occupations. District associations functioned as far-reaching mutual aid societies. Members met newcomers at the dock and offered them a place to stay; provided supplies to aspiring miners, laborers, and farmers; sent money and mail back home; maintained temples and cemeteries; and transported remains of deceased migrants to be buried in their home villages. "In short," summarizes Chan, "these organizations performed all the crucial functions that in China were carried out by extended families, clans, or lineages."[98] The formation of the CCBA, in large part a response to growing anti-Chinese hostility and the recent passage of the 1882 Exclusion Act, enabled ordinary people to call on the combined strength of the district associations to better their position. Indeed, the CCBA would be responsible for hiring lawyers to fight anti-Chinese legislation.[99]

In Oregon, the local Jung Wah Assocation played this role vigorously, but its position within the broader Chinese community was complicated by its function as a labor contractor, negotiating between (and making money from) workers and their largest potential employer, the Northern Pacific Railroad.[100] In fact, while district associations may have advocated on behalf of ordinary folk, they were controlled by merchants who "occupied almost all the available positions of leadership."[101] The *Oregonian* seemed to confirm the less-than-equal relationship between district association leadership and laborers in 1876 when it reported that workers had "emancipated themselves from the bondage of the [Chinese] Six companies."[102] The newspaper's formulation clearly hoped to underscore the effect of American "freedom" on the Chinese workers. Nonetheless, the core idea remains that, although cast as the representative leaders of local Chinese, this merchant elite often acted in their own interests, not those of laborers.

For laboring Chinese in the United States, tongs often provided an associational life that seemed less hierarchical than organizations run by merchants. Whereas district associations may have stressed deference, control, and respectability, tongs were secret societies that emphasized brotherhood and that had roots in antiestablishment agitation. Originating as antigovernment groups in Guangdong, tongs in America "referred to fraternal organizations that bound its [*sic*] members together through secret initiation rites and sworn brotherhood," and they often appealed to migrants who could not claim—or did not want to claim—membership in a district- or clan-based association.[103] Largely because tongs in Portland were intimately connected to illicit activity in the city—especially gambling and prostitution—and because their conflicts sometimes turned violent, they were the most visible variety of Chinese institutional life. But the sensationalism of news coverage should not obscure the fact that, in the first two decades of Chinese settlement in Portland, tongs constituted a vital social formation.

The Chinese Mission School, as it got under way in the city's Good Templar's Building on November 13, 1874, held the potential to join the tongs, the district associations, and the constellation of other social and commercial endeavors that made up the Chinese community in Portland. The school would come to serve a number of functions, but, at the outset at least, participants seem to have been motivated by a few key factors. In a region where hostility to the Chinese was enshrined in law and part of the fabric of everyday life, they found an opportunity for education, a chance for fellowship with other Chinese, the possibility of making white allies, and the promise of respectability, perhaps even social and spiritual (if not legal) equality.

The proselytizing strategy of the mission provides some insight into the desire for education. After considering establishing a purely Chinese-language ministry that would focus on spiritual conversion alone, First Baptist Church's Committee on Chinese Missions, in consultation with missionaries Dong Gong and E. Z. Simmons, "decided to teach English five evenings each week, Thursday evening to be occupied in religious training by the Missionary."[104] The pastor of First Baptist acknowledged the desire for education when he claimed, "The way to reach the Chinese is to bait the hook with the English Alphabet."[105]

To be sure, evangelical uplift required missionary tutelage and supervision, and the school itself, particularly at the outset, relied upon the patronage of white residents for its existence. These factors made the mission a less than ideal place to establish a Chinese-only community institution. However, mission participants initiated meetings that circumvented white surveillance by continuing to convene regularly when the school—and its administrators— went on holiday.[106] And within these meetings, the evangelical message of the equality of souls undoubtedly provided a welcome antidote to the hierarchy of traditional Chinese social organizations, such as district and clan associations.[107]

Moreover, many Chinese would have found the mission to be under much less scrutiny than other community spaces. Indeed, given the growing and seemingly insatiable fascination with the Chinese enclave in the city, it was almost impossible—whether in the mission or out of it—to escape the gaze of white Oregonians. Illicit and semilegal establishments like brothels and tongs consistently attracted the attention of the police. And although the legality of joss houses, restaurants, and the theater was not in question, white authorities also kept an eye on them. These were singularly Chinese spaces in America, and that position, ironically, placed them under enormous scrutiny. "Heathen temples" and joss houses appear repeatedly throughout legislative testimony on the effects of immigration and in ethnographic accounts of Chinatowns. And although large-scale tourism in urban immigrant quarters would not gain great popularity until early in the next century, journalists and city officials often toured these enclaves—usually with white police officers as guides—and published their observations as titillating exposés of a mysterious subculture. Just because the mission school operated under the direct supervision of white Portlanders did not necessarily disqualify it from becoming a foundational institution for the building of Chinese community in the city, for other ethnic establishments and organizations also were subjected to surveillance.[108]

In fact, it was the cozy relationship between the city's white elite and the mission school that may have made it particularly attractive to local Chinese. Mission participants could count many of Portland's most influential citizens as supporters of their school, including two former mayors and a U.S. Senator. The power of these allies could prove invaluable locally and a beyond. White members of First Baptist Church kept an eye out for their Chinese coreligionists as they conducted their business, and, on at least one occasion after the 1892 Geary Act became law, they provided affidavits for Chinese migrants seeking to prove prior residency in the United States upon reentry.[109]

Perhaps as important to Chinese participants as powerful white allies was the opportunity to achieve upward social mobility, respectability, and, perhaps even social equality in the dominant society. An early glimpse at this possibility could be seen when, in a remarkable item, the *Oregonian* reported on the death of Wang Ho, who had become a member of First Baptist. Although not given to referring to the city's Chinese in positive terms, the newspaper nonetheless claimed that Wang Ho had "lived and died a most exemplary Christian."[110]

Seid Back also found a measure of respectability through his association with the mission. Born in China in 1852, Back came to Portland at eighteen and attended the Baptist school where "he embraced Christianity and became an earnest though not fanatical teacher of its doctrines."[111] One late nineteenth-century publication by a regional booster describes Back as an Asian Horatio Alger, coming to this country "penniless" and becoming "the representative of his race in the Northwest, and in private life he can be said to be as prominent as any Chinaman in the United States."[112] In this account, his "constant progress" was based not only on his mastery of English but on his careful study of "the customs and politics of this country," especially Christianity.[113] Yet Back's conversion and his broader social transformation symbolized by his success as a merchant and labor contractor seems to have blinded the authors to other, less admirable aspects of his life, which went unmentioned, including a past conviction for which he was jailed and, in the very same year that his admirers published their account of him, an indictment for opium smuggling.[114]

Perhaps no other individual in Portland symbolized the promise of evangelical Christianity—and the Baptist mission school—more than Dong Gong. Dong's position as the lead missionary in the Portland school did not come without struggles, but he was a living and accessible model of achievement and respectability. Dong's ordination in June 1875 drew evangelical leaders from throughout Oregon and northern California.[115] Earlier that month, he had been chosen to help represent First Baptist Church at the Willamette Baptist Association meeting.[116] Of course, despite these achievements, neither Dong Gong nor Seid Back nor Wang Ho achieved anything like legal or political equality. Nonetheless, for aspiring immigrants, their association with the Chinese Mission School may have illuminated a potential path not just for upward mobility but for a way to earn a modicum of respectability among white Portlanders.

Portland's Chinese established a rich, complex, and dynamic community life. Even glimpsed through hostile or unwelcoming testimony, they had begun to establish key institutions and networks. In the urban settlement on the waterfront of the Willamette, they launched businesses that catered to the needs of their fellow immigrants; they formed mutual aid organizations; they created spaces for social and cultural activities; and, with the help of local Baptists, a number of Chinese undertook to build yet another community institution, the Chinese Mission School. As part of the array of institutions in Chinese Portland, the mission promised the opportunity for social mobility both in China and in the United States and the chance to form lasting bonds of fellowship with each other and with local whites.

On the journey from Massachusetts to North Carolina, Henry Martin Tupper and his wife traveled on the Seaboard Railroad from Portsmouth, Virginia, to

Raleigh. The railroad had been destroyed during the Civil War, and the newly repaired tracks that carried the Tuppers to their destination were part of an early attempt to restore the infrastructure of the vanquished South. Though his efforts were linked to this work to rebuild the physical South and the endeavor to reconstitute the region's government, Tupper maintained a different understanding of "reconstruction." For Tupper, reconstruction began neither with hammer and nail nor with the ballot but with the Bible and with pen and paper. For the northern missionary, the process of reconstruction commenced with his first class in the basement room of the Guion Hotel on the first day of December 1865.

In fact, the building itself was as much a symbol of the era as was the rebuilt Seaboard Line. Designated by Union commanders as a headquarters for blacks who had flocked to the city but who had no place to live, the hotel contained the hopes of freedpeople on the cusp of a new life and the fears of whites—northern and southern—who fretted about the disarray precipitated by Emancipation.[117] The meeting that took place there was, for the missionary Tupper, the first step in bringing about a type of order—to counteract the deleterious effects of slavery and rebellion.[118] For the black churchmen, the meeting meant freedom; it meant access to resources, an education, and a place to worship. It was a meeting and a space that would have been, if not inconceivable, then highly unusual just a short time earlier, but on that early winter day in 1865, out of the political and physical ruin of the Civil War, black mission participants and white missionaries began their reconstruction projects in earnest—together.

Some nine years later, Dong Gong and E. Z. Simmons also arrived in a city suffering from a catastrophic event, and they too undertook what began as a cooperative project—this time among Baptist missionaries, local congregants and elites, and Chinese migrants. To be sure, nothing could or would compare to the immense devastation wrought by the Civil War. Nevertheless, on August 2, 1873, a fire, started by an arsonist's match, decimated twenty city blocks in Portland. The city had experienced fires before; just nine months earlier two blocks had been consumed by flames. But the August 1873 conflagration was, by far, the largest ever to devastate the city.[119]

In the fire's aftermath, Portland's leaders engaged in a process of "reconstruction" not dissimilar from the one undertaken on a national and regional scale in the South. In part, this process entailed rebuilding the physical structures of the city. However, fires represent more than elemental catastrophes that endanger the material vestiges of urban life; late nineteenth-century urban fires were also forces that could destroy the barriers fortifying social structures and unleash instability and chaos.[120] Like in the South, where the Civil War and the ensuing end of slavery made the political, social, and economic role of African Americans a focal point, in Portland, the 1873 fire brought the already conspicuous and growing Chinese population front and center. Despite denials by the anti-immigrant People's Protective Alliance, authorities blamed anti-Chinese agitators, thus exposing a growing hostility that imperiled social stability. The fire itself emanated from the urban Chinatown and swept through the area, seemingly poised to efface the unofficial boundaries that separated Chinese residences and businesses from other parts of the city. Although it never ventured much past the ethnic enclave, the blaze nevertheless was a forceful reminder of the fragility of social relations.

The Chinese Mission School would not open at the Good Templar's Building until November 13, 1874, more than a year after the fire, but planning for the endeavor began in the immediate aftermath. When the first class finally convened, it embodied the hopes and faith of Chinese participants, local white sponsors, and Baptist missionaries. Even as the August 1873 blaze had underscored how vulnerable they remained to white hostility, the city's Chinese who ventured into the classroom fifteen months later demonstrated not only a desire for white protection and patronage but also a faith in the possibility of intra-ethnic congregation, social mobility, and cross-racial fellowship. For city and church leaders like Deacon Douglas W. Williams, who was among the first to propose the mission, the fire's devastating effect on social stability was obvious and direct. Williams's wholesale grocery business stood within the unofficial boundaries of Chinatown and was likely consumed in the conflagration. First Baptist Church itself lay just a block away from the urban enclave, and the flames stopped just two or three blocks short of it. For Williams, especially, the dangers of anti-Chinese hostility, already brewing in Portland and bubbling over in California, were manifest, and, the conflagration hinted at the possibility that the Chinese, like the fire itself, might not be contained by the streets bordering the enclave. For those city and church leaders, the opening of the school offered the chance to demonstrate their command over the city, offering a civilizing mission to control the heathen Chinese while removing the claims of otherness that spurred white violence and arson. And for Baptist missionaries like Dong Gong and E. Z. Simmons the fire brought evangelical opportunity. They could exercise their faith in the redeeming power of Scripture and model a religion that emphasized brotherhood and acceptance more than exclusion while transforming America into a Christian nation.

The disorder that emboldened evangelicals to take action among the Chinese in Portland echoed the larger disarray they perceived in the post–Civil War South. But these "grand and awful times" had more in common than a general similarity of circumstance. Each was a regional variation on a theme. In each case, Baptist evangelicals were responding to the anxieties and disruptions caused by a nation growing into its continental ambitions. Beginning in the mid-1860s, the nation seemed to be realizing its "manifest destiny," reuniting North and South after a bloody and divisive war and linking East and West Coasts with not one but two transcontinental railroads. Yet perhaps ironically, while reunion and expansion signaled the geographic achievement of a nation that stretched east and west, north and south across the continent, the Civil War and the development of the Pacific Coast also created circumstances that threw into question who might constitute the polity of this nation.

Even as Appomattox seemed to indicate that North and South would be bound together and as the formation of the Union Pacific Railroad Corporation and the joining of tracks at Promontory Point, Utah, signified the linking of East and West, the polity of this transcontinental nation threatened a different kind of fragmentation.[121] In its *Dred Scott* decision in 1857, the Supreme Court had denied that any blacks, whether slave or free, were citizens while, under the terms of the 1790 Naturalization Act, Chinese were considered aliens ineligible for citizenship. Both law and tradition placed African Americans and Chinese beyond the bounds of the nation. Yet the end of slavery, along with the political reintegration of the South, had made questions of citizenship and belonging, loyalty and race, central to the ensuing era of Reconstruction.[122] At the same time, the need for labor to exploit the resources and grow the economy of the Far West had attracted Chinese, among others, and, no matter what the intent or desire of this population, enough settled in the territories and states of the region—or perhaps more accurately enough settled enough—to call into question traditional considerations that equated whiteness and national belonging.

In the post–Civil War era, the growing federal government began trying to adjudicate these questions of national membership. In particular, with its provisions for citizenship and equal protection under the law, the Fourteenth Amendment, as it pertained not only to the freedpeople but also to the Chinese, would prove to be a pivotal document. But Emancipation and the migrations and demographic changes of the mid- to late 1860s and 1870s challenged these notions not just of formal citizenship rights but of broader forms of belonging, and the on-the-ground interactions between people, mediated by local and state authorities, were the vital proving ground of post–Civil War and immigration-era social relations where repression and possibility, reaction and radicalism, vied with one another. Indeed, it was through these local, everyday social relations that difference—particularly racial difference—was articulated and rearticulated.[123]

Through restrictive measures, such as the Black Codes and endemic extralegal violence, white North Carolinians and their southern compatriots attempted to reinscribe the social, political, and economic relations that had been so successful during the antebellum era in defining black as slave and white as free. Similarly, Oregon's founders hoped to define their territory as "free" first by excluding blacks and then, as Oregon became a state, by severely circumscribing the rights of both blacks and Chinese. These local assertions of white privilege in North Carolina and Oregon seemed not at all at odds with the tradition of white supremacy that defined American national belonging prior to the 1860s. Indeed, one was an attempt to reestablish the system of slavery that had organized life in the South for more than three centuries while the other was a logical extension of the nation's original naturalization law.

Yet these attempts by local elites to affirm the white supremacist tradition of national membership, while consistent with earlier alignments of national identity and race, took on special significance during this period. Emancipation in the South and Chinese settlement in the West challenged this earlier formulation in unprecedented ways even as the regional articulations of a white supremacist national identity attempted to dampen, perhaps to extinguish, alternate visions of belonging and race evidenced by the actions and aspirations of freedpeople and Chinese. Before Emancipation, economic, political, and legal systems, informal social relations, and disciplinary violence linked all blacks to slavery, reading them out of the national polity as objects—property—rather than subjects. Even free people of color, while not slaves, nonetheless occupied, at best, an ambiguous position, painted by the broad brush of blackness as "others"—"non-Americans in the minds of most American people and in the policies of the government," according to James Oliver Horton.[124] Similarly, both by the legal terms of the 1790 Naturalization Act and by the cultural terms that conceived of them as not "free," Chinese not only were ineligible for citizenship but were also incapable of such a privilege. Indeed, a key element of the notion of Chinese as wholly distinctive from the national polity was the idea, alternately reassuring and menacing to many white Americans, that they were merely sojourners in the United States who had little intention of settling permanently.

In their quest to define freedom on their own terms, however, four mil-lion ex-slaves offered an understanding of blackness that, while rooted in the experience of slavery, was perfectly consistent with full and equal citizenship rights. And as Chinese sowed the seeds of communities throughout the Pacific Coast, establishing homes, business enterprises, and social and cultural insti-tutions, they opened the possibility that "Orientals," in fact, might become a permanent part of the American social landscape, not merely transient and alien figures. In the wake of the Civil War, black southerners, most obviously, sought entry into the nation's polity through formal citizenship and political rights. But their understanding of freedom extended far beyond legal consid-erations, such as the franchise and equal protection under the law, to include access to education and economic rights. Moreover, in institutional choices, such as the attempt to establish autonomous churches and family and com-munity units, and in ideological and cultural forms, such as Afro-Christianity itself, freedpeople made manifestly clear their desire to proceed in this new era as *African* Americans, as a people who desired neither to jettison the traditions and experiences of their slave past nor simply to mimic those—whites—who were already considered free.

Chinese who migrated to the United States, in the meantime, were up-setting a central idea that had marked them as racial others. The establish-ment of Chinese-based institutions and communities in the United States posed the possibility that these "absolute aliens," as *Harper's Weekly* referred to them, might attempt to settle and insinuate themselves into the national polity and, worse still, to thoroughly corrupt the orderly, moral, and Christian settlement of the Pacific Coast as the farthest western border of the nation.[125] While perhaps not as self-conscious as black southerners, in a similar move, Chinese nonetheless relied on their traditions and experiences to shape their institutional, cultural, and communal lives in the United States. As they dis-embarked from steamships that had carried them across the Pacific, Chinese neither forgot their past nor somehow began a conscious effort at assimilating into their new culture. Indeed, a hostile reception militated against any desire to assimilate, and, even as they wanted a modicum of acceptance—perhaps just enough acceptance to be left alone—they began to build lives in America from the tools and knowledge they already carried with them. In this era of opportunity afforded by the end of slavery and the increase of immigration, the hopes and actions of blacks and Chinese did more than make a case for the broadening of the polity. Rather than merely hoping for inclusion, blacks and Chinese were in the process of remaking the social relations that stood at the foundation of the ways in which they had been racialized while simultaneously providing an alternate understanding of the articulation between racial and cultural difference and national belonging.

Baptist home missionaries entered their fields in the South and on the Pacific Coast well aware of the tensions between the reassertions of white supremacy and these new, more heterogeneous imaginings of the nation. Indeed, it was, in part, the potential for disorder arising from these conflicting perspectives that impelled them to these particular sites. Espousing an evangelical nationalism that hoped to both dampen the more virulent strains of white privilege and limit the spectrum of cultural difference, Baptist missionaries, like the populations to which they ministered, embarked on their enterprise with hope and faith in what they believed to be the universal truth of Christianity. And as they endeavored to navigate between and among extremes, their missions became crucial sites for testing new and competing ideas about race and nation.

CHAPTER 3

Callings

And he said unto them, Go ye into all the world, and preach the
gospel to the whole creation.
    Mark 16:15 (ASV)

That ye were at that time separate from Christ, alienated from the
commonwealth of Israel, and strangers from the covenants of the
promise, having no hope and without God in the world. . . .
So then ye are no more strangers and sojourners, but ye are fellow-
citizens with the saints, and of the household of God.
    Ephesians 2:12, 19 (ASV)

And he gave some to be apostles; and some, prophets; and some,
evangelists; and some, pastors and teachers.
    Ephesians 4:11 (ASV)

THE CALLS CAME from different places; the missions emanated from different
institutions. In New York City, officials of the ABHMS offered Henry Martin
Tupper a commission, which he received on July 3, 1865, to work among the
freedpeople in the South.[1] When Tupper and his wife, Sarah Leonard Tupper,
arrived in Raleigh three months later, on October 10, they were outsiders—
Yankees sent by a northern organization. Tupper may have embarked upon his
endeavor with a faith in the righteousness of his mission and with a hopeful

optimism in the desires of black North Carolinians, but if he began his labors in Raleigh with the idea that the local white population would be cooperative, he was quickly disabused of that notion. Indeed, his first approach to the white pastor of Raleigh's First Baptist Church proved less than encouraging. According to one account, when Tupper sought permission to address the black former congregants of First Baptist who were hoping to form their own church and who were temporarily meeting in the basement of First Baptist, the Rev. Thomas Skinner rebuffed him, advising Tupper "to go back home" because the time was "not ripe for a Negro school." When Tupper came back the next morning to plead his case again, Skinner scoffed at the missionary, claiming that no blacks would be interested in meeting because First Baptist already held "the biggest prayer meeting" for "niggers" in east Raleigh. Disappointed but not deterred, Tupper temporarily turned his attention away from First Baptist and to the larger black population around Raleigh.[2]

Dong Gong and E. Z. Simmons arrived in Portland to establish a mission to the city's Chinese as outsiders, too, but they came not at the suggestion of a national organization but at the invitation of the local Baptist church. The mission had been under discussion at Portland's First Baptist Church for more than a year, and, when Dong and Simmons arrived in November 1873, they were welcomed by the church's representatives, and their mission had significant local support. The Rev. D. S. Pierce, two deacons, the church secretary, and a teacher had formed a committee for the Chinese mission; Deacon Douglas W. Williams had secured seed money from the church's Sunday School Fund; and local business and political leaders, some of whom were members of the church, had agreed to back the mission. When the Chinese Mission School gathered for the first time, it counted among its directors and "liberal contributors" former mayor and regional business leader Henry Failing and his business partner and brother-in-law, U.S. Senator Henry W. Corbett.[3]

The differences that attended the origins of the Raleigh mission and the origins of the Portland mission were important. In part, they signified the relative "space" each field occupied in the home missionary imagination. The national organization's attention to the South outstripped its interest in missions among the Chinese, particularly in terms of resource allocation, so it is not at all surprising that the Executive Board would take control of commissioning evangelicals in the South while local Baptists would be responsible for generating resources and support for immigrant missions on the West Coast.[4] The relative size of each population accounts for at least part of this difference.

But the national import of Emancipation and its connection to the aftermath of the Civil War and federal Reconstruction policy ensured the mission to freedpeople a central position in the Executive Board's concerns.

To be sure, the growing Chinese immigrant population alarmed the Executive Board, but the mission efforts among this group, at least initially, nonetheless remained a relatively localized concern. Baptists had been active among the Chinese in California since the 1850s, but the all-consuming crisis of the Civil War and Emancipation diverted funding, personnel, and attention from the Pacific Coast. Pushed to the margins of ABHMS matters, a commissioned laborer of the Society would not renew work among the Chinese in the United States until 1869. Because the vast majority of Chinese in the United States resided in northern California, other parts of the Pacific Coast remained beyond the purview of the national board. Indeed, the growing Chinese Question—and the evangelical response to it—seemed to focus almost solely on the San Francisco area, and, even with the post–Civil War revival of ABHMS sponsorship of evangelical work in the city, local Baptists continued to petition the Society for a larger commitment.[5]

Yet more significantly, the different receptions received by each mission signaled a critical difference in the relationships between the Baptist missionaries and the local elite. Tupper's hostile greeting by Skinner was not at all unusual. The Confederacy had surrendered only six months earlier, and Tupper's appearance in Raleigh marked the arrival of an advanced guard of northerners determined to bring their political, economic, social, and cultural ideas, institutions, and practices to the vanquished South. As early as 1862, the ABHMS had looked forward to the defeat of the rebels so it could undertake "the entire reorganization of the social and religious state of the South."[6] It is not surprising, then, that white southerners such as Skinner would see Tupper as a threat. As historian Paul Harvey observes, "White southern Baptists viewed political and religious reconstruction as the same process in different institutional settings. Just as carpetbaggers had 'stole' the reins of politics, so northern missionaries would seize control of the ecclesiastical government and religious customs of the South."[7] In Portland, on the other hand, local white leaders invited Baptist missionaries to establish the Chinese Mission School, and the endeavor enjoyed significant support from the city's political and business oligarchs. Indeed, the city fathers understood the mission school as a mechanism for social control, rather than an instrument for "reorganization," and thus supported the project through contributions and administrative labor.

These *differences*, then, constitute an important window into the particular and various operations of an evangelical nationalist project that aimed at the universal goal of conversion. Because of the structural position of white northern evangelicals in the South, missions to the freedpeople often could seem to have as much in common with foreign missions as with their domestic counterparts. Indeed, it is no coincidence that northern Baptists embarked on their enterprise in the South as foreign missionaries and mission theorists entered the global expansionist scramble by advocating for evangelical labors abroad as the "moral equivalent for imperialism."[8] American Baptists who traveled to the war-torn South shared with their brethren laboring overseas "a vision of the essential rightness of western civilization and the near-inevitability of its triumph"—a position guaranteed to win them few friends among the "native" elite.[9] The close relationship between evangelicals and local leaders in Portland, on the other hand, suggests a form of missionary paternalism supported by the city's fathers. In this sense, Portland's evangelicals envisioned a more limited change resulting from their efforts than did American Baptists in the South. Whereas northern Baptists in Raleigh and other parts of the former Confederacy hitched their fortunes to federal Reconstruction and its political institutions and goals, Baptists in Portland had no corresponding desire for a broad-based political transformation.

Yet even with these very significant differences, the late nineteenth-century Baptist efforts among black southerners and Chinese immigrants held a great deal in common. The missionaries who undertook and advocates who supported both endeavors were necessarily convinced of evangelical Christianity's power to transform—to convert—individuals and the nation. Although the range of the missions may have differed, both projects endeavored to bring about a conversion that registered not just spiritually but socially as well. Indeed, Baptist home missionaries cast themselves as agents of change and emissaries of the Christian nation. They simultaneously created a conduit for the inclusion of alien populations into the brotherhood of Christianity and the nation while producing a discourse of difference that made that inclusion yet more difficult. The model for conversion (followed by inclusion) pivoted on a notion of uplift, so that even while missionaries engaged in an evangelical project that seemed to mitigate the role of "race" in the quest for spiritual, social, and national transformation, they nonetheless based this project on a proselytizing process predicated on the identification and hierarchical assessment of religious, cultural, and social difference. And missionaries, through this American evangelical interpretation of religious difference, played crucial roles not just in the stated goals of converting the souls and integrating the bodies of blacks and Chinese but also in delineating, elaborating, and perpetuating racial difference through culture and religion.

It is in this respect that the characteristics shared by the two missions illuminate variations on the theme of racial formation. Home missions to blacks and Chinese constituted the mechanisms—termed "racial projects" by sociologists Michael Omi and Howard Winant—through which racial formation occurred.[10] Indeed, these missions, as evangelical nationalist endeavors, were sites where "human bodies and social structures [were] represented and organized."[11] Missionaries, through a language of conversion, national inclusion, and uplift, at once provided an interpretation of their contemporary racial systems (and their histories) and offered a new model for the reorganization of those systems. A comparative inquiry into the two home mission fields, then, opens a window onto the different ways in which blacks and Chinese were racialized by missionaries' evangelical nationalist practices, and it places a religious and nationally based discourse of whiteness at the center of these racial projects.

When the Executive Board of the ABHMS summoned Henry Martin Tupper to New York City to offer him a commission to evangelize among the freedpeople, he was but one religious worker in a much larger enterprise. He joined more than ninety other northern missionaries, assistants, and teachers under the American Baptist banner in the South.[12] While teachers and their assistants proselytized in ABHMS schools, the Executive Board had resolved "to secure the labors of experienced pastors" for its commissions, and Tupper was no exception.[13] In fact, although he had been born into a farming family in southwestern Massachusetts and his parents seemed to discourage his early ambition to receive schooling, Tupper's education and formal ministerial training made him an exceptionally good candidate for missionary work. An 1855 graduate of Amherst College, Tupper studied for the ministry at Andover's Newton Theological Institute.[14]

These educational achievements, it seems, were at least in part driven by his faith, and his activities while at Amherst and Newton provided critical experience and—for the Executive Board of the ABHMS—important credentials. Before attending Amherst, Tupper had experienced a conversion to Christianity and, according to his biographer, first expressed an interest in mission work while a student at the Monson Academy. At Amherst, he reaffirmed his commitment to Christianity: "One Saturday afternoon, he walked twenty miles to the nearest Baptist church and asked for Baptism." Tupper

supported himself in college by teaching "a large Sunday-school class of colored youth." When he moved east to Newton, he continued to teach Sunday
school, moving now to Boston's Dudley Street Baptist Church. In the analysis of Tupper's biographer, these formative experiences in Monson, Amherst,
and Boston were evidence of his calling: "Providence had already opened the
way for him to obtain a varied and practical experience in missionary work."
Whether spurred by "Providence" or by a more material educational and professional ambition combined with an evangelical zeal, Tupper's rise from his
humble farming background provided him with practical experience and evidence of faith—of vocation—that surely made him a highly qualified candidate for an ABHMS commission.[15]

Tupper completed his course of study at Newton on June 26, 1862, as the
Civil War raged. As a seminary-trained minister, he might have awaited an
officer's commission as an army chaplain, but, rather than delay his service,
he enlisted as a private on July 1, 1862, some five days after graduating from
Newton.[16] The extant record provides no direct evidence of why Tupper was
so eager to join the Union cause, but it is reasonable to surmise that he was
moved by the struggle against the slaveholding Confederacy.[17] The egalitarian
tradition of evangelical Christianity that had suffused his work in the black
Sunday school in Amherst surely helped to inspire his enlistment. This, too,
was a calling. Indeed, though it occurred some months after he volunteered,
Tupper's response to the Emancipation Proclamation offers a telling clue.
President Lincoln's decree, freeing all slaves residing in the Confederate territories, took effect on the first day of 1863. Two days later, Tupper scrawled in
his diary, "I am much cheered by the Proclamation of the President. The 1st
of January, 1863 I think will prove one of the most eventful and memorable
days of the century."[18]

Tupper's experience, credentials, and commitments made him an ideal
candidate in the eyes of mission officials, but those same characteristics made
him suspect to the local white elite in Raleigh. The rebuff by Rev. Skinner did
not end in the doorway of the southern pastor's residence. Skinner promptly
contacted the ABHMS Executive Board and assured the governing body that
there was simply no need for a northern missionary in the city. The Executive
Board responded not by dismissing the contention but by dispatching its corresponding secretary, J. S. Backus of New York, and one of its managers, Rev.
E. Lathrop of Connecticut, to investigate Skinner's assertion.[19] Upon arriving
in the North Carolina capital, Backus and Lathrop met with Skinner and "one
of the leading Baptists of the city" to discuss whether or not the freedpeople of

Raleigh, in fact, held enough interest for the ABHMS to support a mission.[20] Significantly, neither Tupper nor any black representative was invited to the meeting. Although no official record of the gathering exists, Backus later sent word of the Executive Board's ruling to Tupper on October 31, 1865: "The Executive Board decide that for the present your field shall be Raleigh, N.C."[21]

This initial episode was a revealing trial of Tupper's faith. Like other northern denominations active in the South, the ABHMS viewed the region as a conquered territory. For northern evangelicals, the Civil War and its outcome had demonstrated the sinfulness of the slaveholding Confederacy, and white southerners had abdicated any moral authority, leaving plenty of opportunities for northern missionaries.[22] Yet particularly in southern cities such as Raleigh, northern missionaries could not merely impose themselves; they, in fact, had to navigate a perilous political and social landscape. The ABHMS Executive Board's response to Skinner's concerns demonstrated Tupper's tenuous position in Raleigh. Not only did the Executive Board take seriously the substance of Skinner's claims, but it also saw fit to seek what amounted to the grudging consent of the southern minister, as well as the other "leading Baptist" present at the meeting. Indeed, the Executive Board, understanding the difficulties that outwardly hostile local clergy would present to Tupper's mission, originally sought to avoid a conflict by suggesting that their missionary relocate to Savannah, Georgia.[23] In the end, Skinner offered nothing more than his blessing, for although Tupper was able to undertake his mission in Raleigh, he failed to gain regular access to the black congregants worshipping at Skinner's First Baptist Church.[24]

Skinner would eventually change his opinion of the American Baptist mission. Twenty-one years after Skinner's complaint to the ABHMS Executive Board, Tupper's mission would be safely established as Shaw University, one of the premier academic institutions for blacks in the South, and Skinner would join the school's faculty.[25] But in the intervening years, the northern Baptist mission in Raleigh would continue to face its share of challenges, including an even less courteous "welcome" than the one offered by Skinner. During Tupper's first year in the city, his wife, Sarah, found a piece of paper in the doorway of the family's house as she was locking up for the evening. The note had a skull and crossbones drawn on it. According to one account, "This was understood as a warning from the Ku-Klux." Believing their cabin—and their lives—to be in danger, the Tuppers spent the night in an adjacent cornfield. The next morning, they returned home to find their cabin unharmed.[26]

Despite these obstacles, Henry Martin Tupper threw himself into his ministry with an energy that may be evidence of the strength of his calling. With no regularly established meeting place and no support from local white institutions or clergy, Tupper went mobile. He sought out groups of African Americans throughout the city and on nearby plantations, preaching to them in their temporary encampments, visiting their homes and schools, and launching regular religious meetings. For example, on October 22, 1865, just a few days after his initial encounter with Skinner, Tupper "preached to the colored teamsters in their camp and established a meeting to be held at 2 P.M. every Sabbath."[27] The next day, he visited fifteen families and a common school, instituting "a meeting for preaching and conference."[28] From mid-October to the end of November 1865, despite having no central place from which to base his operations, the missionary made 137 religious visits to black families, held eleven prayer meetings and established nine others, preached thirteen sermons to hundreds of freedpeople, and officiated at weddings and funerals.[29]

By the beginning of December, Tupper had secured funds from the federal government and had rented a room from the Freedmen's Bureau to hold the first meetings of the class that would evolve into the school at the heart of his mission.[30] With a leased space settled, the missionary next set his sights on establishing a more permanent site, and he drew up plans to purchase property and to erect a two-story building to house a school and a church. He thus turned his considerable energies to fund-raising, and here again the lack of local support made a difference. Missionaries in other fields could turn to local Baptists for substantial financial assistance to establish and maintain their projects. But like American evangelicals overseas, northern Baptists in the South faced an impoverished proselyte population and a local white population that was, at best, unwelcoming.[31]

Without the usual local aid, then, Tupper, like his brethren evangelizing abroad, looked to his "native" land for funds. Extant lists of contributions for the construction of the mission's two-story building shows donations totaling over $1,300.[32] Residents of towns in western Massachusetts, where Tupper grew up and attended church, contributed the bulk of that total.[33] Significantly, four of the eight individual contributors listed were related either by blood or by marriage. The funds donated by Mrs. Earl Tupper, Henry's sister-in-law, were collected from "friends" in Wales, Massachusetts, and another entry specifies contributions from "old acquaintances" from Monson.[34] Finally, Baptist networks also paid dividends. The Sabbath school of Wales Baptist Church collected a total of $75.25, while two prominent brethren, Elijah Shaw and Andrew Porter, gave $200 and $100, respectively.[35] These connections from Tupper's native Massachusetts provided the financial backbone of his early efforts in Raleigh.

To these donations Tupper added grants from the Freedmen's Bureau. The federal agency had provided the very first meeting room for the mission in the Guion Hotel, and he continued to rely on the bureau for critical support. Not only did the bureau supply rent for the mission's temporary accommodations, but, according to Shaw University scholar Wilmoth A. Carter, it gave Tupper $2,400 toward the building of the new school and church structure.[36]

Finally, African Americans added a large percentage of their modest incomes to help establish the mission. Soldiers of the Twenty-seventh Colored Regiment, stationed in Raleigh, donated $65 to the endeavor while black residents of the city contributed some $300. For the black troops, this small contribution held great symbolic significance. The soldiers were liberators who fought not only for freedom but also for equality, and they must have noted the precariousness of both conditions in the months following the Civil War.[37] Those who helped the fledgling mission likely shared the concerns of an officer of the First Colored Regiment, also stationed in Raleigh. "With the present loose way of administering the [loyalty] oath and extending pardons and political privileges to rebels, North Carolina is not capable of governing herself within the Union," he warned. "There are not troops enough here now, and I am satisfied there will be trouble before Spring."[38] Black troops, like those who were stationed in Raleigh and who contributed to the Baptist mission, understood that Emancipation did not necessarily lead to equality, and they surely saw the church and school as a fundamental institution in their continuing struggle for their idea of freedom.

The $300 donated by local black residents also held great symbolic value. To be sure, given the destitution of the post–Civil War black population, the sum was, in and of itself, significant. In interviews conducted by the Works Progress Administration, ex-slaves recalled the terrible poverty in Raleigh. Tina Johnson moved to the city from Georgia immediately after the war: "We comed ter Raleigh 'fore things wuz settled atter de war, an' I watches de niggers livin' on kush, co'nbread, 'lasses an' what dey can beg an' steal frum de white folks. Dem days shore wuz bad."[39] Patsy Mitchner remembered the joy of Emancipation being tempered by the bitterness of having little economic opportunity: "Slaves prayed for freedom. Den dey got it dey didn't know what to do wid it. Dey wus turned out wid nowhere to go an' nothin' to live on. Dey had no 'sperence in lookin' out for demselves an' nothin' to work wid an' no lan'."[40] Yet despite bleak prospects, freedpeople nonetheless found ways to save and to contribute to individual endeavors and community institutions that supported their commitment to post-Emancipation autonomy. The $300 accumulated and donated by ex-slaves in Raleigh represented one of a broad spectrum of ways in which, as historian Sharon Ann Holt has argued, former slaves "marshaled and applied resources of time, labor, and cash, resources developed within household economies" to produce "discretionary income" for essential organizations outside the household.[41] Later, black students at the mission school would save scrupulously to raise money for tuition, even though their funding for tuition was often supplemented by ABHMS sources. In 1881, when Frank Freeman, who had been born into slavery in 1857, decided to attend Shaw University, he relied on $47.75 he had saved through austerity to pay his initial fee, and, even with tuition subsidized by ABHMS funds and other philanthropic sources, he continued to work while a student "to help pay my way."[42] The hard work, sacrifice, and capital supplied by freedpeople demonstrated their commitment to the church and school at the center of the mission and made the fulfillment of Tupper's calling possible.

In Raleigh, Tupper capitalized on the enthusiasm of local blacks. In February 1866, with their aid and with the aid of northern benefactors and philanthropists, he and African American Baptists in the city organized Second Baptist Church and planned to purchase a lot for his proposed schoolhouse and church building.[43] In the meantime, he continued his theological class, adding students and sessions. By the end of his first year in North Carolina, the first story of the building had been completed, Tupper opened the school with three teachers supported by the New England Freedman's Aid Society, and the missionary claimed some 250 souls who attended the day school and another 100 who attended at night.[44] Although he referred to this educational ministry as the "primary department," it was, in reality, a mixed classroom in which students received fundamental education, such as literacy, as well as scriptural training. It would be two years before the Raleigh mission began to focus more exclusively on theological and higher education in accordance with the ABHMS Executive Board's 1866 decision to stress ministerial over common school instruction.[45]

Unlike the majority of its efforts in the South, American Baptist home missions to the Chinese usually began when local residents or congregations initiated evangelical programs and later petitioned the Society for support. Portland was no different in this respect. Although the ABHMS Executive Board counted the mission as an important part of its evangelical project and eventually would provide financial support, it was Portland's First Baptist Church that issued the call for a Chinese mission. It was a call made in response to the growing Chinese population and the perceived dangers that seemed to attend this demographic fact; it was a call that echoed and was linked to Baptist efforts in northern California; it was a call issued, in small part, to compete with the city's Congregationalists, who had established a Chinese mission in February 1873; it was a call heeded not just by Dong Gong and E. Z. Simmons but by First Baptist's leaders and Portland's elite.[46] Indeed, it was this last characteristic that most set it apart from ABHMS labors in the South.

Douglas W. Williams, deacon at First Baptist Church and one its members since its reorganization in 1861, took particular note of the fire from arson that decimated much of Portland's Chinatown in August of 1873. The location of his wholesale grocery business, in a section of the city heavily populated by Chinese, meant both that he was familiar with this group of city residents and that his business was probably lost in the fire.[47] When Wiliams moved to appropriate funds from the Sunday school budget to establish the mission, he may have reminded his brethren that their church dodged a similar fate by only a few blocks—a sure sign that *something* must be done about this dangerous presence in their midst.

Williams found in the congregation's pastor at that time a sympathetic ear. Rev. A. R. Medbury had been ordained at and served as pastor of First Baptist Church in San Francisco before moving to Oregon in June 1872.[48] In San Francisco, Medbury led a congregation long acquainted with mission work among immigrant Chinese. The formal ABHMS Chinese mission in San Francisco began in 1869, but, more than a decade and a half earlier, in 1854, J. L. Shuck, under the auspices of the Southern Baptist Convention, had established a domestic ministry in northern California.[49] From his base in Sacramento, where he helped found the first Chinese Baptist church in the United States, Shuck ranged widely throughout the region.[50] He became pastor of Sacramento Baptist Church and eventually resigned his pastorate in early 1860 after suffering serious injuries in a riding accident. He would continue to work as an itinerant missionary in the area, ministering to Chinese and white populations.[51] In the meantime, however, the San Francisco Baptist Church had established a locally sponsored mission to the Chinese. By the time the ABHMS commissioned a missionary to work in San Francisco in 1869–70, its Committee on Missions among the Chinese on the Pacific Coast reported that "as many as one hundred and fifty" gathered "each Sabbath in the First Baptist Church, San Francisco" to be "taught by members of that church."[52]

Once taking the pulpit in Portland, Medbury hinted that his pastorate would be open to initiatives like the Chinese mission school that his congregation in California had so successfully sponsored. Indeed, in his inaugural sermon, he chose chapter 8 of St. Paul's letter to the Romans as his text.[53] Although there is no extant version of the sermon, important themes from this scriptural passage stand out. Most fundamentally, it is significant that Medbury preached from Paul—the first evangelist. More specifically, Paul's epistle begins with an expression of the universal grace of Christian belief and concludes with an assertion of the transcendence of God's love, which unites all: "I am persuaded, that neither death, nor life, nor angels, nor principalities, nor things present, nor things to come, nor height, nor depth, nor any other creature, shall be able to separate us from the love of God, which is in Christ Jesus our Lord."[54] Emphasizing the universal possibility for redemption through conversion and focusing on the brotherhood of all Christians, Medbury provided a foundation for evangelizing among Chinese immigrants who, to much of his congregation, must have seemed beyond the pale of American Christianity. Having heard Medbury's sermon, Deacon Williams would have felt confident that his pastor would support his proposal for a Chinese mission.

But Medbury brought to Portland more than his expansive understanding of Christianity's redemptive and salvific powers. He also brought knowledge, experience, and contacts. As the Portland church began to plan the mission in August 1873, he called upon his Bay Area colleagues to suggest a suitable evangelist; he also specified the most important qualification, insisting that the missionary be able to preach in Chinese.[55] American Baptist records indicate that a handful of European American missionaries already had been involved among Chinese home missions, and others, commissioned primarily through the Southern Baptist Convention's Foreign Mission Board, possessed experience in China (and language skills); yet it seems that either Medbury insisted or his San Francisco brethren understood his request to mean that only an ethnic Chinese missionary would do. In any case, Medbury, Williams, and others were disappointed to learn that no "suitable Chinese convert" was available, and it would be almost nine months before the ABHMS missionary in San Francisco, John Francis, forwarded Dong Gong's name to Portland, recommending him "as an exemplary Christian."[56] By then, however, Medbury had already advised First Baptist of his intention to leave Portland for evangelical work in Wisconsin. When he and his family decamped for the Midwest in July 1874, the congregation put aside its plans for the Chinese mission.[57]

First Baptist, however, would soon issue its call again. In October 1874, Medbury's successor, Rev. D. S. Pierce, revived the plan to establish a mission "aimed at . . . the conversion of the Chinese."[58] Pierce, unlike Medbury, had little practical experience to prepare him for this undertaking; his previous posting in Laramie, Wyoming, afforded him, at best, limited contact with Chinese.[59] Nevertheless, Pierce's evangelical Christianity provided him with a strong ideological framework for encouraging a mission. His inaugural sermon to First Baptist had stressed "the universality of religion" and the "progress that Christianity is making among the leading nations of the earth and the influence of individuals."[60] Preaching from the Book of Malachi, Pierce emphasized the universal, perhaps imperial claims, of Christianity: "For from the rising of the sun even unto the going down of the same my name shall be great among the Gentiles; and in every place incense shall be offered unto my name, and a pure offering: for my name shall be great among the Gentiles, saith Jehovah of hosts."[61] For Pierce, the transcendent message of God's grace made difference—national, ethnic, racial—surmountable. Christianity was universal.

Once again, Douglas Williams took the lead as First Baptist renewed its evangelical calling. In early October, Williams secured money from the church's Sunday School Fund, and the congregation established a committee to oversee the proposed mission school.[62] The congregation also directed Pierce to inquire if Dong Gong's services were still available. Upon receiving word that Dong was, indeed, interested in the Portland job, Pierce not only offered him a six-month commission but also requested that Rev. E. Z. Simmons, the new head of the ABHMS Chinese mission in San Francisco and former China missionary, accompany Dong to Portland to help establish the enterprise.[63] Simmons would return to California after a week and a half, but Dong, as the primary missionary at the new school, remained.

Yet even with Pierce's unquestioned pastoral support, it is significant that Douglas Williams was an instrumental figure in the establishment of the Chinese Mission School. As their coreligionists in the South had been demonstrating for a decade, a committed evangelist could accomplish much, but proselytizing was made more difficult if the local elite—church elders, business leaders, politicians—refused to support the mission. In Portland, the support of prominent local merchant and church deacon Williams was just the tip of the iceberg.

Historian Carlos Schwantes has observed that, by the late nineteenth century, "Portland had become a city noted for . . . its God-fearing respectability . . . [and] a more structured society . . . dominated by the Ladds, Corbetts, Failings, and other first families."[64] It is no particular surprise, then, that First Baptist enjoyed a close relationship with the city's aristocracy. Indeed, the Failings not only were (quite literally) the first family of First Baptist, they were also one of the city's leading families. Active in business and politics, the Failings—especially patriarch Josiah and eldest son Henry—embodied the ideals of elite moral stewardship that marked the calling of evangelical nationalism at the heart of the Chinese mission.

Josiah, with his wife and children, had migrated to Portland from New York City in 1851, and he quickly established a wholesale mercantile firm, J. Failing and Company. Within a year, he was elected to the City Council; the next year, in 1853, he became mayor. But Josiah's engagement in the city's life extended beyond formal politics. The year after being elected mayor, he hosted the organizational meeting to found a Baptist congregation. Failing and other Portland Baptists worried that the young city (it had been incorporated only in 1851) was falling prey to the irreligion, immorality, and disorder that northeastern evangelicals and home mission supporters claimed marked western settlements.[65] Hoping that a formal church, with regular worship and moral leadership, would extend the benefits of Protestant culture and turn the tide of impiety and tumult, they called a "meeting of the friends of a Baptist Interest in the City. . . . The present condition of Society in Portland," they asserted, "seems to indicate to us as Baptists that it is our duty to make an Effort to Sustain Baptist Worship in this city."[66]

Josiah Failing would be listed as the church's first constituent on membership rolls—with his wife and daughter enumerated second and third, respectively—and the connections between the Failings and First Baptist Church were strong and enduring.[67] In 1860, for instance, when First Baptist struggled to maintain congregants, the Failings remained the only constant.[68] Curiously, Josiah and Henrietta's sons did not join their parents or sister as founding members of the church, but they nonetheless played active roles in First Baptist affairs.[69] Indeed, Henry was a trustee of the church, and James participated as the congregation's collection agent. They both followed in their father's footsteps by working on the committee devoted to the Chinese mission.[70]

Older brother Henry, especially, would also match his father as a prominent businessman and civic leader, further connecting the church and its mission to secular Portland. Following his father into public service, Henry held multiple appointed offices, including a seat on Oregon's Water Committee, regent of the state university, trustee of the Deaf Mute School in Salem, and trustee and treasurer of the Children's Home.[71] Like his father before him, he served as the city's mayor, winning two consecutive elections beginning in 1864 and gaining election again in 1873.[72]

When Josiah retired from the family business in 1864, Henry assumed control of J. Failing and Company. Six years earlier, at age twenty-four, he had married Emily Phelps Corbett, and, in 1869, he and Emily's brother, Henry W. Corbett, purchased First National Bank of Portland, the region's most important financial institution.[73] In 1871, Henry Failing and Corbett—a future U.S. Senator—joined forces again, transforming the family firm into Corbett, Failing, and Company. The two partners, along with Henry Failing's brothers, Edward and James, now headed the leading wholesale mercantile business in the Pacific Northwest.[74]

Henry Corbett was not a member of First Baptist Church, but a number of his business associates, like the Failings, were. Corbett, for instance, sat on the first board of directors of the Oregon Railway and Navigation Company with the church's forty-third member and one of its founding "incorpora-tors," attorney Joseph N. Dolph.[75] Significantly, Dolph and Henry Failing maintained a relationship not just in their religious lives but also in their business affairs, eventually serving together on the Board of Directors of Henry Villard's Oregon and Transcontinental Company.[76]

These associations confirmed social status, reinforced civic standing, and created a network of political and business power. Portland's aristocracy shared economic, political, and social interests; it also held a common vision for the city, region, and nation. Men like the Failings, Dolph, and Corbett were ardent Republicans who believed that a properly ordered society, with men of commerce at its apex, would lead to progress.[77] The overlap between religious and secular associational life proved indispensable as the city's elite attempted to implement its vision as society's stewards. It is indeed telling that the links among Portland's philanthropic efforts mirrored its commercial and personal connections. As a trustee and treasurer of the city's Children's Home, Henry Failing, for example, could count on his business partner and brother-in-law to be a generous donor.[78]

The Chinese Mission School stood as a central institution in elite efforts to stave off retrogression and ensure orderly progress. In fact, local leaders came together to make certain that the institution was launched in good

health. Dolph, Corbett, and Henry Failing all served on the board of directors, and they were reported to be "liberal contributors."[79] Other important
figures in Portland commerce and politics also contributed to the mission, including James Failing, city auditor and clerk and transportation entrepreneur
W. S. Caldwell, and Oregon Central Railroad Company vice president W. L.
Halsey.[80] And Henry Failing provided the critical link between the fledgling
school and its original home in the Good Templar's Hall Building, just up
Alder Street from First Baptist.[81] Two years before the school's first class convened there, Failing had purchased an interest in the building.[82]

For an elite preoccupied not only with the accumulation of wealth but also
with the consolidation of power and the maintenance of social order, the mission to the Chinese was a perfect outlet. In the face of growing anti-Chinese
agitation and in the aftermath of the August 1873 fire, elite control over the
city must have been sorely tested. The ability to contain and to convert the
immigrant population—and to protect it from violence—would underscore
the influence and command of these leaders. The school represented the centerpiece of this containment strategy and signified an exemplary expression of
missionary paternalism embodied by the moral and civic authority of church
and city leaders.

The support of these leaders proved vital. The mission attracted a sizeable
student population almost immediately. Originally, Medbury had hoped that
preaching would occur only in Chinese, but when Dong Gong and E. Z. Simmons met with the church's Committee on Chinese Missions, "It was decided
to teach English five evenings each week, Thursday evening to be occupied
in religious training by the Missionary."[83] Within weeks, the mission offered
separate morning and evening Sabbath schools, a Tuesday evening service, and
a school that met every night. Dong Gong preached in Cantonese and English, and students studied Scripture as they learned to read English. Songs—
especially hymns—played an important role in the curriculum.[84] English
classes were soon supplemented with instruction in other secular topics, such
as geography and math. The more comprehensive course of study was the first
step in a proposed "permanent college for Chinese instruction."[85]

Significantly, although anti-Chinese activities in the city did not stop,
First Baptist Church and the mission's supporters seem to have been successful in establishing the social order they envisioned and in demonstrating the positive effects of the project on their participants. By 1878, when
the ABHMS suspended its missions in California due to white protests, the
Executive Committee of the Society boasted, "The mission in Portland, Or-

egon, is undisturbed by this question. It is maintained and fostered by the Baptist Church in that city, and commands the sympathy and respect of the community."[86] That same year, the ABHMS, which, in previous years, had contributed general and educational funds, took over responsibility for the school's missionary's salary.[87]

The 1878 suspension of ABHMS activities among Chinese in California would prove temporary. The very next year, the ABHMS would appoint a Chinese evangelist, Chew Yow, in Oakland, and, in the meantime, the Southern Baptist Convention's (SBC) Home Mission Board continued to support work in San Francisco.[88] Dong Gong's fellow traveler, E. Z. Simmons, who would remain in San Francisco under an SBC commission until 1880, was joined in 1878 by Jesse B. Hartwell, another returned China missionary. When, in 1884, the SBC concluded that it could no longer afford to maintain its domestic work among the Chinese, the ABHMS assumed control of the San Francisco mission and all related projects.[89] That same year, the Society named Hartwell the superintendent of Chinese missions on the Pacific Coast, and he supervised teachers at mission schools in San Francisco, Stockton, and Chino, as well as missionaries in Fresno, Oakland, and Portland.[90] A decade after the founding of the Oregon mission, the ABHMS could boast of a regional network of schools, missions, and churches for the Chinese.

It took even less time for the Society to establish a similar complex of institutions among blacks in the South. Within a year of the Raleigh mission's December 1865 founding, the Executive Board counted some fifty ordained ministers that it had commissioned throughout the South and almost a hundred black churches that it supported.[91] It also "sustained schools at Washington, Alexandria, Culpeper, Fredericksburg, Williamsburg, Richmond, Petersburg, Portsmouth, Raleigh, New Orleans, Murfreesboro, Nashville, Albany, and Ashland."[92] The 1869 rechristening of the North Carolina school as the Raleigh Theological Institute was part of a broader push within the ABHMS to focus energy and resources on establishing more permanent (though perhaps fewer) institutions throughout the region, joining efforts in Washington, D.C.; Richmond, Virginia; Augusta, Georgia; New Orleans, Louisiana; and Nashville, Tennessee.[93] By the next year Tupper had raised enough money from a single benefactor to place the school on a more secure footing, changing the name to "Shaw Collegiate Institute" to reflect the generosity of Elijah P. Shaw of Massachusetts, and, in 1874, Shaw extended its mission, completing the Estey Building to house female students, again echoing a broader trend of the Society. Indeed, it was also in 1874 that the ABHMS commissioned Joanna P. Moore as its first female missionary (other women had been "missionary assistants," "teachers," or wives) to work among freedwomen. Within ten years, as it was incorporated as Shaw University, the Raleigh school had joined a constellation of ABHMS-affiliated projects throughout the South that included the Wayland Seminary in Washington, the Colver Institute in Richmond, the Benedict Institute in Columbia, the Nashville Institute, the Augusta Institute, and Leland University in New Orleans, as well as scores of lesser satellites, such as mission schools, churches, and prayer meetings.

Within these regional networks in the South and on the Pacific Coast, missionaries, whether itinerant evangelists, Bible-school teachers, or theological institute instructors, engaged in the work of proselytizing. They heeded Christ's call to "go ye into all the world, and preach the gospel to the whole creation." But conversion was tricky business, especially conversion as mandated by the evangelical nationalist ideology of the American Baptists. If evangelical Christianity should be the common thread binding all Americans, then conversion should endeavor to alter the spiritual *and* material lives of proselytes. Indeed, Baptist evangelicals found it impossible to disentangle religious and worldly matters, and their mission projects reflected this ambitious, transformative aim.

Elijah C. Branch, a missionary who worked in Memphis, Tennessee, even before the end of the Civil War, demonstrated the overlap between spiritual and temporal goals. In addition to conducting prayer meetings, overseeing Sabbath schools, and making family religious visits, he was superintendent of School Number 1 in Memphis, where he taught basic literacy, arithmetic, and geography as well as religious education. He also helped distribute food and supplies to the poor. "But my work is not all in the school," he wrote. "Out of school, I visit the sick and help the needy. While in one hand I have carried the basket of provisions to feed the hungry, with the other I have dealt out '*specifics*' both for souls and for bodies."[94]

Moreover, no matter how deep their faith in the ultimate truth of Christianity and its salvific powers, these latter-day Pauls were equally convinced that, for their potential proselytes, there was nothing obvious about Christianity's truth or power. It is no coincidence that in reports from the field, missionaries referred to their "labors." Proselytizing required more than the mere revelation of transcendent truths. If the scales were to drop from the eyes of former slaves and Chinese, then missionaries would need to develop programs designed to attract and maintain each group's sustained attention and tailored to attend to specific needs.

A critical first step in mission work, then, required a thorough assessment of the particular conditions that attended each group, and this assessment was based on a fundamental understanding of difference between missionaries and potential converts. While it may seem simple enough to dismiss this difference as merely the gulf between Christian missionaries on one hand and heathen Chinese or blacks on the other, British historian Susan Thorne's observation that conversion was predicated on the "inevitably pejorative nature of missionary constructions of heathenism" is instructive.[95]

The judgment that assumed the necessity of transforming black and Chinese populations in the first place presupposed their lesser spiritual and social condition, and this presupposition was followed by assessments that required the identification and characterization of deficiencies in target populations. Indeed, American Baptist officials and missionaries set about ascertaining the needs of African American and Chinese communities by trying to establish the essential—and inferior—character of both populations. They carefully catalogued religious practices, social relations, familial customs, material condition, and behavior, circulating their findings in the religious press, sermons, and speeches. As they produced this literature to garner support for, justify, and explain their labors, they ironically succeeded in also producing a type of knowledge about blacks and Chinese. In a literature that purported to reveal key characteristics of black and Chinese communities and cultures, evangelicals thus established what Joan Jacobs Brumberg has called a "missionary ethnology."[96]

This literature effectively reduced Chinese and black religious life, social relations, and culture to a set of descriptions expressed in a vocabulary of uplift. Such ethnographic portraits produced static representations of what came to be understood as the normal—even natural—state of African American or Chinese immigrant life and lifestyles. Missionary ethnology took on even greater weight because the evangelicals were themselves men and women who had extensive personal experience among black and Chinese populations about whom they were reporting. According to James C. Thomson, Jr., Peter W. Stanley, and John Curtis Perry, for example, missionaries were "the largest group of Americans who experienced China directly between 1842 and 1942," and they "became prime communicators of the one civilization back to the other."[97] These accounts thus carried the imprimatur of expertise.

Unsurprisingly, religious practice occupied a central place in the missionary ethnology of ex-slaves and Chinese.[98] Evangelicals' observations of African

American services featured descriptions of strange rituals expressed in tones of frank bewilderment. Ellen Adlington, a teacher from the North, witnessed a religious gathering of blacks and related being "screamed at in a wild ignorant half rhapsody." She bemoaned that "not a word [was] said of the commandments."[99] American Baptist missionary Jonathan W. Horton, working at Port Royal, South Carolina, confessed that he was "very much puzzled [about] what to do about the religious feeling of these people."[100] Even as northern Baptist missionaries witnessed men and women practicing a religion that was nominally Christian, the emotional expressions of belief differed greatly from the orthodoxies to which they were accustomed.

While Ellen Adlington and Jonathan Horton experienced exasperation at what they witnessed, Joseph T. Robert, head of the ABHMS school in Georgia, understood the "utterances and . . . tears" during black worship as evidence of "intense interest in [the] study of the Holy Scriptures."[101] For Robert, the "eminently emotional and imaginative" qualities freedpeople evinced during religious services were evidence of their "unabated fondness for the study of the Bible."[102] And this observation underscored a critical redemptive quality missionaries saw in the strange behavior of African American Christians: devotion. Northern evangelicals thought ex-slaves lacked orthodox belief and practices—a void to be filled by ABHMS schools and formally trained ministers. But they also believed that black southerners possessed an emotive devotion to Christianity on which few missionary observers cast doubt. E. G. Trask, a missionary laboring in Tennessee, marveled that African Americans' enthusiasm for worship was rivaled only by their willingness to sacrifice to build religious institutions. He remarked that "for everything [freedpeople] eat or wear they have to pay enormous prices, and their opportunities for obtaining money with which to pay are very limited, the sufferings in consequence of their poverty are very great, and yet at their meetings last Sabbath they contributed four dollars."[103]

Meanwhile, as missionaries observed the Chinese, one trait stood out above all others: their "heathenism." "Heathenism" became shorthand for a comprehensive set of ills that beset the Chinese population in Asia and the United States. Bereft of Christianity, Chinese people and their nation had been left in the darkness of a retrograde civilization. Evangelists proselytizing among the Chinese in America found evidence of irreligion—and lack of civilization—everywhere. Missionary accounts led readers on tours of "heathen temples" and opium dens and "revealed" the extent of prostitution and gambling in American Chinatowns.[104] One colorful account by a home missionary detailed a temple "for the worship of heathen deities" in San Francisco. In this "miniature" version of a "house of gods," "darkness" reigned, and congregants worshipped not Christ but idols.[105] Depicting a world to which most white Americans had no access, missionary ethnology described a culture and a people mired in superstition and immorality and not yet redeemed by Christianity.

Whereas missionary efforts among ex-slaves aimed at altering nominally Christian practice, evangelical endeavors among the Chinese hoped to replace completely non-Christian religions, and evangelical assessments of these religions remained central to descriptions of the "Chinese character." Historian Carl T. Jackson, for instance, observes that missionaries credited Confucianism with both negative and ostensibly positive attributes.[106] Confucianism, as described by missionaries, was the source simultaneously "of the Chinese people's haughty attitude toward outsiders and mindless adherence to tradition" and of their "rational" mind.[107] The first American Baptist woman to travel to China with her missionary husband confirmed (and contributed to) this ethnology's negative assessment of the Chinese when she published her widely disseminated memoir. Henrietta Hall Shuck claimed that "pride" and "self-righteousness" were two of "the prominent characteristics of the great Confucius."[108]

If missionaries, in their observations of African Americans, identified a positive trait in black devotion, then evangelicals working among the Chinese might have found a similarly encouraging attribute in the supposed rationality imparted by Confucianism. But just as the emotional manifestations of devotion provided missionaries with evidence of black difference, Confucian rationality, coupled with the arrogance so many claimed to observe, underscored an essential characteristic that distinguished the Chinese. Even their professions of faith were suspect, for their cerebral bent meant that converted Chinese tended to practice a decorous yet unfeeling—perhaps even unbelieving—form of Christianity.

This representation of the Chinese contrasted directly with the missionary ethnology of blacks, whom evangelicals considered to be enthusiastic but overly emotional and wholly unorthodox. Baptist leader and university president E. G. Robinson noted, "The Mongol, with his Confucian ethics, will make of the gospel religion rather than piety, while the African, with his emotional nature, will make, of the same gospel, piety rather than religion."[109] While the Chinese might have developed a rational understanding of Christianity, they lacked the fundamental ability to believe. Blacks, on the other hand, clearly believed in Christianity, but they had not developed the ability to understand the meaning of Scripture.

Significantly, these missionary assessments of Chinese and black religion possessed a remarkable consonance with the ascendant biological racialism of the late nineteenth century. In 1892, for example, Joseph Le Conte, a professor of natural history and geology, a member of the National Academy of Sciences, a president of the American Association for the Advancement of Science, and a charter member of the Sierra Club, applied evolutionary theories to matters of racial difference, arguing that blacks had little biological capacity for social and cultural development outside of the control of whites and, therefore, had been particularly suited for slavery.[110] After Emancipation, Le Conte argued, blacks still required "some form or degree of control by the white race."[111] As he made his argument, Le Conte contrasted blacks and Chinese in a racial hierarchy, asserting that "inferior races may be divided into two groups—viz., those which are inferior because undeveloped, and those which are so because developed, perhaps highly developed, in a limited way or in a wrong direction. . . . The Negro is the best type of the first group, and perhaps the Chinese of the second group."[112] Although evangelical nationalists espoused a faith in the ability of all people to come to Christ, be transformed by Christianity, and, therefore, theoretically be included in the nation, missionaries' focus on cultural difference lent itself to the elaboration of racial hierarchies grounded in biology. Through a discourse of pious yet backward freedpeople and coldly intelligent and formalistic Chinese, missionary ethnologies added a culturally and religiously shaded layer to late nineteenth-century efforts to solidify the racialization of blacks and immigrants.

The discursive links between religious and cultural difference on one hand and biological racialism on the other were only part of the evangelical contribution to the articulation of race in the late nineteenth century. Baptist home missionaries also connected their endeavors in the United States to the work of American evangelicals abroad. In rhetoric, in practice, and especially in the depiction of the objects of proselytizing as cultural and racial others, they saw their national project as part of a broader, worldwide mission. The process by which domestic evangelicals identified the objects of their domestic project with "foreign" populations marked Chinese and African Americans as aliens even within the territorial boundaries of the United States. Baptist home missions, in short, played a key role in representing Chinese and blacks as racial *and* national others.

American Baptist mission advocates insistently made connections between domestic and foreign ambitions. In its 1878 annual report, for example, the Executive Board of the ABHMS declared, "Whenever Home Missions succeed, there manifests itself not the spirit of Home Missions only, but Foreign likewise. . . . He who wishes well the world's evangelization, will take care that the spirit of Home Missions is nourished, and that the basis of all evangelical influence is broadened by their successes."[113] The previous year, the Women's Baptist Home Mission Society (WBHMS), an independent but associated female organization, had made clear its domestic mandate "to carry forward the work of Christian women for the evangelization of the heathen and semi-heathen people and homes in our country."[114] But the male-run ABHMS was quick to remind supporters that the WBHMS's domestic emphasis would play a crucial role in attempts by American evangelicals to bring Christianity to "the uttermost parts of the earth."[115]

Missionaries themselves also connected their labors in the United States with evangelical work abroad. Pioneering female missionary Joanna Moore had originally intended to minister to the "heathen" in India, but family responsibilities prevented the schoolteacher from traveling overseas. Instead, moved by the 1863 testimony of a man who had recently visited an encampment of former slaves on Island Number 10 on the Mississippi River, Moore dedicated herself to missionary labors among black southerners. Nevertheless, this lifelong home missionary acknowledged the link between her early desires and her eventual vocation. "I gave up preparation for the Foreign Field in 1855, because my parents very much needed me," she observed. "And yet in one sense I have been a foreign missionary ever since."[116]

Moore's sense of this "foreign" endeavor in the American South is elucidated in her memoir. Almost immediately upon arriving, she came to see a connection between her efforts in the American South and Christian missions in Africa. She provides numerous instances of raising money for African missions, linking the fate of Christian freedpeople in the United States to the conversion of Africans.[117] Moore also almost certainly found the war-torn South and its African American inhabitants to be unfamiliar, even alien. The expectations had been set even before she embarked on her mission journey, for as she listened to stories of Island Number 10, exotic images of blacks mapped easily onto common understandings of the Asian heathen among whom she originally had hoped to work: "There passed before my imagination a panorama of bondmen, tied down with cords of ignorance, superstition, and oppression."[118] Moore's odyssey first to Island Number 10 and then throughout Arkansas, Mississippi, Louisiana, and Tennessee confirmed this sense of foreignness.

Sarah ("Sallie") Elizabeth Stein also worked domestically among a population she deemed alien. Taking up her home mission commission as a teacher at the Baptist Chinese Mission School in Fresno, California, on May 15, 1888, Stein also understood her U.S.-based efforts to be connected closely to foreign evangelical labors.[119] A former schoolteacher like Moore, Stein viewed her posting in California as a continuation of the religious work that had taken her to Guangdong, China, for eight years before her arrival in Fresno.[120] It is not surprising, then, that her observations about her domestic mission inevitably drew upon comparisons with her endeavors abroad. Stein, for example, glumly observed that Chinese residents of Fresno, despite living in a religiously more salubrious environment, still, like their countrymen in China, possessed "hearts . . . of superstition and idolatry."[121] She was, in part, acknowledging that she ministered to a population that seemed to be just as alien as those to whom she attended in China and that endowed her home mission work in Fresno with a sense of the foreign.

But the links between overseas evangelical expansion and domestic missions were more than rhetorical. Dozens of Baptist missionaries joined Sallie Stein's trans-Pacific movement. In fact, during her commission in Guangdong, she labored alongside E. Z. Simmons and R. H. Graves, both of whom had already worked among the Chinese in the United States. They were following a pattern that originally had been established by J. L. Shuck, the first Baptist domestic evangelist to the Chinese in California and a returned China missionary. Indeed, Graves and Simmons both did two stints in Asia separated by domestic commissions in San Francisco.[122] It was during his tour in San Francisco that Simmons accompanied Dong Gong to Portland to help establish the Chinese Mission School.

The Hartwell family—of San Francisco, Tengchow (Penglai), and Guandong—exemplified this China-U.S. missionary connection. In 1884, the ABHMS would tap the family's patriarch, Jesse Boardman Hartwell, to serve as its superintendent of Chinese missions on the Pacific Coast. The Society based its choice on the fact that he had been working in the SBC's Chinese mission in San Francisco for six years, but his twenty years' experience in China under the SBC's Foreign Mission Board surely influenced their decision as well. Once in California, Jesse worked alongside his two surviving daughters, Nellie and Anna. Born in China to Hartwell's first wife, they both held positions as teachers at the San Francisco Chinese Mission School. By the spring of 1888, when twenty-five-year-old Nellie set sail for southern China as an SBC missionary, she had spent enough time at the school to form close relationships with the Chinese who attended classes.[123] Younger sister Anna would soon follow Nellie overseas after graduating from the Baptist Missionary Training School in Chicago in 1891 and spending a year as her father's assistant in San Francisco.[124]

While the Hartwells, Simmons, Graves, Stein, and others moved back and forth across the Pacific, Baptist missionaries in the post-Emancipation South rarely traversed the Atlantic, despite Joanna Moore's reflections about Africa and African Americans. Nevertheless, missionaries and officials linked labors in the South to efforts to evangelize Africa. In 1882, mission official Henry Lyman Morehouse insisted upon the close relationship between black southerners and the conversion of Africa. He argued that missionary and educational endeavors in the South were particularly important because it was within institutions founded by these efforts that "the missionary spirit for the evangelization of Africa is fostered . . . and the sympathies, the prayers and the contributions of the freedmen are being evoked for their pagan kin across the sea."[125]

Morehouse's contention revealed a common assumption. American Baptists generally asserted rather than demonstrated the link between African Americans and Africa. In fact, Morehouse's use of "pagan kin" as the operative bridge across the Atlantic is an instructive juxtaposition. It suggests both a cultural evaluation of the religious state of Africans and a connection to black Americans based on lineage or blood. This supposed affinity was founded not just on a common non-Christian cultural origin but also on kinship—perhaps even biology. Direct comparisons between the spiritual and social condition of African Americans and Africans reinforced these assessments. One female mission official, for instance, asserted that black women "realize[d], all too bitterly from the depths of their own sad experiences that Africa lies all about them, and that the ignorance and superstitions of their own homes must be done away with first of all."[126] When Joanna Moore claimed to be a kind of foreign missionary, she was thus contributing to a discourse that moved blacks beyond the boundaries of the nation and marked them as aliens.

This process was perhaps even more straightforward in home missions to the Chinese, for the depiction of "foreignness" was central to their exclusion. As in the case of African Americans and Africa, white evangelicals believed that Chinese who resided in the United States would play a special role in the conversion of China. In part, this belief was grounded in the observation that many Chinese in the United States returned eventually to China—a fact that home missionaries seized on during the 1870s and 1880s, especially, as they found their efforts stymied by the anti-Chinese movement and as proselytizing and institution building became more difficult.[127] In 1875, for example, a committee of American Baptist officials noted, "the great majority of Chinese emigrants have a fixed purpose of returning to their native land. . . . [A] convert won to Christ, from among the Chinese in America, is a native helper for China."[128] Chinese return migration made domestic missions even more important, for they were crucial to the evangelization of China.

The identification of Chinese in America with foreign populations abroad became a pivotal representation within a racializing discourse. To be sure, rates of return migration, in addition to being an outgrowth of anti-Chinese hostility, reflected the desire of migrants themselves. Yet it is critical to note that while Europeans who journeyed to the United States often experienced comparable or even greater rates of return, contemporary and subsequent scholarly accounts generally distinguished between European "settlers" and Chinese "sojourners."[129] Chinese were marked as outsiders, interested only in exploiting the economic opportunities of the United States before returning home to enjoy their riches; they were, therefore, undeserving of legal equality.[130] Representations of Chinese as sojourning workers in the United States also linked them to contract—and less-than-free—labor that stood in striking contrast to the ideals of post–Civil War free labor rhetoric.[131] The sojourner discourse was thus instrumental in paving the way for legal immigration restriction, and formal exclusion strengthened cultural notions that racially marked Chinese as aliens.[132]

Home missions became a central site for the formulation and elaboration of these mutually reinforcing ideas. As missionaries sought to answer the call of evangelical labors, they engaged in a process that required them to delineate fundamental differences between themselves and their potential proselytes. In so doing, they contributed to a discourse of cultural and religious difference that ostensibly opened the possibility for black and Chinese inclusion within a Christian nation but that simultaneously lent itself to reinforcing growing racialized and biologically based notions of difference. In part, this occurred through essentialized missionary assessments of black and Chinese "character," culture, and religion that mapped easily onto the growing literature on biologically based differences. It also occurred through an evangelical discourse that identified blacks and Chinese as "foreigners" even within the borders of the nation.

*   *   *

Significantly, especially as more women entered mission work during the late nineteenth century, the tensions generated by the racial exclusions abetted by evangelicals' notions of cultural and racial difference and the promise of national inclusion proffered by conversion pivoted increasingly on gender. In fact, even as African American and Chinese populations attracted more attention from home missionaries, female evangelicals took on greater importance both practically and rhetorically. Baptist women established two national organizations in 1877, the WBHMS (based in Chicago) and the Woman's American Baptist Home Mission Society (WABHMS) in Boston, and the WBHMS created the Baptist Missionary Training School for female evangelicals in 1881. Joanna Moore had anticipated the movement of women into formal domestic evangelizing when she entered the field in November 1863, and she received the first commission granted by the WBHMS soon after its founding. By 1880, Moore would be one of thirty-two female missionaries, assistants, and teachers working in the South.[133] Neither was Sallie Stein alone when she arrived in Fresno in May 1888 under a WABHMS commission to replace Frances Potter. She met her coworker, Mrs. Alanson D. Smith, at the mission school and joined at least seven other female Baptist missionaries ministering to Chinese in northern California.[134]

The institutionalization of female Baptist mission work was part of a larger movement that saw native-born, white, middle-class evangelical women extending the reach of their activities beyond the traditional notions of the home. Like other Protestant women, Baptists relied on their standing as the moral centers of the home and the home's standing as the moral center of society to advance an expanded concept of the domestic realm, and, for female missionaries, the home was a unique site of access.[135] Thus, the Chicago-based women's society endeavored "to promote the Christianization of homes," and its sister organization in Boston asserted that "the elevation of . . . women, and . . . the creation of truly Christian homes, where virtue and piety shall flourish, is emphatically the work of Christian women, and *only* theirs."[136]

Yet because home missions were considered to be essential paths not just for religious conversion but also for national inclusion, female evangelicals could play an expanded role in secular matters.[137] As domesticity occupied a more central position in this process, female missionaries became primary agents in defining who might be considered worthy of belonging to the nation. This was what Joanna Moore had in mind when, in the midst of explaining the proper role of mission women, she declared, "The prosperity of our

Nation depends upon our homes and home is what mother makes it to a large extent."[138]

The emphasis on domesticity meant also that mission efforts focused increasingly on female proselytes. Joanna Moore began ministering to women and children almost right away, visiting homes and creating Sunday and Bible schools. By the late 1870s, she was exploring the possibility of establishing "a training school for colored women," and, in 1885, Moore launched her "first real boarding school for women" in a "rented house." In this school and others "for wives and mothers," the course of study focused on the home and family, training female students in the domestic virtues of proper "housekeeping," "laws of health," and "social purity and temperance." And to keep the goals of women's mission work explicit, Moore held regular "Mothers' and children's meetings, where all questions pertaining to the duties of wife and mother and child will be discussed and carried to God in prayer."[139]

Moore's work supplemented the larger labors of the northern Baptist–sponsored colleges and seminaries. In fact, by the time she established her first school, Baptist-affiliated institutions, like the Wayland Seminary in Washington, D.C., and Shaw University, were already admitting women, and Sophia B. Packard and Harriet E. Giles had established the Atlanta Baptist Female Seminary. With the obvious exception of the Atlanta school, these colleges and seminaries had originally been concerned with creating a class of male leaders, especially ministers. Women's classes were added because male leaders could only inhabit good Christian homes if they had good Christian spouses.

At Baptist seminaries and colleges the emphasis was never entirely on domestic or industrial education.[140] It is significant, however, that, as the Jim Crow regime forced its way into power, more and more philanthropic foundations that funded black educational institutions began to propound theories of black suitability for industrial rather than classical education, and this shaped the types of classes and programs these schools offered. Shaw University, for instance, maintained its liberal arts and theological programs, but its administrators recognized that a major benefactor, the John F. Slater Fund, preferred funding technical programs, and this part of the school's curriculum began to expand as early as the 1880s.[141]

On the Pacific Coast, "rescue missions" aimed at prostitutes in San Francisco appear to have been the most common—or at least the most publicized—form of engagement between white female missionaries and Chinese women. Presbyterians, Congregationalists, and Methodists created mission homes for women who sought refuge from prostitution.[142] In these missions to "fallen" women, the interlinked ideals of domesticity, moral purity, and respectability took center stage.[143]

However, Baptists did not engage in formal rescue missions, and the demographic particularities of the Chinese population in America complicated the ideal of women's work for women, for cultural practices and systematic exclusion created a severe sex-ratio imbalance.[144] Nevertheless, Baptist women did make an effort to reach Chinese homes, and, especially as a small American-born generation of Chinese women developed, they even began to organize classes exclusively for young women and girls.[145] In 1885, for example, a fellow missionary in San Francisco reported that Janie Sanford was making regular visits "among women and children."[146] But evangelicals hoped also to organize schools, and Baptist devotion to domestic training can be seen in female missionaries' tenacious desire to create programs for Chinese women.

There is little extant evidence of what exactly occurred in these classes. However, if we use the rhetoric of women's missions, the programs of Baptist missions in the South, and Peggy Pascoe's study of the Presbyterian rescue mission in San Francisco, it is likely that the educational program consisted of training in the proper elements of middle-class womanhood. The curriculum most probably included prayer and Bible study for piety, supervision to ensure purity, and lessons in cooking, housework, and child care to instill domesticity.[147]

It is significant, though, that a good part of women's missions on the Pacific Coast entailed working with male proselytes. But even in these female missions to men, respectability and gender remained at the center of training programs. American evangelicals painted Chinese with the broad brush of "heathen" and all that designation's accompanying ills. This ostensibly religious designation, however, had social manifestations, including the allegedly tyrannical treatment of women by Chinese men—a characteristic few missionaries failed to note. Many complained, for instance, that Chinese social relations made the domestic education of women—in fact, *any* education of women—nearly impossible and thus prevented the creation of Christian families and homes. Such was the case in Portland in 1875, when exasperated Baptists explained that it was "not safe to undertake" a female training class, "owing to the prejudice of the Chinese to teaching women."[148]

In addition to catechism, then, missions to Chinese men would begin with instilling proper respect for women and would result in the "manly" acceptance of women's domestic education. As one missionary observed, after lamenting that Chinese women were prevented from such training, only "the teaching of Christian truth" could lead to "a noble and outspoken manhood in behalf of every good word and work."[149] If, as Peggy Pascoe has argued, female rescue missions were to allow "degraded" women to regain their moral purity, then missions to Chinese men were to instill reverence for Christian womanhood, perhaps even to create marriageable men for rescued women.[150]

Female missions in both fields created unprecedented opportunities for blacks and Chinese. In the South, missionary investment in educational institutions would have a lasting effect, and mission officials understood this as a primary goal of their project. Black proselytes and white missionaries alike knew that teachers were community leaders, and Baptist-trained women emerged in leadership roles.[151] As Henry Morehouse remarked, "A well-qualified Christian teacher . . . is . . . a great power for good in the community,—second only to the educated preacher of the Gospel."[152] As Jim Crow and Judge Lynch strengthened their grip on the South, African Americans found refuge in missionary schools and churches. The message of hope that had pervaded these institutions in the heady days of Reconstruction shifted to a more cautious strategy of community building and sustenance, but black schools, especially, would, as Raymond Gavins has argued, foster "an attitude of protest against Jim Crow" and would later serve as the staging ground for a more concerted assault on the system.[153] Chinese rescue missions most obviously provided women the chance to better their social condition by escaping exploitative sex work.[154] And missions to Chinese men held the possibility of educational attainment and access to white sponsorship and resources.

Moreover, beyond even the social possibilities they opened to clients and potential clients, Baptist home missions could foster sustained interracial, intercultural contact. Historian Evelyn Brooks Higginbotham asserts that female-centered evangelical work could result in an "unlikely sisterhood" between white and black women. She argues that missions "created structured avenues along which black and white women traveled together, heard each other's voices, and learned of each other's struggles and values."[155] Similarly, Pascoe has written convincingly of the emotional bonds that Chinese women and white female missionaries developed.[156] The links between mission men and women and clients also served a more practical purpose, particularly as the veil of oppression and restriction descended on the Jim Crow South and Exclusion Era Chinese America, for the friendships, acquaintances, and other relationships forged in mission communities could provide blacks and Chinese access to limited resources and might offer a modicum of protection from the worst abuses of white supremacy.

Yet these avenues that held such promise for mobility and interracial "dialogue" and "communication" traversed a white supremacist social landscape, and the power of missionaries as producers of cultural and racial knowledge should not be underestimated. In fact, female home missions produced a discourse of difference that marked blacks and Chinese as outsiders—a discourse that complemented the elision of foreign and domestic fields. Neither the desire to convert nor the process itself provided a neutral conduit for inclusion. Conversion hinged on the delineation of essential differences between mission women and proselytes, and the evangelical goal of "elevating" target populations to respectability assumed their lesser condition.

No other set of ideas and practices illustrates the limits of home mission contact better than the emphasis of missionaries on gendered notions of respectability. On the Pacific Coast, where missionary ethnologies by evangelicals laboring in China buttressed ideas about heathen immigrants, the supposed paths for inclusion were articulated in a vocabulary that made it clear that clients would find it difficult to truly break the bonds of their cultural tendencies. Even rescue missions—perhaps the starkest example of evangelical labors as a conduit for social (as well as spiritual) uplift—contributed to this discourse of difference. As historian Nayan Shah notes, as early as the mid-nineteenth century, "white politicians, missionaries, and physicians castigated Chinese female prostitution as a leading threat to the moral and social order."[157] Missionaries' focus on this dimension of sexuality and gender played a key role in the racialization of Chinese women. In fact, historian George Anthony Pfeffer has argued that the press's "presumption that every Chinese woman is a prostitute"—an image developed in large part through missionary ethnologies—was a key factor in the racial logic of immigration exclusion even prior to the 1882 Exclusion Act.[158]

Missionaries also produced images of Chinese men in the United States that foreclosed any possibility of attaining the characteristics of American manhood.[159] The initial assessment of Chinese as patriarchal in the extreme gave rise to a secondary discourse of manhood that emphasized the subordinated position of Chinese men to white women. In practice, it seemed, requiring Chinese men to submit to female missionaries as their social and moral betters was the most common method of instilling proper respect for female domestic purity and piety. This gender disciplining appears vividly in a widely distributed WABHMS pamphlet. In this leaflet, a fictional home mission woman relates her triumph of converting Lee Jip and the tragedy of Lee Jip's accidental death by trampling.[160] The relationship between Helen Dickinson, the missionary, and Lee Jip (whom she calls Gypsy) is emotionally close, but it seems even closer than the intimacy required of evangelical conversion. In his "bright, winning face and soft, gentle eyes," Lee Jip is "more childlike than an American boy of half his age."[161] Dickinson's language suggests that the relationship is one of mother to son, even more than missionary to proselyte. She models a maternal relationship that reinforces a hierarchy that maintains white female moral authority and the subordinate position of Chinese men.

The parable also points to two ideas that place this depiction of Chinese men within a broader context of fixed national and cultural difference. Helen's nickname for Lee Jip—"Gypsy"—is not pure whimsy; it is a direct allusion to the "sojourner" representation of Chinese—they were unsettled, never intending to stay or become citizens. And that Lee Jip perishes, even after accepting Christ, suggests that while evangelicals could be spiritually successful, the next step in home mission ideology—inclusion in the Christian nation—remained futile. Chinese men were simultaneously too autocratic, patriarchal, and heathen and not manly enough to be included in the nation.[162]

Female missionaries in the South also participated in this double-edged process. Even as their work opened institutional support and possibilities for working alongside black women, it also produced a vocabulary of difference pivoting on domestic respectability. "Cleanliness and purity" were at the center of Joanna Moore's catechism, and she went to great pains to educate black women about the "laws of health, including proper food, clothing, exercise, cleanliness, and care of the sick."[163]

Moore was not alone in her preoccupation. A flurry of reports from mission women in 1879 and 1880 only underscores the central position of domestic cleanliness and its necessary corollary, filth-laden black clients, in evangelical literature. In these accounts, even households led by Christian mothers needed "enlightening as to the efficacy of soap-suds."[164] A missionary's description of a former slave woman illustrated what female evangelicals were up against: "I think I never saw a person so wretchedly dirty as one of these women was. Her filthy garments hung in tatters; her face was bedaubed with grease and coal-dust, her hands indescribable."[165] The repetition and dissemination of these images went hand-in-glove with a developing discourse that intertwined moral, cultural, hygienic, and physical difference as central to definitions of the black race.[166]

The emphasis of female missionaries on the fundamental and gendered differences of Chinese and black clients complemented the discourse that linked domestic and foreign evangelical efforts. Taken together, these aspects of Baptist women's home mission work illustrate what Amy Kaplan has referred to as two different but subtly linked notions of the term "domestic."[167] On the one hand, female home missionaries represented the growing number of trained women entering evangelical work, signaled the expansion of the domestic sphere, and exemplified domesticity and respectability as key signifiers for conversion. On the other hand, as evangelicals ministering to blacks and Chinese, they played a central role in setting the standard of respectability that divided civilized from savage and defined the "domestic" against the "foreign."[168] They related Chinese immigrants and African Americans to populations beyond the territorial borders of the nation and marked those who resided in the United States as alien others. Although mission women tended to emphasize culture rather than biology, this demarcation of cultural difference, pivoting on who might be included in the nation, resulted in a culturally constructed racial discourse.

Baptist home missions among blacks in the South and Chinese on the Pacific Coast exposed both the promise and the limits of the ABHMS evangelical, nation-building, and racializing project. For white evangelicals, the desire to create a Christian America had led them to a conclusion full of radical possibility. Despite the recent model of black slavery and the long-standing 1790 Naturalization Act, which restricted citizenship rights only to those immigrants who were "free whites," the ABHMS believed that its evangelical nationalist project should be expanded to include freedpeople and the Chinese in America not just as coreligionists but as fellow citizens. Yet internal ideological contradictions and, especially, external opposition limited the application of this belief. Nevertheless, through its vigorous labors, the ABHMS provided important tools to African Americans and Chinese immigrants as *they* sought to dismantle the hierarchy of race.

In 1882, ABHMS corresponding secretary and official historian Henry Lyman Morehouse declared, "The Gospel breaks the shackles of hierarchy."[169] Morehouse's words evoked the promise and possibility of an evangelical Christianity that ministered to Chinese immigrants in the aftermath of the Chinese Exclusion Act and to African Americans in the post-Reconstruction South. He believed that the acceptance of Christianity by men and women of diverse backgrounds would reduce social differences through assimilation. Yet Morehouse's simple statement of faith concealed a more complex process in which the hierarchy of race, rather than being eradicated, was rearticulated through religion. And while adhering to the Baptist faith in divine providence and the power of Scripture, Morehouse neglected to credit the most influential earthbound opponents of racial hierarchy—African Americans and Chinese immigrants themselves.

CHAPTER 4

Congregation

And they continued steadfastly in the apostles' teaching and
fellowship, in breaking of bread, and in prayers.
And fear came upon every soul: and many wonders and signs were
done through the apostles.
And all that believed were together, and had all things common.
  Acts 2:42–44 (ASV)

Let us break bread together on our knees (on our knees),
Let us break bread together on our knees (on our knees).
When I fall on my knees with my face to the rising sun,
O Lord, have mercy on me.
  "Let Us Break Bread Together" (traditional)

HENRY MARTIN TUPPER'S optimism found its measure in ambition. Within
a year of the first meeting of the American Baptist mission school in Raleigh,
the northern missionary who headed the institution hoped to raise a building to house the school and a church—a permanent structure that would
symbolize the lasting transformation of the souls and lives he had been called
to convert. To realize his ambition, Tupper turned to friends from his native North. But he also turned to his putative charges. Few freedpeople could
afford outright cash donations to the endeavor—although some significant
pledges did arrive—so the black participants of the Raleigh Baptist mission

contributed something familiar: They gave their labor. Soon they would be asked, literally, to help build the mission school by making bricks and laying them. But for now, as the mission hoped to increase its building fund, they worked as performers. In December 1866, students from the mission's Sabbath school took to the stage. No extant program of the concert survives, but from the record that does exist it is clear that students performed hymns and other religious songs before an audience of benefactors, potential sponsors, and curious white residents of Raleigh. They sang to commemorate the mission's first anniversary and the Christmas holiday.[1]

Almost nine years later, Chinese participants at the Baptist mission school in Portland also contributed their labor to an evangelical effort by taking to the stage. At first, organizers planned a simple public "Spelling Match," but by the evening of April 26, 1875, participants had transformed the program into a full slate of song, prayer, addresses, and recitations. Each class demonstrated reading and recitation exercises in English. They also sang hymns, such as "The Morning Light Is Breaking," closing the exhibition with a rendition of "Jesus Loves Me" performed by the entire school. Mission participants made cash contributions when they could, and they soon would be asked to pay a tuition fee to attend the school, but on this occasion they were called on to demonstrate their religious and secular scholarship "to defray the expenses of the Mission," and the money raised by their performance was "applied for the payment of the organ now used by the Chinese church."[2]

The Raleigh concert and the Portland recital had more in common than providing economic support for their respective evangelical institutions.[3] Each marked a significant institutional milestone and a holy day. The Raleigh show coincided roughly with the first anniversary of the mission's first class and with Christmas, while the Portland exhibition followed closely on the heels of Easter and was a celebration of the first baptisms of mission participants. Missionaries and teachers in both Raleigh and Portland intended the concerts to demonstrate the ameliorative effects of evangelical uplift and the efficacy of mission efforts. In North Carolina, men who only recently had suffered under the material, moral, and spiritual depredations of slavery appeared transformed by mission classes as they entertained with religious songs. In Oregon, as Chinese students performed exercises in English oratory and sang hymns, they too provided evidence of their spiritual and social conversion. Portland's *Oregonian* took note of the intended message when it reported that the 1875 exhibition "passed off with credit to the scholars, and showed that the efforts put forth to teach the Chinese were not all in vain."[4] The concerts signaled to mission advocates, potential benefactors, and skeptics alike that Baptist home mission projects were capable of transforming the lives of blacks and Chinese. Former slaves and heathen aliens were now on their way to becoming respectable Christians, perhaps even worthy of citizenship.

But performances like the 1866 concert in Raleigh and the 1875 recital in Portland were still more complex. Even as the exhibitions were meant to show that they had been spiritually and socially altered—*converted*—by Baptist missions, the black Sunday school and Chinese mission school students transformed the meanings and aims of the events through their participation. Like the missionaries who organized the concerts, black and Chinese participants were, in part, motivated by the material possibilities engendered by their performances. They, too, wanted to raise money to create and sustain churches and schools. But their support for and participation in the endeavors underscored their hope that they would eventually lead the institutions for which they labored.

And while students were also most certainly proud of their religious and academic acumen, their message of evangelical transformation likely contained subtle critiques of their assumed inferior status. In slavery, black southerners had become accustomed to reinterpreting received ideas of Christianity and Christian authority as masters and southern evangelicals sought to inculcate slaves with a form of Christianity that emphasized obedience and subordination.[5] This tradition of rearticulation survived Emancipation and served freedpeople especially well in their relations with the missionaries. In Raleigh, the December concert was, in part, a celebration of Christ's birth, but black performers also surely referenced the communal festivities associated with the traditional break from labor during slavery, and, given the high rate of rural-to-urban migration, perhaps even alluded to the revelry of the Jonkonnu (John Canoe, John Kunering, John Cornu) rituals rooted in West and West Central African yam festivals.[6] And as they showed how much they had learned from the missionaries by singing hymns together—a crucial component of late nineteenth-century Sunday school and mission pedagogy—they also asserted their new status as freedpeople, demonstrated a form of fellowship with each other, and signaled notions of equality and freedom to fellow blacks.[7] If the choir, or the missionary direction of the choir, was influenced by the growing fascination with African American spirituals, then the messages of fellowship, freedom, and equality—the message of hope—were even greater, as students sang songs that referenced West African communal religious practices, like the ring shout, and whose lyrics identified the singers as a chosen people of God for whom justice would soon come.[8]

For the Chinese in Portland, it is more difficult to detect similar "hidden transcripts," for there is little evidence to suggest the development of a uniquely Chinese tradition of Christianity in late nineteenth-century America.[9] Nevertheless, the mission school participants, like their counterparts in the South, signaled broader ideas of Chinese and Christian fellowship and claimed public space as they performed. Singing hymns and reciting Scripture and lessons together, they reinforced and displayed the bonds of community that had been forged in classes, prayer meetings, and church services.

The feeling of congregation conveyed by the mission participants in Portland and in Raleigh reverberated beyond the walls of the buildings where they performed. The black Sunday school students in Raleigh and Chinese mission Mission School students in Portland had been praying together, learning together, and sometimes living together, nurturing the intimate sense of fellowship fostered by evangelical Christianity and at the foundation of community formation. As they took to the stage for their concerts, they publicly revealed those bonds of black community in Raleigh and Chinese community in Portland. They also showed those who did not participate in Baptist missions the possibilities for inclusion and acceptance that Emancipation or immigration might hold, especially if mediated by mission institutions. On one level, concert participants communicated to other African Americans and Chinese that they too could aspire to full spiritual—and perhaps even social and political—equality with whites. On another level, through their actions, they demonstrated the value of coming together to consolidate the fragile forms of community facilitated by Emancipation and immigration.

These snapshots of community formation that come into focus while examining mission exhibitions hardly do justice to the significance, complexity, and scope of the networks crafted by black and Chinese Baptists. In these early, celebratory moments of mission development, hope for social equality radiates. Yet even before the storm clouds of legalized segregation and Exclusion gathered, black North Carolinians and Chinese Oregonians found such hope dimmed by uncertainty. As they performed at their respective concerts, each group found itself in the midst of extraordinary social ferment. The Raleigh recital took place as the post–Civil War status of blacks remained, at best, ambiguous, perhaps most starkly marked by the rumors of a black conspiracy and uprising that had circulated throughout the state the year before, and, more to the point, as the state legislature was in the process of passing its harshly restrictive Black Codes.[10] In Portland, performers took to the stage in the wake of an upsurge of anti-Chinese agitation in the city and throughout the Pacific Coast.[11]

In this context, the fellowship displayed, as well as the broader networks that these acts of camaraderie and community represented, took on great significance—a significance that would only grow as Jim Crow and Chinese Exclusion gained momentum. Historian Earl Lewis has written insightfully and eloquently of the importance of black forms of "congregation" during segregation. As the repressive white supremacy of Jim Crow sought to distinguish between blacks and whites in a separate and unequal system, "congregation . . . symbolized an act of free will, whereas segregation represented the imposition of another's will. Slyly, modestly, blacks . . . substituted the one for the other in daily dealings, adroitly inverting the language of oppression."[12] But black southerners were not the only group who faced systematic differentiation and exclusion; Chinese, too, felt the oppression of segregation. And they, like their black counterparts, sought to turn the language of white supremacy on its head by emphasizing their will, their agency, through community formation.

The constellation of institutions, associations, and formal and informal networks established by aspiring black and Chinese Baptist mission participants repudiated white evangelical notions of inferiority and subverted the condescension of missionary discourse and practice. In these spaces for religious expression, education, and community, African Americans and Chinese challenged the deference demanded by their roles as mission "proselytes" while at the same time accepting the resources—financial, intellectual, and religious—of the missionaries. Accepting the mission enterprises into their lives, they seized opportunities for education, support, protection, and autonomous space, thereby rearticulating the missionary discourse of uplift.

Blacks and Chinese who emerged from mission institutions became leaders. Their mission educations encouraged them to see themselves a separate, culturally elite class, the moral stewards of their flocks.[13] But, in significantly different ways, mission-educated African Americans and Chinese modeled alternate visions of community leadership. Black Baptists who attended the ABHMS mission in Raleigh were rooted in the communities in which they labored, and the critical importance of churches and schools within these communities gave teachers and ministers institutional platforms from which to lead. The relationship of mission-educated Chinese to their unconverted countrymen in the United States was more ambiguous, for their embrace of Christianity appeared to mark a fundamental break from the cultural and class traditions of other Chinese in America. Nevertheless, Chinese converts formed a small but important community. Although lacking the same institutional

and traditional foundation as their black brethren, they still provided fellowship for one another in local settings and in extended networks, represented
the sense of possible "progress" to white elites, and modeled striving and accomplishment for their non-Christian countrymen. As the hope and faith in
Emancipation and immigration gave way to the fear and struggle of segregation and exclusion, as Jim Crow muzzled the greatest weapon—citizenship
rights—that black southerners possessed in the fight against white supremacy,
and as Chinese settlement and claims to national belonging were blocked at
the port of entry, their cultures of congregation, where blacks and Chinese
could literally and metaphorically break bread with one another, became the
training ground for leaders who not only extended the networks further but
who also symbolized the fulfillment of black and Chinese aspiration.

African American and Chinese performances in exhibitions may have been
the most public forms of support for their respective home missions, but these
activities were by no means the only ways that they helped to create Baptist churches and schools. Indeed, in perhaps the most basic, even mundane,
way—their early and enthusiastic participation in evangelical programs—they
established the foundation for lasting institutions. But they did more than
merely partake in classes, prayer meetings, and services offered by white evangelicals. Black and Chinese participants shaped mission programs to suit their
own needs, creating spaces and institutions in which to express and pursue
ideas of freedom, equality, belonging, and hope.

In the South, freedpeople took full advantage of the evangelical overture
presented by northern missionaries like Henry Martin Tupper. In part, this re-
ceptiveness indicates a shrewd assessment of the material support for community institutions available to ex-slaves after the end of the Civil War. Though
they may have felt the full weight of condescension implicit in uplift ideology
and missionary ethnology, they nonetheless *chose* to participate in mission
programs.[14] In fact, Tupper's charge to spread the gospel, convert souls, and
establish meetings, churches, and schools held great power for black North
Carolinians. During the antebellum era, the efforts of southern ministers and
slave owners to convert slaves to Christianity through "plantation missions"
had resulted in the widespread dissemination of Christian belief. Although
differing in many ways from the intended social control and obedience of the
missions, as the historian of religion Albert J. Raboteau notes, "by the eve of
the Civil War, Christianity had pervaded the slave community. . . . Not all
slaves were Christian, nor were all those who accepted Christianity members

of a church, but the doctrines, symbols, and visions of life preached by Christianity were familiar to most."[15]

For a number of reasons, the Baptist denomination resonated with African Americans.[16] First and foremost, its tradition of congregational autonomy was crucial for those wishing to worship without worrying about the authority of whites.[17] This tradition not only enabled a measure of independence from hierarchical denominational structures, it also allowed more social and cultural space for variations in worship. The greater freedom of worship merged with the emotional content of evangelical religion to provide increased room for practices that resonated with traditional African religions.[18] The role of ministers or preachers as local leaders of each congregation also appealed greatly to men and women coming out of slavery. In bondage, the slave preacher had taken on enormous authority as a community leader.[19]

This compatibility was not lost on Baptist missionaries and officials, who excitedly commented on it as they savored the prospect of bringing their message before such a receptive audience. Noted the Executive Board of the ABHMS in 1865, "A very large portion of the colored people of the South are Baptists in their church relations, or their religious preferences."[20] The year before, the ABHMS missionary in Port Royal, South Carolina, had estimated that "seven-tenths of the ten or fifteen thousand colored people in Port Royal are, and for many long years have been, Baptists in their preference, and thousands of them by profession, no one will deny."[21]

And, indeed, Tupper's arrival in Raleigh occasioned great interest among black residents of the city and its environs. Former slaves from throughout the region sought Tupper's services as a minister and an evangelist as he established religious meetings, presided over Sunday schools, and attempted to organize black churches. In particular, they engaged the missionary to perform religious rites, such as marriage ceremonies. Toward the end of his first autumn in Raleigh in 1865, Tupper kept a schedule that saw him marrying ex-slave couples every three days.[22] In the aftermath of slavery, the confirmation of marriages by the civil government held great practical value, for legal sanction legitimized freedpeople's children, qualified spouses for soldiers' pensions, and prepared couples to partake in the possible reapportionment of land.[23]

Yet the desire of former slaves to have their marital unions—either newly made or reaffirmed—acknowledged by an authority with both civil and religious standing signified something deeper. Most obviously, African American couples sought to exercise a newly won basic civil right. Under slavery, the illegality of slave marriages, the forced conjugality between nonconsenting partners, and the disruption of marital and other family ties through slave sales not only marked the choice of freedpeople to marry as a poignant counterpoint to the unfreedom of bondage but also made such decisions forcefully assertive political acts.[24] Even after the North Carolina legislature, as part of the state's Black Codes, passed a law that required ex-slaves to register marriages with county clerks or justices of the peace, the high level of compliance constituted a choice made by freedpeople to formalize marital bonds and reaffirm ideas of marriage that had been held during slavery.[25]

It was no coincidence that ex-slaves sought Tupper's services as a minister to sanctify their matrimonial bonds. A ceremony officiated at by a clergyman, as much as the marriage itself, served as a declaration of hard-won freedom. During the antebellum era, slaves had developed and practiced a religion that fused African traditions with the Christianity propagated by evangelical plantation missions. Afro-Christianity was shaped by the punishing oppression of servitude, the emancipatory faith and egalitarian spirit of African and Old Testament theology, and the relentless zeal for freedom of the slaves themselves. White evangelicals had engaged in plantation missions during the 1830s and 1840s that were sanctioned by slave owners and that emphasized social control and obedience, but slaves transformed the Christianity they received and practiced it beyond the gaze of masters.[26] This "invisible religion" constituted an opportunity for significant, though usually clandestine, resistance to the slave regime.[27] In the period immediately following Emancipation, the public expression of faith, especially those marking crucial moments in the life cycle, signaled that black religious expression—and the hopes and desires to which it gave voice—would no longer remain hidden.[28]

For ex-slaves, the Christian rite of marriage helped to define the contours of freedom in more specific ways as well. In the aftermath of slavery, as white North Carolinians sought to limit the rights, control the mobility, and compel the labor of blacks, the state held a greater interest in marriage. "To keep freedpeople from threatening civil society," writes historian Laura F. Edwards, "they had to be brought into it. To be brought into it, they had to be married." Even as African Americans sought the state's recognition of their matrimonial bonds, conservative white leaders and the laws they advocated tended to emphasize the obligation, not the rights, of marriage.[29] Yet the very choice of a minister like Tupper over a county clerk or a justice of the peace to confer the rite demonstrated freedpeople's faith in Christianity and their skepticism of the state. For these former slaves, the hope in freedom lay as much with the emancipatory and redemptive higher power of Christianity as with civil institutions.

But black participation in the Raleigh mission entailed more than engaging Tupper to officiate at special rites and services. Freedpeople flocked to prayer meetings organized by the missionary and welcomed him into their homes for religious visits, thereby underwriting the missionary's efforts. As Tupper noted in an early letter to the ABHMS corresponding secretary, "I have been visiting the colored people in their homes. They welcome me with the greatest cordiality. . . . I find plenty to do and am welcomed by every colored man and listened to with much apparent interest."[30] This interest blossomed within months, and, by February 17, 1866, black Baptists in Raleigh joined the northern missionary in organizing Second Baptist Church.[31] The 1866 Christmas concert was an effort to raise funds for a building that would house Second Baptist as well as the mission school.

However, Tupper's sanguine reports to the Executive Board concealed the degree to which his attempts were challenged, frustrated, and reoriented by black Baptists in the city. In other words, like many missionary-generated documents, Tupper's dispatches emphasized the success of his efforts and all but ignored freedpeople's efforts to tailor them to their needs. A closer examination of the genesis of Second Baptist reveals that not all African American Baptists in the Raleigh area necessarily welcomed his efforts. In fact, although Tupper hoped to lead the black members of the city's white-run First Baptist Church to form their own congregation with him at the helm, the black congregants of First Baptist elected to remain. Their reasons for staying are unclear, but three years later, in 1868, some two hundred black members of First Baptist formed their own church under the leadership of Henry Jett, an African American lay preacher. Both the timing of the creation of the newly formed First Baptist Church, Colored, and Jett's leadership suggest that black worshippers were interested in more autonomy than they believed a white northern missionary would have afforded them.[32]

The refusal to join Tupper and the subsequent formation of a separate black-run church put the white missionary on notice. Although Tupper's affiliation with the ABHMS and his links to northern philanthropy meant that he could harness substantial resources—especially money and personnel—to attract potential proselytes, Tupper was also continually vulnerable to ex-slaves seeking to form their own churches under their own leadership. In fact, the move by Jett and his fellow congregants of First Baptist Church, Colored, was not at all unusual. Both contemporary observers and subsequent historians have commented at length on the exodus of black members from white-run churches.[33] Tupper thus needed to deliver the services desired by prospective black participants. He also needed to remain vigilant. Even as a missionary, minister, and teacher influenced by evangelical uplift ideology and acutely aware of his position as a religious leader responsible for the moral stewardship of his flock, he depended upon black involvement as a marker of missionary success and was obligated to take care not to overstep the bounds of his authority, lest his flock depart. Black Baptists could always vote with their feet.

Evangelicals in Portland were also acutely aware that the Chinese to whom they hoped to minister were capable of voting with their feet. If they had anticipated that the Chinese would be mere objects to be molded by Scripture, mission supporters at Portland's First Baptist Church were quickly disabused of that notion even before the opening of their mission school. Dong Gong, the Chinese missionary laboring in San Francisco whom they hoped to hire to oversee their project, proved a tough and able negotiator. After learning of Dong's availability, the recently established Committee on Chinese Mission Work at First Baptist instructed Rev. D. S. Pierce to offer Dong a job "for six months at $25.00 per month, also to pay his passage to Portland, and to procure an outfit for the School." Dong quickly informed the committee that he would accept the job, but that twenty-five dollars a month was insufficient, especially "if he [was] to devote his whole time to the work." Although records never reflect a comment on Dong's demand that his salary be increased sixty percent to forty dollars per month, the Chinese Mission School's budget indicates that First Baptist acquiesced.[34] Dong's insistence on receiving more money not only exemplified shrewdness on the part of the Chinese missionary, it also signaled his striving for equality.[35]

Supporters of the mission from First Baptist Church worried about the will not only of their new Chinese missionary but of their potential proselytes as well. Originally, Rev. A. R. Medbury had planned that the mission would preach to the Chinese exclusively in their own language, and he and Pierce, his successor, emphasized spiritual conversion as the primary aim of their efforts. However, when Dong Gong and E. Z. Simmons arrived and met with First Baptist Church's Committee on Chinese Missions, they decided that English language instruction was a necessary part of the curriculum. The mission school soon supplemented the English language classes with instruction in other types of secular education, including geography and mathematics.[36]

In part, the broadly transformative aims of the evangelical nationalism espoused by Portland Baptists explain the expansion of the school's curriculum from pure catechism to secular subjects. If the Chinese Mission School was to minister to the minds and souls of its students, then it was necessary to provide an education in a wide array of topics. But the more extensive curriculum was also a result of the desires of the Chinese in the city. Indeed, teachers and administrators observed that the most effective way to attract souls for conversion was to offer training in English and other types of secular learning. The sentiment was made plain when Rev. A. S. Coats, who assumed the pastorate of First Baptist in 1877, closed the school's third annual exhibition by paraphrasing mission theorist Joseph Cook: "The way to reach the Chinese in America is to bait the hook with the English Alphabet."[37]

That significant numbers of Chinese in Portland availed themselves of the mission, whether for the bait of English or the hook of Christianity, convinced white evangelicals and supporters that their goal of social and spiritual transformation was attainable. The Chinese Mission School's first monthly report indicates that an average of fifty-nine students attended every evening while the morning and evening Sabbath schools averaged thirty-one and thirty-three students, respectively. Fewer students went to the evening school during the second month, owing in part to "the disastrous fire in the Chinese part of the City and the extreme cold weather," and from mid-February to mid-March 1875, the school experienced yet another dip in participation. By February 1875, however, participation had settled at between thirty-five and forty students. Moreover, the baptisms of Sam Song Bo, Lam One, Sid Que, Wong Sam, Wo Gow, Lai Tin, Loung Jue, Wong Tehung, Wong Haw, and Foong Pay Fang the day before the April 1875 mission school concert were evidence of the project's success.[38]

While the extant record leans heavily toward how missionaries understood Chinese participation in the mission, such a narrow interpretive perspective misses an opportunity to understand the role of the school in the lives of its students and in the broader context of Chinese Portland. Just as Dong Gong had aspired to equal pay for his services as a missionary, the Chinese who attended mission programs sought a recognition of spiritual equality and even made a claim for civic belonging. The annual concerts embodied these aspirations. In part, the Chinese affirmed the hopes of the white sponsors of the mission school by modeling the spiritual and social transformation they desired. It was therefore both fitting and significant that Dong Gong, during the first annual concert, emphasized the degree to which his spirit had been altered by Christianity when he announced that no Chinese religion or philosophy "can stir my heart nor satisfy my conscience like the New Testament."[39]

But in taking to the stage to demonstrate their command of hymns, spelling, oration, and geography, Chinese students provided a counterexample to the dominant racial thinking of the time. Displaying the changes engendered by their mission education, Chinese participants made clear that the biological designations of unalterable racial characteristics were wrong—that education and conversion could overcome blood. They also offered an alternate image of the Chinese to white observers. The missionary ethnology of Baptist evangelicals portrayed the Chinese as aloof and, therefore, difficult to convert. Not only did their perceived arrogance make the emotional commitment to Christ more difficult, but Chinese conversions that did occur were made suspect by a perceived tendency to profess faith without truly embracing Christianity. Warned one Baptist missionary, "I can see about me a great tendency to paganize Christianity. . . . Christianity, grafted upon a pagan stock, will never produce the fruits of the Spirit."[40]

In particular, the hymns performed at the concert displayed a critical part of the religious pedagogy designed to penetrate the hearts of potential converts and "produce the fruits of the Spirit." Singing was an important feature of the mission's Sunday and night school, providing an activity that students found engaging and that teachers, missionaries, and ministers believed would provide the necessary emotional atmosphere to lay the foundation for a genuine conversion experience.[41] Through song, Chinese mission participants did more than learn the catechism. They highlighted their emotional capacity and countered popular ideas of them as unfeeling and spiritually indifferent.

Chinese also used these public exhibitions to demonstrate their fellowship with white, evangelical Portland. Linked by a common religious language, they asserted their membership within the larger Christian community. The public celebration of the first ten Chinese baptisms in the city marked by the first concert symbolized this sense of congregation. But such public events represented the largest—and most peaceful—interactions between the city's Chinese and white inhabitants. To be sure, dozens—even hundreds—of quotidian interactions occurred each day without incident, but the numerous, often spectacular, episodes of harassment and violence against the Chinese seemed to set the tone for race relations in the city. Against the backdrop of growing—and more virulent and violent—anti-Chinese animosity in northern California, which was featured regularly in local newspapers, the climate in Portland seemed ominous indeed. But the apparent embrace of Chinese Christians by the city's elite—by families like the Failings and the Corbetts—and by institutions like First Baptist Church represented a refuge from the rising tide of white supremacy. The concerts, of course, may have been extraordinary events, but there is evidence to suggest that the acceptance of converted Chinese by the city leaders extended beyond these exhibitions. In 1878, for example, Portland's newspaper, not given to characterizing Chinese in particularly positive terms, marked the death of First Baptist Church convert Wang Ho by proclaiming that he had "lived and died a most exemplary Christian."[42] The ability to find a common connection to the city's elite must have been a high priority and a source of great comfort.

Black southerners' dreams of freedom also found expression in Baptist missions. However, although they shared with their Chinese brethren on the Pacific Coast an evangelical language of spiritual equality and a faith in education as the path to individual and collective improvement, the specific contours of African American engagement with Baptist efforts and the communities and institutions that resulted from that engagement differed significantly. A critical outcome of Chinese participation in the Portland mission was their newfound ability to connect with the city's white leaders and fellow evangelicals and to signal the possible benefits of conversion to fellow converts or potential converts. For black mission participants, the benefit could be even more far-reaching, extending deeper into African American communities. Those who joined the Baptist mission in Raleigh would emerge as leaders not just within churches or as those deemed respectable by whites but within the broader framework of black religious, social, educational, and religious life in the late nineteenth-century South.

Black North Carolinians who chose to affiliate with the ABHMS and with Tupper's Second Baptist Church in Raleigh occupied an awkward position, for in doing so they broke with their black neighbors, who had left white-led congregations to form their own independent churches, such as First Baptist Church, Colored. But ABHMS proclamations that the organization hoped to control the schools and churches it established only until local black Baptists and their communities had been "elevated" enough to take over, in addition to the Society's material support and links to Reconstruction-era institutions, influenced many African Americans to cast their spiritual and educational lot with Tupper's mission. While not affording the same prospects for autonomous worship and institutional control as an independent school or church, the ABHMS project nonetheless provided a modicum of space for black expression and fellowship.[43]

However, those who elected to worship and learn under the auspices of the ABHMS-run mission had to negotiate the hierarchical assumptions of evangelical ideology. They had to balance their desire for continued access to northern Baptist largesse and the wish to maintain the bonds of black community and culture that had brought them together in the first place with missionary programs designed to transform their spiritual and material lives. As northern white evangelicals sought to "elevate" ex-slaves by encouraging them—perhaps even coercing them—to conform to their religious, gender, and social norms, black Baptists sought ways to reconcile such efforts with their pursuit of self- and group improvement.

It was not that black mission participants rejected wholesale the ideas of evangelical transformation and uplift. Rather, they differed with white evangelicals over the desired outcome of their social and spiritual conversion. Missionary officials envisioned the graduates of schools like Shaw as an elite leadership class that would help lift the mass of blacks from ignorance, immorality, and poverty. They quite astutely recognized the authority and respect accorded to plantation preachers during slavery and in the immediate aftermath of Emancipation. "In the colored preachers," asserted the Society's Executive Board, "we see a class of men, who, by the simple purity of their lives, have won the confidence, love, and respect of their people. These preachers are the leaders of all social movements among the freedmen. If we can lead and elevate them, we may through them hope to elevate the mass of the people."[44] But if white officials intended this group of educated black ministers and teachers to engage in a similar form of uplift to that practiced by white missionaries, they underestimated the extent to which this leadership class was connected to the communities from which its members came.

To be sure, many beneficiaries of mission education inherited the condescending and hierarchical assumptions of evangelical uplift. One black student at an American Baptist mission school, for example, spent his summer vacation, like so many of his fellow students, teaching and preaching throughout the countryside. During the course of his travels, he witnessed an African American religious revival. His depiction of the event for ABHMS officials echoed the patronizing tone of the white missionaries' own ethnographic accounts: "Such awful[,] disgusting, and unchristian and heathenish practices are carried on that the strongest words in the language are perfectly tame and meaningless when one would attempt to describe the scene."[45]

At least in part, this unnamed student's description, like all missionary ethnology, was intended to emphasize the distance—and difference—between uneducated folk and himself. But in reality, the difference was less pronounced than he described. There was precious little room for such distinctions in the daily interactions between black ministers and teachers on one hand and ordinary blacks on the other, especially in the first decades after the Civil War. William Warrick, for example, lived with his wife and two grown children. Warrick's status as an educator and religious leader among black residents of Raleigh was clear. He had headed the Miles School for ex-slaves in the heart of the city, and he would soon become the sole ABHMS-commissioned black missionary there. Yet community status and professional standing alone were not enough to realize the aspiration of economic independence for his family. In fact, though Warrick's children followed their father's example and worked as teachers, they found it impossible to strike out on their own. The salaries of the three employed family members were crucial to supporting the entire family, as was the unpaid and often hidden labor and production of William's wife, Louisa.[46]

Charles and Barbera Manley also shared their home with their grown children. Charles was a minister, but any sense of superiority this leadership position may have afforded him was surely tempered by the presence of his laboring children in his home. Daughter Pattie was a domestic servant for a white family while sons William and Sidney worked as laborers. Similarly, although school teacher Jefferson Hinton may have been considered a role model, community leader, and respectable professional, he remained connected to the vast majority of black workers in Raleigh despite his education, profession, and status, for his wife was a domestic servant.[47] Although they may have been accorded more respect within their communities and their relationship to the means of production differed from those of laborers, black ministers and teachers were rooted within black communities. Indeed, the status and opportunities afforded by education, while providing the training and the stamp of expertise, did not necessarily translate into economic mobility or independence.

The intimate connection between these aspiring leaders and their communities was grounded in more than proximity and kin. As they struggled through post-Emancipation poverty, their experiences kept them linked to their humble origins. George L. White, who would later become a force within the African Methodist Episcopal Zion church and a national advocate for black education, excelled at the ABHMS school in Raleigh during the 1880s and eventually graduated with honors, but he also struggled to pay his tuition. This son of former slaves worked as a janitor to pay for his education. For White, as for many other emerging educators, professionals, and ministers, family and broader community efforts created the circumstances that enabled him to attend Shaw. Before venturing to Raleigh as a student, he had attended public schools and the State Normal School in New Bern where he lived with his widowed mother. The family undoubtedly could have benefited greatly from White's entrance into the workforce. Yet it was decided early on that he should concentrate on his studies while his mother shouldered the burden of providing for the family.[48]

The aspirations of these men, then, represented something more than individual striving, and their accomplishments signaled something greater than individual attainment. It was within the families of nascent leaders that the impact of these collective hopes was first felt. This was certainly the case for Caesar Johnson, one of Shaw's first graduates and a leading black Baptist in North Carolina. Born into slavery in 1840, Johnson became a denominational leader even before attaining formal theological training at the ABHMS school in Raliegh. In 1867 he had joined other ex-slaves to establish the state's black Baptist Educational and Missionary Convention, and he labored as a missionary for the ABHMS until entering Shaw in 1872. At Shaw, he augmented his knowledge and honed his ambition. While still a student he helped establish a statewide black Baptist association. After graduating, he remained in Raleigh where he gained prominence as a minister.

Even with this impressive record of accomplishment and as his career flourished, Johnson's family represented both the modest circumstances of post-Emancipation blacks and the aspirations he inspired. Johnson lived with his older sister Fannie Montgomery and his younger brother Jacob Montgomery. Fannie, who was ten years older than Caesar, had lived two-thirds of her life as a slave and was illiterate. Jacob, however, was some fourteen years younger than his brother and had come of age in those heady post–Civil War years. With both the general sense of possibility engendered by Emancipation and his brother's specific example to inspire him, Jacob followed Caesar to Shaw and would eventually be appointed by the school's faculty to be one of the honored assistant teachers.[49]

These models of hope and accomplishment extended beyond individual families and served as a basis for broader imaginings of what might be possible in the post-Emancipation world. American Baptist projects, such as Shaw, were crucial institutions as this group of new leaders ascended to prominence. In part, the men and women who entered these schools would offer their lives as examples in what historian Kevin Gaines has called "the struggle for a positive black identity in a deeply racist society."[50] Caesar Johnson, George L. White, and their classmates and fellow alumni would influence men such as J.

A. Kenney, an 1896 graduate of Shaw's college department who stayed in Raleigh to attend Shaw's pioneering Leonard School of Medicine. Kenney may not have been born into slavery, but his long journey from his family's rural Virginia home to his position as the resident physician at Booker T. Washington's Tuskegee Institute and an officer of the National Medical Association—a journey that traversed farm labor, waiting tables, public common schools, and Shaw University—was one that they would have recognized as familiar. Kenney's path, like the ones charted by Johnson, White, and others, represented a model of possibility in the transition from slavery to freedom. Spurred by post-Emancipation striving and connected to personal and family experiences in slavery and poverty, these individuals sought progress and improvement not just for themselves but for the communities in which they were rooted.[51]

In Oregon, the transformative possibilities offered by the Baptist home mission promised progress and improvement, too, and a number of Chinese residents of Portland could claim to be models of respectability courtesy of their participation in the mission school. As in Raleigh, the example of individuals held collective consequences. Students' achievements established exemplars of the promise of evangelical conversion. Sam Song Bo was among the first mission school students to relate his Christian experience and detail his belief in Christ, becoming a member of First Baptist Church. Baptized three days later at a special church meeting, Sam soon expressed interest in continuing his studies beyond the mission school. Unable to pay for additional schooling, Sam appealed to First Baptist for help. A few months later, "It was unanimously agreed to send Bro. Sam Song Bo to McMinnville College." The church's commitment to Sam was not a fleeting enterprise; he enjoyed its support for more than two years while he completed his studies. Sam's ambition and the opportunities provided by the mission and First Baptist illuminated a world of possibility to other mission participants and to other Chinese in the area.[52]

In addition to converts like Sam, Chinese ministers and missionaries—especially, in the early years of the mission, Dong Gong—served as models and leaders for those who ventured to the mission school and for those who were looking for a means by which to improve their circumstances. Dong's spiritual conversion in San Francisco had marked a broader transformation that gained him the trust and respect of white evangelicals. Throughout his tenure at the Chinese Mission School, he was held in high esteem by the school's benefactors and his fellow administrators. During the first two school exhibitions, he addressed the audience directly as *the* representative of Chinese Christianity.[53]

Yet while Chinese ministers, missionaries, and other successful converts might have modeled the benefits of conversion to their "heathen" country-men, their relationship to this broader, non-Christian population in Portland remained complex. In contrast to the black population in the South, Chinese in the United States had no tradition of or even familiarity with Christianity. They had few institutional sites, such as local churches, from which to de-velop as community leaders among non-mission-based populations, and they possessed no shared, syncretic language of collective redemption and promise with those who had no formal Christian training. Consequently, converts and leaders like Sam and Dong held fewer links to non-mission-affiliated Chinese. In fact, conversion required proselytes to renounce their "heathen" past and embrace Christianity in a way that set them apart. To be sure, it was both the mandate and desire of converted Chinese to proselytize among their fellow countrymen, so it was in their evangelical interest to maintain a relationship with non-Christians. And although many students lived together at the mis-sion, the mission itself was located within a Portland neighborhood heavily populated by Chinese. Nevertheless, Christian Chinese leaders were marked by their conversion in a way that emphasized their difference from rather than organically connected them to others in the city who hailed from China.

Significantly, even the benefits that accrued to elite-sanctioned, mission-affiliated Chinese leaders were fraught. Despite the authority invested in him by white evangelicals, Dong's position within the mission made it clear that he was something other than an equal. Indeed, he struggled to achieve full influ-ence over the mission project. As the sole designated missionary and an or-dained minister, Dong led worship services and Bible studies, though he never held any other responsible official position. At the mission school's founding, First Baptist Church's committee announced, "Dong Gong has charge at pres-ent," but quickly added that William Dean would be "appointed to mor-row evening" as "Director of the School." It would take an additional seven months for Dong to be added to the church's supervising Chinese Mission Committee.[54]

But this unequal partnership with white evangelical leaders was only part of the difficulty that Chinese mission participants faced. More so than in the South, the "elevation" of some Chinese by mission education or conversion strained their relationships with their still "heathen" countrymen. Whereas African American southerners emerging from slavery could lay claim to an emancipatory tradition of Christianity formed during slavery and adroit enough to appear to accommodate more orthodox forms of belief, Chinese converts had no similar heritage of Christian rearticulation. Rather than transforming and adapting the catechism of missionaries, Chinese converts seemed to adopt the worship and theological assumptions of white evangelicals, echoing, more often than not, the themes and premises of missionary ethnology. Dong Gong, for example, commented disapprovingly on the "idol worship," superstition, and insularity of the city's Chinese residents.[55] Moreover, while mission-educated blacks held deep ties to their communities, Chinese converts found themselves separated from the broader Chinese population. In 1876, the Portland school's secretary reported that mission participants not only had lost jobs with Chinese-owned businesses but also had been assaulted.[56]

In part, this difference between black and Chinese experiences can be explained simply by the fact that mission-educated African Americans left places like Shaw and found sanctioned, institutional spaces within black communities from which to lead. They took up pastorates in black churches or found jobs as teachers within black schools. Chinese mission participants, on the other hand, had no equivalent structural link to the broader community. In Chinese communities, a mission education and, to a greater extent, Christian conversion might have been perceived as a kind of apostasy that pushed converts to establish their own institutions and networks that existed at a distance from other ethnic associations and organizations.

Chinese community and associational life in Portland developed around institutions and establishments that, at best, elicited the disapproval of respectable Christians. The "joss house," or temple, in the heart of the city's Chinatown was, of course, beyond the pale to converted Chinese. And though the city's evangelical and respectable elite commented on them far out of proportion both to their community importance and to the size of the clientele, opium dens, gambling establishments, and brothels all had their place in the social and leisure life of Chinatown; these places of business, too, were off limits to converts. Even seemingly innocuous—though crucial—institutions, such as Chinese district associations were places that Christians and proselytes felt less than comfortable going to for fellowship or calling on for help. Indeed, while district associations frequently engaged in what might appear as culturally neutral activities such as dispute resolution, employment services, and immigration and return migration logistics, they also shipped the remains—sometimes after exhuming them—of deceased migrants back to their native places in China. This funerary practice was both essential for the fulfillment of traditional and Confucian rituals and, in the eyes of Christians, one of the ways in which unconverted Chinese were most obviously "heathen." With conversion, whether because they no longer wished to associate with un-Christian practices or because they were no longer welcome, Chinese converts looked to alternative, Christian-based associations for fellowship and mutual aid.[57]

Nevertheless, opportunity and upward mobility did not entirely isolate mission-educated Chinese from their countrymen. As noted earlier, the Baptist school was located in a Portland neighborhood with a heavy concentration of Chinese, and mission residents thus lived among others from China.[58] Perhaps more importantly, the mission and its fellowship provided non-Christians with another social option. And although the hierarchy of Christians and "heathens" was very much part of the catechism, so was a language of the equality of souls that must have held great appeal for laboring migrants who felt the full weight of the condescension and disdain not just of white Americans but of Chinese merchants and labor contractors as well.

Moreover, even as their new faith inspired skepticism and disdain from other Chinese, their new evangelical belief encouraged them to seek new souls and to make contact with the unconverted. Indeed, the Chinese leaders who helped run the mission school worked as organizers, literally taking to the streets to preach and creating institutions for their countrymen beyond the purview of First Baptist Church, the ABHMS, and the Chinese Mission School. In 1877, for instance, even as the Executive Board of the Society assumed responsibility for his salary, Dong Gong began to broaden his evangelizing beyond Portland to other parts of Oregon and Washington Territory. He traveled widely, ministering to Chinese populations in isolated (but nonetheless significant) rural, coastal, and mining settlements. Through this itinerant work, Dong established regular meetings that, although ostensibly religious in nature, also provided opportunities for social congregation. These recurrent meetings held the potential to evolve into churches or other community institutions. In collaboration with the white-run Baptist church in Salem, Oregon, Dong organized a mission school that thrived. He also aided Baptist missions and prayer meetings among the Chinese in Oregon City, Albany, Astoria, and The Dalles in Oregon, as well as the Puget Sound area in Washington Territory.[59]

These efforts were part of a much broader network of Chinese Christians. Through their individual travels and their proselytizing journeys, students and leaders linked the Chinese Mission School in Portland to other churches, schools, missions, and prayer meetings throughout the Pacific Coast and across the ocean to China. Dong exemplified this web. Like many others who traveled to the United States from China before 1882, Dong came to California as a laborer. In San Francisco, he found work as a cook but also began attending classes at the city's Baptist mission. Although the extant record is silent as to his initial motivation, Dong appears to have embraced Christianity quickly, and he was baptized by missionary John Francis. When he, like many of his countrymen, returned to his family in China, Dong continued his religious education at a mission school run by Baptist missionary and theologian R. H. Graves in Canton (Guangdong). Upon Francis's urging and with Graves's recommendation, Dong soon returned to California, this time as a missionary. Although he had originally intended to travel with his wife, the missionary arrived alone in San Francisco and joined Francis and Lee Key in their evangelical labors. He was not in town long, however, when the call came from Portland, where he was to work for more than seven years. In early 1881, Dong returned to China to be reunited with his wife and children. But even there he continued his missionary commitments and called upon his Chinese brethren in Portland to contribute "several hundred dollars" for his evangelical work and a chapel that he supervised.[60]

Dong was not the only Chinese evangelical laboring on the Pacific Coast. Lee Key and Fung Chak both were responsible for mission activities in San Francisco, and after Dong left Portland, Fung moved north to take his place. He would remain in Portland for two years, eventually returning to China, just as Dong had. In all, three different Chinese evangelicals would lead the Portland mission.[61] All of them would also spend time in San Francisco and other parts of California as missionaries, joining the five other Chinese brethren who held official positions in Baptist institutions on the Pacific Coast, and at least Dong and Fung also proselytized and led churches in China.[62]

The role of these Chinese evangelicals differed in distinctive ways from their white brethren. Most obviously, they were the visible representatives of the larger Chinese population on the Pacific Coast. And as converted Christians, they held a particular status as "respectable" Chinese who had close contact with white evangelicals, teachers, and elites. This access, along with their standing as missionaries and ordained ministers, also provided them status within Chinese Christian communities. From their position as leaders, then, Chinese missionaries such as Dong and Fung mediated between local white elites and interested Chinese to carve out critical religious, educational, and social space. In fact, they helped to establish an important and interconnected array of institutions, ranging from prayer meetings to schools and churches.

For Chinese Christians, the significance of this network went well beyond the establishment of specific institutions. Once in place, these evangelical institutions became important reference points for a mobile population. Carrying a letter testifying to membership in the Baptist mission or church in Canton or in another U.S city or town assured converted Chinese a warm welcome into the Portland community. Fung Chak, for example, noted in 1881 that he, the mission school, and First Baptist Church had "received three Chinese by baptism [and] two by letter."[63] If mission residents chose to leave the city, they received a similar letter that they could present to a Baptist institution at their destination. This was the case with Sid Que who, shortly before returning to China from Portland, was given a "letter of recommendation . . . signed by the Pastor and the Clerk [of First Baptist Church]."[64]

Converts who came into contact with one another through mission projects also created their own meetings and societies, independent of white-run or white-sponsored churches or evangelical organizations. As historian Wesley Woo has discovered, Chinese Christians in San Francisco organized the interdenominational Youxue Zhengdaohui in 1871. Although they first met at the Chinese Presbyterian Church, the chief organizers appear to have been Baptist acquaintances and acolytes of the Baptist convert and preacher Fung Seung Nam who had held an ABHMS commission from 1869 until his death in 1871. Eventually, Youxue Zhengdaohui fragmented into separate denominational units, but each entity had similar rules and goals. According to Woo, they conducted their own worship services and study groups without white evangelical supervision. Among the important directives, the requirement to "love one another" loomed large.[65]

To be sure, Chinese had other associational resources upon which to draw during their travels. Family and district organizations remained perhaps the most important form of institutionalized organizational structure for migrants and immigrants between southern China and the Pacific Coast of the United States. But for Chinese converts, church membership provided benefits that these other associations did not. The connection to an explicitly Christian organization with links to the city's elite gave them the basis to appeal to white patrons for protection. In 1875, for example, First Baptist Church member Captain Nathaniel Ingersoll revealed at a church meeting that one of the mission's ten original converts was scheduled to sail back to China aboard the *William H. Bessee*. The *Bessee* was captained by one of Ingersoll's acquaintances, and the church, voting as a whole, moved to have Ingersoll write to the ship's captain. The letter requested that the captain "hunt up our Brother and give him words of cheer and comfort while on his voyage."[66]

"Brotherhood" in the Baptist church provided more tangible benefits than "words of cheer and comfort," especially as the movements for immigration exclusion succeeded. As legislation restricted immigration and forced Chinese residents of the United States to register with the federal government and, in most cases, to confirm that they were "persons other than laborers," having relationships with respected white members of the community proved to be an invaluable asset. In 1894, in compliance with the 1892 Geary Act, which extended the terms of the original Chinese Exclusion Act for another ten years, Wong King submitted an application for a certificate of residence. His application, which was eventually granted, not only contained a physical description and a "photographic likeness"; it also included affidavits from people who could vouch for his status as merchant and that he had resided in the United States at the time of the Geary Act's passage on May 5, 1892. Although the actual affidavits are no longer extant, it appears that Wong's witnesses included members of First Baptist Church where, though not a member, he attended the mission school.[67]

As with their Chinese brethren on the Pacific Coast, mission-educated blacks in the South did more than merely lead by example. Beyond their individual achievements and their positions as role models within black communities, men and women who attended ABHMS schools helped forge vital institutions beyond the purview of the formal mission itself. In the increasingly virulent white supremacist environment of the South during the 1870s and 1880s, black Baptists laid the groundwork for a loosely connected constellation of schools, churches, and denominational institutions, which extended beyond religious organizations to include public schools and governmental and social service entities. As one Shaw graduate noted, "We have sent out hundreds of teachers who are now doing service in our public schools, scores of ministers who are now preaching the gospel, and dozens of men in other walks of life."[68]

As students, the men and women who attended the Raleigh school, like their counterparts at other ABHMS institutions throughout the South, often took to the countryside during summer vacations. They earned money and gained valuable experience as they preached and organized educational and religious meetings for more isolated populations. As with the congregations, classes, and meetings that Dong Gong established in Oregon and the Pacific

Northwest, these assemblies and congregations constituted valuable community resources. But while Dong, in addition to building links in a Chinese Christian network, could offer potential proselytes a kind of respectability that might earn them favor with or protection from local elites, the arrival of a black Baptist missionary in an isolated rural town often heralded the organization of a meeting or a class or, in some cases, a church that would be run entirely by local blacks. In addition, graduates of Shaw and other schools, after receiving formal theological training, often worked as missionaries in nearby areas or around the state.[69]

But many of the graduates of Shaw's theological course of study had their greatest influence from the pulpits of autonomous black churches, leading perhaps the most important institutions within African American communities. One survey of Shaw's graduates, published in the wake of the December 1907 Clifton Conference on black religious life, listed no fewer than seven graduates leading congregations in central North Carolina alone. Five other graduates were ordained ministers who listed their occupations primarily as teachers, but they also held pastoral positions.[70]

Shielded from white interference, black churches, including those led by Shaw-educated ministers, continued to foster the emancipatory Christianity that had developed during slavery. But in the new era of African American freedom and citizenship and the subsequent white reaction, this religious tradition took on new meaning. In fact, the messages of endurance, deliverance, and eventual justice that had resonated in the antebellum period began, again, in the post-Reconstruction period, to have a special significance. And the theological concern with the promise of freedom, along with the increasingly circumscribed social and political space for blacks, meant that churches held a vital public dimension as well. Church buildings were used for more than worship; they housed schools, libraries, meetings, concerts, and clubs, and church membership overlapped with extended families and civic and fraternal organizations.[71] As both spiritual and community institutions, black churches fostered and sustained ideologies, practices, and organizations that gave meaning and shape to freedom.

Black ministers trained at Shaw also helped organize and lead larger denominational associations. The North Carolina State Convention (Colored), for instance, formally linked disparate Baptist congregations, and provided a single, powerful voice as well as an effective organizing infrastructure. By the mid- to late 1870s, Shaw graduates emerged as the organization's most prominent leaders. In 1877, just a year before becoming two of the first six graduates of Shaw after its incorporation, Caesar Johnson and N. F. Roberts were elected to major posts within the convention. Johnson was the president while Roberts served on the Executive Board; both demonstrated their commitment to educational endeavors such as the one they pursued at Shaw by sitting on the Committee on Education. Fostering the growth of black churches, missionary enterprises, and schools, the convention lay outside the authority not only of local white Baptist organizations but of the ABHMS as well.

But the influence of Shaw-trained men and women extended beyond religious institutions. Just as church buildings could serve more than one purpose, graduates of the Raleigh school found their calling in endeavors beyond the pulpit. Many, like Rev. C. S. Brown, placed their faith in education well as in Christianity. Brown had been a convert to the power of education before arriving at Shaw in 1880. Born in Salisbury, North Carolina, during the final years of slavery, Brown was educated at a freedmen's school after Emancipation. He completed the course of study and went to work at the recently established national cemetery in town to help support his family, all the while continuing his schooling and eventually earning a teacher's certificate. Brown then embarked on a career as an educator and taught at a Stokes County school before pursuing his studies at Shaw. Within a year of his graduation from Shaw in 1885, he assumed leadership of the Waters Normal Institute in Winton, North Carolina, an academic institution established in 1886 "by the Colored Baptists of Hertford, Bertie, and Northampton counties, North Carolina."[72]

Brown's tenure at Waters reveals how the web of relations he entered at Shaw could both provide him a position of leadership and help him to build an important community institution. At Waters, Brown called on the connections he had cultivated in Raleigh to encourage funding from the ABHMS. It seemed to work, for at least one source claimed that "Waters Institute received the largest amounts from the Home Mission Society given to any similar school in the State, which enabled the school to so far outstrip the other secondary schools of the State."[73] He also drew on his classmates and acquaintances from Shaw to staff the school. Of the seven other faculty members, four had attended the Raleigh mission institution. W. P. Graves had undertaken the collegiate course while Miss Addie L. Hall, Miss Mamie S. Roberts, and Mrs. Meander S. Sessons had attended the Women's School and had lived at Estey Hall.[74]

These connections were nurtured at Shaw. Students spent time together in classes, worshipped together at religious services, and lived together in dormitories. The personal relationships and sense of fellowship fostered in the congregation of mission school life extended beyond Shaw's physical boundaries to these formal and informal networks. C. S. Brown and his faculty may have established a particularly successful school, but other Shaw alumni like them also built educational institutions throughout North Carolina and the South. These foot soldiers were vital combatants in the battle to provide black southerners educational opportunities, but Shaw was equally successful in turning out field generals as well. Both John O. Crosby and John Whitted, for example, were graduates of the Baptist college, and each served as the head of a state normal school for blacks. Crosby would eventually be appointed the first president of the State Agricultural and Mechanical College for blacks.[75]

Whether as teachers at secondary or common schools in local communities or as administrators at regional, state-run schools, black educators provided a model of aspiration and success for others to follow; they also helped to create lasting and valuable institutions. Significantly, the overlapping sacred and secular training that they received at mission schools like Shaw meshed neatly with two facets of black life in the post–Civil War South. The training of moral stewards, a concept at the heart of the evangelical nationalist ethos, made good sense to a population for whom, under slavery, black preachers had been important leaders and for whom education was a key to social improvement. And the emancipatory message of Afro-Christianity encouraged participation in a broader, civic struggle for social and political equality. It is therefore not surprising that the educational leaders who emerged from Shaw also maintained positions as ministers, or that educators also carved out niches for themselves as political leaders. John Whitted pastored the Warrenton Baptist Church while he ran the state normal school.[76] John Crosby also pulled double duty as a pastor and school principal in Salisbury, but his activities led him beyond the church and the classroom to the Republican Party meeting hall. When he arrived at Shaw he had already been active in party politics as a member of the Union League and as a patronage appointee as the Fairfield County (South Carolina) census taker. Later, as a teacher and the pastor of a church in Warrington, North Carolina, Crosby was elected as a delegate to the state Constitutional Convention.[77] Thomas O. Fuller may have been the quintessential man of education, religion, and politics. Before moving to Tennessee in the first years of the twentieth century, Fuller, who earned two degrees from Shaw in the 1890s, served as the principal of the Shiloh Institute (originally Warrenton High School), led a Baptist church, and became the only African American elected to the North Carolina state legislature in the hotly contested election of 1898.[78]

Yet the impulse that led men like Whitted, Crosby, and Fuller to engage in civic and religious activities differed in a crucial way from the evangelical nationalist idea of stewardship that mission officials hoped to impart. Even as they seemed to echo missionary-derived themes of racial reform through elevation, their actions, their connections to the students they taught and congregations they led, and their belief in the egalitarian aims of evangelical Christianity and the new era of freedom tempered the condescension toward and demands for deference from their brethren. In other words, through their belief in a *black* evangelical nationalism and their social and political practice, they offered a more democratic vision of black leadership. The mission-educated ministers, principals, and politicians may have been, to use historian Glenda E. Gilmore's formulation, the "black Best Men" who "believed that in order to continue to enjoy 'manhood rights,' as they referred to the franchise and officeholding, they must conform to middle-class whites' definitions of manhood."[79] But by establishing, managing, and propagating schools, churches, and other educational institutions and by actively participating in the political process, they challenged racist assumptions about the intellectual limitations of blacks as well as missionary contentions that they were not yet ready for leadership roles. In essence, their example undermined a significant part of the ideological foundation on which white evangelical uplift was based.

Although the valorization of middle-class respectability may have been both part of their mission training and part of their rhetorical repertoire, black leaders who had been educated at Shaw and other Baptist institutions had a broader spectrum of ideologies and experiences from which to draw, and they balanced the hierarchy of uplift with a commitment to material and structural change. Waters Normal Institute Principal C. S. Brown, for example, expressed a vision of respectability based not on the morals and manners of ordinary African Americans but on their economic autonomy and political equality: "I have urged my people to buy land—farm land; and the result is that the colored people own about one third of all the land in this county, and pay one third of the public taxes. We have here at Winton perhaps more colored registered voters under the amendment than at any other voting precinct in the state."[80]

Of course, black and Chinese leaders, and the networks they helped to create and maintain, did more than offer different visions of respectability and challenge assumptions of missionary uplift. They also provided alternative models of the very meaning of race. In their activities as community leaders and by setting examples of aspiration and achievement, black and Chinese Baptists countered white supremacist notions about the limited capacity of "inferior" races. And as blacks and Chinese imagined their relationships to their ancestral homelands in different ways and extended their evangelical networks beyond the borders of the United States, they also attacked racialized assumptions of foreignness that buttressed these ideas of inferiority and that provided a basis for unequal treatment. This broader understanding of "race," embedded in social and political contexts and historical tradition as opposed to pseudoscientific theories, served as a critical countervailing idea to the biological and cultural essentialism of white supremacy.

Even as missionaries discursively linked blacks and Chinese to foreign lands, thereby emphasizing their alienness, the objects of this discourse deployed alternate models that built on but altered central ideas of missionary ethnology and notions of cultural and racial difference. Black Baptists, in ways perhaps similar to their white counterparts, saw a close link between their lives and the lives of those in Africa. African American Baptist minister and antislavery activist L. A. Grimes asserted in 1866 that "the colored men have Africa on their minds. They wish to evangelize the land."[81] And, during the 1880s, Shaw graduates J. O. Hayes and Lula C. Flemming linked the home mission project of black Baptists in North Carolina directly to Africa as they embarked on work in Liberia and the Congo Free State, respectively.[82]

Motives that drove Grimes's contention and the commitment of Hayes and Flemming are more difficult to discern than those of their Chinese brethren. In part, black evangelicals like Grimes, Hayes, and Flemming, to be sure, had absorbed depictions of Africa as a "dark" and "heathen" place. These images were central to missionary ethnology of the time, and they likely hoped to deliver their ancestral homeland from darkness by spreading the light of American Christian civilization.[83] But black missionaries balanced these hierarchical assumptions with an equally powerful, if somewhat more abstract, sense of genuine identification with colonized Africans, resulting in what historian Sylvia Jacobs has described as a "fairly widespread sense of obligation for Africa."[84]

William W. Colley took up this obligation in 1875. A graduate of the Baptist-run Richmond Institute, Colley traveled to Liberia and Nigeria as an assistant to W. J. David, a white Southern Baptist, and soon became one of the most ardent voices calling for the increased involvement of black Baptists in Africa, especially through the creation of an African American foreign mission organization.[85] His pleas began within a year of his commission when he expressed his hope that "the colored brethren will begin their work in Africa this year, either by sending a man or supporting one. This is *their* field of labor."[86] He continued his calls upon his return to the United States in 1879 and was largely responsible for the founding of the black Baptist Foreign Mission Convention the following year. He returned to Africa in 1883 as one of the first missionaries appointed by the new body.[87]

In part, Colley's call to support more black evangelicals in Africa stemmed from his understanding that "race" linked African Americans and Africa. Yet his notion of race differed in subtle but important ways from the relatively straightforward ideas of biological—blood or kin—foundations asserted by white missionaries. To be sure, it would be far too simple—and incorrect—to say that Colley and his black American brethren saw in their potential proselytes an essential commonality. Indeed, as historian James T. Campbell has argued, African American mission advocates' "identification with Africa" was generally "self-referential," equating "heathenism with slavery" and "missions with emancipation," thus inspiring "feelings of affinity and obligation."[88]

But Colley's experiences in Africa, especially on the eve of the British conquest of southern Nigeria and as Liberia's independence faced the threat of British and French imperialism, also honed his sense of identification with blacks on that continent while sharpening his understanding of the white supremacy he faced in the American South. Indeed, his proselytizing partner, a white Mississippian, provided a handy experiential link, for W. J. David had few qualms about expounding on the superiority of whites. It may be too strong to argue, as Sandy Dwayne Martin has, that the affinity that Colley and other black evangelicals felt with Africa constituted "a proto-pan-Africanism."[89] However, his upbringing and education in Virginia, his strained interactions with David, and his witnessing of European colonialism provided a foundation to begin viewing "race" in broader terms. Although perhaps tempered by discourses of kinship and uplift, the identification of Africans and African Americans was nonetheless based on common experience and social and political position. In other words, Colley's work in Africa was providing him with the tools from which to forge a sense of racial identity not out of biology but out of social relations.[90]

For Chinese Baptist missionaries such as Dong Gong and Fung Chak, the efforts to proselytize abroad meant that they confronted directly the popular stereotype of Chinese as sojourners who had no desire to settle permanently in the United States. In fact, they were not the only converted Chinese to preach and practice the Gospel on both sides of the Pacific. Numerous others followed the same transoceanic path, and the vestiges of their movements can be found in more tangible form than ABHMS records. As they traveled, they organized Bible studies, Sunday schools, religious meetings, mission schools, and churches. They worked regionally throughout California, Oregon, and the Washington Territory in locations as far south as Los Angeles and in towns and hamlets like Astoria, Oregon. In China, they staffed American-run missions as "native helpers" and "Bible women" and became pastors of their own congregations. From irregular religious meetings to full-fledged churches, these institutions—whether autonomous or semiautonomous—provide evidence of a network created by and for Chinese Christians that traversed the Pacific Ocean.[91]

Seen in light of the dominant sojourner discourse, endemic in contemporary popular, political, and evangelical literature, that placed Chinese in the United States squarely—if metaphorically—beyond the bounds of the nation, this network of Chinese Baptists suggests a rearticulation of the idea of belonging within a framework of American home and foreign mission efforts. It was both as simple and as complex as making a virtue of a vice. The barriers to American national belonging established by both informal and state-sponsored methods were formidable, and, given the ways that missionary ethnologies reinforced this sense of foreignness, men such as Dong Gong advanced another idea of belonging that transcended the nation as the primary form of social and political organization and made faith the sole marker of belonging.

Especially in the mostly male Chinese world in the United States, this process of rearticulation occurred through social practice. To be sure, Baptist missionaries and converted Chinese held a view of domestic respectability in which the husband-and-wife relationship was an integral element. But the daily lives of Chinese in America provided a visible alternative to this discourse. Although judged uncivilized, illicit, and immoral by evangelicals and subsequently deemed deviant by social scientists, homosocial domestic arrangements—boarding houses, mining camps, and the like—were the everyday reality for Chinese men in the United States.[92] And they themselves understood their domestic lives as something other than perverse or deviant. These natives of southern China were part of a longer and broader tradition of split-household families in which male migrants journeyed abroad, in search of economic opportunity, and the homosocial associational lives of Chinese men in America mirrored similar dynamics in cities in China, bound together by a variety of secret societies and brotherhoods with long histories of their own.[93] The experience of Chinese men in the United States might be seen not as abnormal but rather as merely an extension of traditional practices, and Chinese men's participation in mission networks suggests an adaptation of these practices to new forms.

Significantly, blacks and Chinese also contested gendered notions of domestic respectability in ways that drew less on transnational perspectives and more on alternate practices and traditions. The actions of African American Baptist women, for example, constituted a kind of oppositional politics that attempted to combat racist structures and images by claiming the markers of respectability—education, manners, piety, purity—usually reserved for whites. Mission-educated women appropriated evangelical rhetoric about the singular importance of Christian wives and mothers and used it as a justification for a more active role within their marriages and a more public and political position within society at large. When a Baptist mission official claimed that "if we educate young men for the ministry, and leave them to make marriages with heathen women, we practically nullify all our efforts to elevate the race, by leaving young minds to be molded by ignorant, superstitious women," he hoped to underscore the bounded domestic space over which Christian women were to preside.[94] But black women reinterpreted the meaning of Christian marriage to move beyond these circumscribed positions. As Glenda Gilmore has observed, educated black women, such as those who attended Baptist schools, tended to see marriage as a "civil enterprise" in which "the ideal . . . was an 'industrious partnership'" that could enter the realm of formal politics through a delegate-husband model in which "male voters often saw themselves as representing their wives . . . as family delegates to the electoral sphere." When black men were stripped of the franchise, black women assumed greater political roles, relying on their connections to and experiences of interacting with white women to enhance their position as state clients during the Progressive Era.[95]

On the Pacific Coast, appropriation of the missionary rhetoric of respectability also could be subversive. Women who entered rescue missions used the institutional support of evangelicals to insist upon less exploitative gender relations, including marriage, with Chinese men.[96] Moreover, much like black mission participants in the South, Chinese women who were "rescued" offered a compelling example of purity, piety, and self-respect that countered racist images. Chinese men, too, could offer models of educated and respectable manhood that provided counterexamples to the proliferation of anti-Chinese representations. Sam Song Bo, for example, could demonstrate individual ambition, Christian morality, and evangelical zealousness that won him the financial support of many of Portland's leading white residents and, thus, enabled him to pursue his education beyond the city's Baptist mission school.

African American and Chinese mission participants contested the racialized ideas engendered by the home mission project. They countered these racist ideas through social and discursive practices that displaced the American nation as the primary engine of and model for evangelical belonging and subverted home missionaries' notions of domestic respectability. Because evangelicals' racialized notions of difference were deployed through nationalism and socially sanctioned gender roles, African Americans and Chinese in the United States challenged those ideas on the very same terrain. In this sense, then, the antiracism of mission participants hinged not on a narrow sense of racial rearticulation but also quite necessarily upon the rearticulation of national and gender discourses and subjectivities as well.[97]

Sometimes consciously, often simply through their actions, black and Chinese Baptists transformed the racial discourses espoused by missionaries. African Americans, first in the contest over the meaning of freedom and then as the vice grip of Jim Crow tightened, hoped to remake blackness, loosening it from its associations with the degradation (and depredations) of slavery. Indeed, the creation of black churches and the maintenance of distinctive forms of Afro-Christianity exemplify this rearticulation of race that, unlike the missionary ethos of assimilation by uplift, could accommodate cultural difference while also modeling an alternate mode of national and religious belonging. Chinese, in the meantime, attacked the "sojourner" representation that became the rationale for depriving them of naturalization rights. In part, their very actions belied the racial stereotype of unassimilability as they settled in increasing numbers and created their own communities and institutions, but they also rearticulated the notion of the sojourner by constructing a trans-Pacific network of Chinese Christian churches and missions that modeled a new identity—one that undermined the evangelical nationalism of white missionaries and replaced it with a transnational, cosmopolitan Christianity that focused on the equal brotherhood of all Christians.

Yet while there are many similarities between the two cases, especially the ways in which both blacks and Chinese looked to mission projects for valuable resources, there is also a crucial difference. Put simply, African Americans, formally citizens by virtue of the Fourteenth and Fifteenth Amendments, could make a legal claim on the state and on the nation that Chinese immigrants, barred from naturalization since 1790, could not. This difference was borne out by the different uses to which they put their forms of congregation. Particularly in the years before the veil of segregation descended on the South, black Baptists used their overlapping networks and ideologies of education, religion, and politics to make their freedom dreams come true. In contrast, Chinese, unable to become citizens, looked at alternative notions of belonging that did not require, or perhaps even transcended, state approval.[98] In large part, this difference explains the enduring nature of the racialization of Chinese as "perpetual aliens." It also provides a conceptual foundation for understanding the violence and rigor of the legal maneuverings that formally relegated blacks to second-class citizenship status. Because black southerners had been granted "insider" status by Emancipation and the Reconstruction amendments, white southerners had to create a means by which to render them "outsiders." Finally, it provides a way of understanding why African Americans could prepare their communities for an assault on the white supremacist system in the United States in a way that the Chinese population in America could not.

CHAPTER 5

Conflict and Community

Then said they unto him, Say now Shibboleth; and he said
Sibboleth; for he could not frame to pronounce it right: then they
laid hold on him, and slew him at the fords of Jordan. And there fell
at that time of Ephraim forty and two thousand.
Judges 12:6 (ASV)

THERE SEEMED TO be no such thing as a straight line for white missionaries or for black and Chinese mission participants. Mission theorists, officials, and advocates posited a linear equation to describe the progression
from "heathen" to Christian American—merely add a mission education
and inspire conversion. Black southerners certainly desired the short-
est possible path from slavery to freedom, from freedom to equality; and
Chinese—whether sojourner or settler—most assuredly hoped for the most
direct route to Gold Mountain and all that it represented. A cursory examination of official ABHMS records might indeed suggest a steady and
upward trajectory of progress. The Raleigh mission had established Second
Baptist Church early on, and, in 1875, the Society, missionary Henry Martin
Tupper, and other supporters helped solidify the educational project by in-
corporating Shaw University. And the Chinese Mission School in Portland
had, by 1877, achieved firm enough footing for the Executive Board of the
American Baptist Home Mission Society to commit resources to the local
project while supplementing missionary Dong Gong's salary so he could

serve as the Society's designated evangelist not just in Portland but for Chinese throughout Oregon and Washington Territory.

Yet a closer look at the extant evidence reveals a less constant movement. Missionaries, blacks, and Chinese—each group found the path they traveled, whether to salvation or to freedom or to security or to all three, bedeviled by discord. In fact, Baptist projects in Raleigh and Portland faced serious obstacles that threatened their existence and challenged the definition of mission-based communities. Home missions may have been arenas where participants could come together in fellowship and congregation, but conflict framed these sites.

On one level, the Raleigh mission and the Portland school were objects of controversy among local blacks and Chinese in their respective cities. In Raleigh, the initial challenge presented by the refusal of black congregants at First Baptist Church to follow white missionary Henry Martin Tupper's lead to form an all-black congregation was succeeded by a series of convoluted legal actions over Tupper's legitimacy as pastor of Second Baptist Church. Tangential to the everyday affairs of the mission school, this controversy developed over the other arm of the ABHMS project in the South—the church. In Portland, the murder of two Christian converts by fellow Chinese residents of the city cast issues of belonging into high relief. In both locales, conflicts among blacks and among Chinese helped define the contours of community, exposing questions of class as points of tension and underscoring the contested nature of identity and belonging. Black and Chinese mission participants were presenting new identities, based in part on the status that an association with educational institutions and white missionaries could bring. These new identities, while perhaps serving as a basis from which to draw community leaders, also constituted a source of conflict within the larger freedpeople and Chinese populations in Raleigh and Portland, respectively.

On another level, the relationships between local whites and American Baptist institutions marked the contours of mission-rooted communities that bound missionaries and participants together. While the historical record reflects remarkably few instances of outright action taken toward mission institutions in either Raleigh or Portland after the mid-1870s, in both cities histories of white supremacy saturated the environment and shaped every encounter between those associated with Baptist missions and local whites. But the position of the American Baptist home mission in Raleigh differed considerably from the position of the evangelical project in Portland. In particular, Henry Martin Tupper, Second Baptist Church, and Shaw University, especially in the early years, had no direct relationship to Raleigh's elite whereas Portland's Chinese Mission School enjoyed the sponsorship and protection of that city's leading citizens.

The difference here is crucial. While Chinese in Portland were by no means immune to hostility, discrimination, and violence, the mission school's links to local power provided an extra measure of insulation from the worst forms of anti-Chinese agitation brewing up and down the Pacific Coast. Nevertheless, while the more subtle form of elite control exercised by Portland's leading citizens through the Baptist mission differed in method and general effect from the naked hostility exhibited by North Carolina's white leaders who tended to be hostile to Raleigh's mission, the intent—discipline, control, and the maintenance of power—remained the same. This comparison, then, provides important insights into the various forms that white supremacy could take.[1]

For black and Chinese mission participants, congregation and fellowship, to be sure, remained critical and compelling reasons for their involvement in Baptist evangelical projects, but their participation did not come without cost or controversy. Although the "contests of faith" that characterized all missionary-proselyte relations lay below the surface in Raleigh and Portland and were rarely explicitly articulated, proselytes and missionaries encountered other challenges that helped to define the boundaries of their mission-based communities.[2] In particular, both missions experienced disputes internal to proselyte groups and over the constituency of each. Although these disagreements took substantially different forms in North Carolina and Oregon, they both resulted in a brighter line between the black residents of Raleigh and Chinese residents of Portland who participated in American Baptist missions and those who did not.

The significance of these conflicts lies in the tensions created by the aspirations of mission participants. In their hopes to fulfill the promise of Emancipation and immigration and in their attempts to protect themselves from the worst abuses of the resurgent white supremacist nation, blacks and Chinese availed themselves of mission programs and churches to rearticulate meanings of racial difference. Based on the spiritual and social transformations promised by evangelical Christianity, this valorization of themselves as respectable may have been somewhat lessened by the sense of collective responsibility held by both sets of incipient leaders, but it nonetheless remained a source of potential conflict. An examination of two cases in which disputes did, in fact, arise sheds light not just on the limits of these Baptist communities but also on the fundamental difficulties faced by this class of mission-affiliated blacks and Chinese as they attempted to balance the hopes and fears that accompanied their developing sense of collective identity and responsibility.

Henry Martin Tupper and his ABHMS sponsors may have expected him to minister to a single, monolithic African American community in Raleigh, but he quickly found that this overly simplistic idea had no relationship to reality. Tupper's early attempt to lead black worshippers out of the city's First Baptist Church failed, most likely over questions of black leadership and autonomy. Throughout the mid-1870s, during the period when Shaw's supporters and managers sought to incorporate the school and eventually succeeded, Tupper's Second Baptist Church—the congregational arm of his evangelical endeavors that he and black Baptists had established in 1866 and which housed the early school—confronted what chronicler Wilmoth Carter has referred to as a "crisis of legitimation."[3] In early January 1874, as Tupper prepared for a northern tour with a group of singers from Shaw, the church and Tupper's school "were turned into the street after having occupied the building for more than seven years with their right to do so unquestioned."[4]

The eviction of the church and school came as a result of a lawsuit filed by a group of men who had been excluded from Second Baptist Church for transgressive behavior, but who still claimed to be the church's trustees.[5] The plaintiffs in *Gideon Perry and Others v. H. M. Tupper* asserted that they, not Tupper, held the right to the property on which the church stood. The court case was contended on a variety of legal claims, but beneath the legalities lay a more fundamental concern about just who constituted the members and leaders of Second Baptist Church. Although Tupper and his African American associate pastor, Augustus Shepard, claimed stewardship over the black congregation, the plaintiffs produced evidence that over one hundred congregants had been meeting at an alternate location.[6]

Each of the plaintiffs in the lawsuit had been a leader in Second Baptist Church, and each was dismissed from the congregation and replaced as trustee after an accusation of transgression. Significantly, the exclusions occurred in two general waves that provide some insight into the reasons for the complaint. The first wave began when Gideon Perry was accused of stealing lumber from the church in the fall of 1867. Later that year, Abraham Nickols, one of the church's original trustees, was charged with not being of sound mind, and the church revoked his right to speak during meetings, as well as his leadership position, in early 1868. In 1871, Ed Jones's wife complained to the church that he had visited a brothel, and her account was corroborated by associate pastor Augustus Shepard, who had witnessed Jones leaving the establishment. On January 8, 1872, Jones was dismissed. Hilliard Williams's difficulties with Second Baptist bridged the two periods of dismissals, for he was removed as trustee on December 28, 1869, when an entirely new board was elected, but remained a member of the church until his exclusion on October 21, 1872.[7]

In fact, on that fall day, Joel Evans and Hardy Cross joined Williams as members of Second Baptist who were deemed disruptive and who appear to have been purged from the church. Williams and Cross had been condemned for intemperance while Evans was censured for "disorderly conduct," which included an attempt to lead the congregation through unskilled preaching and evincing "hostility toward students in the school who were studying for the ministry."[8] The charges against Williams, Cross, and, in particular, Evans hint at a struggle over leadership—and membership—within Second Baptist.

This insinuation of conflict is corroborated by accounts of the contentious church meeting that occurred on September 25, just one month prior to the ouster of Williams, Evans, and Cross. The referee who investigated the claims and counterclaims of the 1874 lawsuit found that preceding the September 1872 meeting, "considerable disturbance had arisen among the members of said church, many of them being much displeased with their pastor [Tupper], the defendant."[9] The referee's report notes that one week before the fateful meeting, the missionary and minister "said, in conversation with Hilliard Williams, Joel Evans, Abram Nichols [sic] and Hardy Cross, that the church was his own, and he intended to govern it as he pleased."[10] This dissatisfaction with Tupper's leadership bubbled to the surface at the September 25 meeting when Joel Evans took the floor and refused to yield to Tupper, Shepard, or the church secretary. In the midst of the confusion, Abraham Nickols announced "that all who desired a black man for a preacher should come over to his side of the house."[11] No action was taken, although the degree to which sentiment among people at the meeting favored Nickols's appeal cannot be known because, without an official motion to adjourn, the secretary of Second Baptist, Sherwood Capps, closed the meeting. The investigating referee hints that Capps's actions came as a result of pressure from Tupper.[12]

It must be noted that, while Tupper was named the defendant in the case and although the referee indicated dissatisfaction with him as the church's pastor, the missionary had tried to defuse the situation many months earlier when he stepped down from the pulpit and promoted Augustus Shepard. When a significant faction of worshippers at Second Baptist requested that he return to the head of the church, Tupper assented.[13]

Nevertheless, whatever Tupper's earlier intentions, the dissident members almost immediately established an alternate site and new leadership and declared their congregation not an offshoot but the true Second Baptist Church. They met in homes and other locations, worshipped at Joel Evans's house, and, although contested by Tupper, Shepard, and other stalwarts, claimed that two-thirds of the congregation had followed their lead, including all of the deacons and all of the trustees except one.[14] In the meantime, the group of worshippers led by Tupper and Shepard continued to conduct business as Second Baptist Church, expelling Williams, Evans, and Cross right away.

Legally, the suit was thus a dispute over who could claim the right to the appellation of Second Baptist Church of Raleigh. The case itself continued through various appeals and pleadings (in addition to at least two additional suits) until 1877 when it was resolved in favor of Tupper, Shepard, and the ABHMS. Yet the conflict went far deeper than merely litigation over a name. In dramatic fashion, the divisive and bitter quarrel highlighted questions concerning the American Baptist mission's constituency, leadership, and authority. Although often obscured by fragmentary extant documentation and the less than impartial nature of the most complete existing account, the issues at the heart of the contentious legal battle deserve a closer look.

Perhaps the most fruitful way of understanding the matters at stake in the controversy over Second Baptist Church is through a detailed examination of the various accounts—primary and secondary—of the lawsuit. Henry Martin Tupper laid out his version of the story in a handwritten document dated January 8, 1877.[15] In this rendition, Tupper placed blame for the lawsuit not on the plaintiffs but on Thomas Pritchard, the white minister who had succeeded Thomas Skinner at First Baptist Church. Attributing Pritchard's animosity to political machinations, Tupper muted any mention of a desire for black leadership at Second Baptist and, thus, dismissed the possibility that the dissident congregants had taken action on their own behalf. In fact, he referred to the plaintiffs as "half a dozen ignorant colored men" who were being used as "tools."[16]

Wilmoth Carter, in her comprehensive study of Shaw University, relies on Tupper's account. Her findings echo the missionary's rendering of the controversy, and she attempts to strengthen the case for political intrigue by further undermining the credibility of the plaintiffs.[17] Taking the cases of exclusion at face value, Carter dismisses each dissenter as intemperate, crazy, disorderly, or "licentious."[18] Most significantly, in Carter's chronicle, Abraham Nickols, who challenged the congregation to appoint a black preacher, was "deranged," and Joel Evans, who expressed the desire to preach to and lead the church and who ridiculed students studying for the ministry, was "a hard drinker" and "profoundly ignorant."[19]

The referee's findings and at least one report of the North Carolina Supreme Court, however, take a different perspective. These accounts point to a conflict over Tupper's leadership of the congregation. Although the exact nature of this friction is not mentioned, the report hints that it stemmed from the desire of the plaintiffs to have a black minister lead the church. Not only did the dissident worshippers meet at the house of the man who had derided educated black ministers and demanded an African American preacher, but Tupper's highhanded behavior was also at issue.[20]

Certainly Thomas Pritchard was no advocate of Henry Martin Tupper or the ABHMS, and the mission during its early history was hardly free from harassment by local white elites in the highly charged political and racial climate of Reconstruction North Carolina. Nevertheless, the evidence suggests that divisions among black congregants of Second Baptist, more than white political intrigue, played the crucial role in the church's leadership crisis. Tupper sought to maintain control over the congregation that housed his school, and when he began to hear of disgruntlement over not having a black minister, he quickly attempted to appoint his African American associate, Augustus Shepard.

The dispute turned not just on the question of whether black leadership would be permissible but also on the *nature* of black leadership. Joel Evans's words and actions suggest that the ABHMS desire for an educated clergy lay at the heart of much of the conflict. Evans had done more than call for the congregation to be led by an African American pastor; he had scorned the black students studying for the ministry at the ABHMS-sponsored school. The disdain evinced by Evans and, presumably, the others who followed him suggests that the call of northern white missionaries for an educated clergy was not wholly embraced by black Christians after Emancipation. Indeed, in slavery, black preachers had wielded great authority as religious and political leaders. The insistence on ministers formally trained in theological programs devised by European Americans threatened not only to erode the power of individuals but to undermine the emancipatory and revolutionary possibility at the very foundation of Afro-Christian ideology by discrediting its most articulate orators and promoters.

In fact, the very nature of the political controversy referred to by Tupper and, later, Carter underscores the degree to which the dissidents questioned the white missionary's authority to impose his preferred criteria for a suitable pastor. Although of secondary importance to the desire for a minister of the dissenting congregants' own choosing, the contentious politics of Reconstruction North Carolina weaved its way through the story. The administration of Governor William W. Holden from 1868 to 1870 and the presidential election of 1872 set the stage. Holden had been appointed Reconstruction governor by Republican President Andrew Johnson. He was most noted for raising militia troops from the western part of the state to quell Ku Klux Klan activity in Caswell and Alamance counties. This bold move led to vigorous Democratic Party opposition and resulted in Holden's dubious distinction as the first governor to be removed from office by impeachment.[21] On the national stage in 1872, Horace Greeley, a former Whig with reform credentials, won the Democratic Party nomination and threatened to sweep the corrupt Grant administration out of office. Although he previously had denounced the Ku Klux Klan and supported enforcement of laws in the South, by the time of the nomination he had become a sharp critic of both Reconstruction state governments and the freedpeople.[22]

During the campaign of 1872, one of Greeley's advocates visited North Carolina to speak on his behalf, and Tupper made his way to see the speaker.[23] The missionary's public support of Greeley apparently did not sit well with many of the black members of Second Baptist. The Republican Party, after all, had been the party of Lincoln, and members of the church questioned whether they wanted as their minister someone who could support a Democratic candidate for president running on a platform to end Reconstruction.[24] Cross, Evans, and Williams, apparently concerned over Tupper's politics, sought and received a meeting with former Governor Holden.[25] Shortly after this meeting, the three dissidents established their own claim to Second Baptist. Thus, the controversy within the church overlapped with contentious politics, but issues of authority and autonomy lay at the heart of the dispute.

The actions of the dissidents, particularly Evans's antagonism toward those studying for the ministry and toward mission-educated ministers, also suggests a significant division, turning on the idea of respectability, among Raleigh's black Baptists. As Glenda Gilmore has so convincingly argued, educated, "middle-class" black men worried that the behavior of poor, young, and uneducated African Americans compromised their manhood and thus their claims for racial equality.[26] The feeling, it would seem, was mutual. While perhaps less interested in the relationships between manhood, respectability, and racial equality, the dissident Baptists nonetheless understood the importance of establishing, maintaining, and protecting their own institution, and they most certainly bristled at the characterizations of them as easily fooled dupes and ignorant dolts that constituted the stock repertoire of white missionary ethnology and perhaps the language used—and increasingly so—by those hoping to lead the race into the new age of Emancipation.

Here, then, was a series of incidents that gestured toward the limits of mission-trained black leadership. As Evelyn Brooks Higginbotham has demonstrated, "Respectability demanded that every individual in the black community assume responsibility for behavioral self-regulation and self-improvement along moral, educational, and economic lines. The goal was to distance oneself as far as possible from images perpetuated by racist stereotypes. Individual behavior . . . determined the collective fate of African Americans."[27] Aspiring leaders who trained at American Baptist mission schools endeavored to engage the post-Emancipation period by creating new identities that modeled the capacity of black Americans to accomplish achievements equal to those of white, middle-class Americans. Yet in establishing themselves as, to use Gilmore's formulation, the black Best Men and Best Women leading their race into the next century, mission-educated African Americans entered a process fraught by white supremacy. Indeed, even as they hoped to represent the race, they were keenly aware that the mark of blackness enabled white Americans to look to *any* black man or woman as representative.[28]

While the controversies over proselyte membership and participation in the Raleigh mission were litigated through the judicial system and were linked to high politics, the Chinese experience in Portland took a decidedly more violent, extralegal turn. With a significantly less deeply rooted tradition in Christianity, Chinese immigrants had disputes concerning the mission school that had little to do with clashing claims to congregational authority. Rather, the conflicts had even more sweeping—and often more dire—implications. In its broadest sense, the discord among immigrants over the mission school turned on a choice between two seemingly mutually exclusive loyalties.

In stark contrast to the protracted legal disputes in Raleigh, the controversies over Chinese mission participation in Portland took the more dramatic form of periodic violence—and threats of violence—against immigrant converts. Although the discord in North Carolina included its share of vitriol, there is no indication that it ever resulted in direct physical confrontation. In

Oregon, this was not the case. On numerous occasions, church records and the city's major newspaper allude to attacks on and threats to Chinese Christians, including at least one murder. These moments—though difficult to discern fully in the fragmentary extant sources—suggest the difficult choices facing students and demonstrate one way in which the boundaries between the mission-based communities and outsiders developed.

Numerous immigrants passed through the doors of the Baptist Chinese Mission School. Although early figures give an exaggerated impression of the number of participants, subsequent records indicate a fairly regular attendance rate. It is impossible to ascertain whether or not the same students attended classes from day to day or week to week, but intermittent conversions celebrated by the school and First Baptist Church point to a relatively stable constituency. For this group of immigrants, choosing to attend classes and perhaps converting to Christianity were not easy decisions.

The mission's managers never explicitly spelled out the requirements of participating in the school. Nevertheless, it seems apparent that missionaries, teachers, and sponsors all desired students to forsake "heathen" beliefs and embrace Christianity. This spiritual transformation was signaled by more worldly markings, such as a change in behavior, and no two activities demonstrated conversion more than renouncing traditional Chinese belief and demonstrating their earnest faith in Christ by street preaching. In an early annual report of the Chinese Mission School, for example, the school's managers noted that immigrant participation in the school had resulted in "a strong and increasing moral and civilizing influence" and that most of the students "have already renounced the idol worship of their ancestors."[29] The report also observed that missionary Dong Gong had begun a program of street preaching with many of the students, and together they would address, in particular, passengers on ships coming from and going to China.[30]

Both the renunciation of a central Chinese religious practice and public evangelizing may have set students and converts in the good graces of their new Christian patrons, but those acts alienated them from their fellow immigrants. Almost immediately, students began to experience disapproval from family members and other Chinese residents of the city. Jennie S. Briggs, the school's secretary, informed the trustees, the ABHMS, and other supporters in 1876 that mission participants had "borne persecution," including "several" who had been fired by Chinese employers, one who had experienced a "cruel scourging," and another who had been pelted with stones.[31] Later that year, the *Oregonian* confirmed reports that Chinese converts and students were often spurned by the rest of the immigrant population. The newspaper reported that two pupils of the mission school "lost good positions as clerks with their heathen relatives, and considerable money for their course. They were offered larger wages if they would recant, and refused entrance to the store because of their firmness."[32]

As the "cruel scourging" alludes to and the stoning demonstrates, community discipline could often turn violent. During no other time was this more evident than in 1878. In the spring of that year, two Chinese men, Moy Luke and Ah Sam, were charged with kidnapping a woman named Wong Ho, and Chinese residents of Portland followed the case with great interest.[33] So, too, apparently, did the city's white readers of the *Oregonian*, for the newspaper reported on the lurid details of the case and editorialized on Chinese criminal gangs and the treatment (and, implied the paper, prostitution) of women.[34]

During the trial, Rev. Dong Gong acted as an interpreter, presumably because, by virtue of his position (and his faith), he had been deemed by authorities to be the most trustworthy Chinese resident in the city.[35] Certainly, Dong's working relationship with many of Portland's most powerful men, including Josiah and Henry Failing, Henry Corbett, and Joseph Dolph, placed him in a unique position to act as intermediary—in a variety of capacities—between immigrants and the state. To many Chinese, however, Dong's position at the mission school and his cozy relationship with the city's elite was anything but an endorsement. During the trial, he was assaulted by four men "known to belong to the Moy Luke faction."[36] Apparently, the attackers, as allies of the defendants, perceived Dong to be biased in his duties. According to the *Oregonian*, they believed Dong to be a stern critic of Chinese prostitution in the city.[37] Perhaps they recalled that the mission had sheltered two women seeking to escape coercive relationships just a few years earlier.[38] To the defendants' supporters, Dong's loyalty lay with the mission, First Baptist Church, and the state, not with his fellow immigrants.

With the trial's guilty verdict and sentencing of the defendants to the penitentiary, threats to the well-being of Dong and mission school participants seem to have subsided temporarily. But less than six months after the assault, another, more grisly attack shocked the Chinese Mission School, First Baptist Church, and the city. In early October 1878, a "young Chinese Christian named Chin Su Ying was shot twice, his head cut open and one of his hands nearly chopped off" at the city's joss house.[39] Although not connected to Dong's beating, the gruesome murder cast an ominous shadow over the school, and mission officials speculated that the slaying, given its location and the victim, was motivated by anger over Chin's conversion.[40]

In fact, rumors of a large-scale plot against Chinese mission participants, impossible to substantiate, swirled around the evangelical institution.[41] The manager of the joss house and several major Chinese merchants, however, denied the existence of any such intrigue. It is clear, however, that Chinese Mission School officials—and, one imagines, students—took the stories of conspiracy quite seriously. The annual report of January 1, 1879, noted, "The lives of those attending [the school] have for months been threatened."[42] Although the crisis appears to have subsided, it is not possible to determine whether the allegations were true or what occurred to decrease the threat against the Chinese students and Dong Gong. The conspiracy could not be proved, but the previous instances of violence and discipline seem to support the view of mission officials. Whether real or imagined, enough had occurred to validate the concerns of mission participants.

The sharp division between Chinese residents of Portland underscores the emergence of a developing new class within the immigrant population. The Chinese Christians affiliated with the Baptist mission school were working out a new identity, and they made their decisions at a dear price as they risked alienating family, friends, and employers. Often they were cut off from these other networks of support, forcing them to rely even more on the community of coreligionists at the home mission. In similar fashion to the nascent African American leadership class developing in mission schools throughout the South, Chinese converts hoped to bridge the gap between the dominant white society in which they lived and their fellow immigrants with whom they shared experiences of movement and marginalization. But among these incipient cultural brokers the multifaceted promise of acceptance and protection by local elite whites, inspired by a faith in the egalitarian hope of evangelical Christianity, was too attractive to pass up in the contest over loyalties and faith.[43]

Yet even as the extant evidence of the hostility of Portland's Chinese toward their mission-affiliated countrymen is rife with menacing images of assault and murder, it is important to note that the decision to join mission-rooted communities may have been a little less straightforward than the heroic choice to forsake one's "heathen" traditions and compatriots. Indeed, as in the South, Chinese mission participants were aware that they were marked by racial difference and therefore vulnerable first and foremost to white supremacist violence and discrimination.

In fact, conflicts among blacks in Raleigh and among Chinese in Portland over questions of authority, leadership, loyalty, and respectability were not the only disputes to affect the mission-rooted communities. Although Shaw University's position in Raleigh remained quite different from the Chinese Mission School's place within Portland, white supremacy also influenced both evangelical projects and the communities they fostered. Surprisingly, in the extant record, there are relatively few discernible instances of overt action directed against either institution after the 1870s. The gap in evidence is likely attributable, at least in part, to the fact that relatively few documents from either school—and especially from students at either school—have survived.

A cursory examination of mission records suggests that perhaps black and Chinese accommodation and white tolerance, not outright conflict, characterized the relationship between mission participants and the disposition of those associated with Baptist missions in Raleigh and Portland. However, what appears to have been accommodation did not preclude conflict. It merely characterized the struggle first by black and Chinese mission participants to find places for themselves within white supremacist societies and then to maintain institutions in the face of almost overwhelming opposition.

Both Baptist missions had been established amid relatively dramatic demographic changes and within dynamic, generally adverse racial climates. The ABHMS project in Raleigh, initiated by a northern missionary and Union Army veteran and directed toward former slaves, had experienced opposition from the local white population practically from the very first day. In Portland, the Chinese Mission School, established with the aid of members of the local white elite, encountered less direct antagonism as an institution, but had its origin in anti-Chinese agitation. As Reconstruction gave way to white-led Redemption and, eventually, Jim Crow in the South and as agitation in California and Oregon against immigration mounted and ultimately resulted in immigration exclusion, mission institutions, buffeted by local expressions of these developments, became sites of self- and community preservation for African Americans and Chinese immigrants. As racial discord sharpened the contrast between whites and nonwhites, the mission-based communities, determined to survive, went to great lengths to prove their respectability and thus acceptability within both cities.

In Raleigh, the hierarchical notions of difference embedded within the evangelical nationalist project met their match in the desires of black mission participants and, in a more limited way, in ABHMS missionary Henry Martin Tupper's own good intentions. Even accounting for the developing gulf between the black Best Men and Women educated at the mission school and the black masses whom they hoped to represent and uplift, the leaders who trained at the Baptist mission possessed a vision of a broadly inclusive society that most certainly threatened to accomplish "the entire reorganization of the social and religious state of the South."[44] Committed northern white missionaries played no small role either. By explicitly ministering to African Americans and linking the spiritual mission of evangelical Christianity with the social and political goals of Emancipation and Reconstruction, Henry Martin Tupper's mission endeavored to educate a black Christian citizenry and to train ministers and teachers to be its leaders.

As the social, economic, and political structure of the antebellum era seemed increasingly likely to be turned upside down, white leaders and others in Raleigh reacted harshly, and Tupper and the ABHMS mission came under almost immediate fire. The evangelical from Massachusetts not only was warned away by Raleigh's most prominent white Baptist minister, but as noted earlier he and his wife encountered a threat by the Ku Klux Klan. "Radical" Reconstruction led by Congress reversed many of the limits imposed by the Black Codes during those difficult first years, but political maneuvering, legal actions, and extralegal intimidation against blacks and their advocates still existed in North Carolina's capital city, perhaps even worsening after the withdrawal of federal troops in 1877. The ABHMS mission, as an institution initiated by a northern evangelical and former Union Army soldier and unambiguously devoted to promoting black freedom and citizenship, continued to endure opposition in its first decade or so of existence.

In 1870, for instance, Tupper, with the aid of the Freedmen's Bureau and donor Elijah Shaw, was poised to purchase property for the mission's grounds. According to Tupper, before the transaction could be completed, the reason for the purchase—to house an African American school—soon came to light, "and the whites at once set to work to prevent us from obtaining possession of the property."[45] Although he had made arrangements for an initial payment of 20 percent, he was soon informed that the total amount—some $20,000—was required. After traveling to New York and convincing the Executive Board of the ABHMS to deposit the remaining $16,000, Tupper found that banks from New York to Raleigh "refused to have anything to do with us."[46] In the meantime, he discovered that a number of influential white residents of Raleigh had raised $14,000 "to stand a lawsuit if it became necessary to prevent us from obtaining the property."[47] In the end, Tupper, as an agent of the ABHMS and with funds from his benefactor, purchased another property.

And though only fragmentary and indirect, the comments of one southerner appear to indicate that the residents of Raleigh were somewhat less than obliging to Tupper and his mission. One critic noted that teachers at Shaw were a "most forbidding New England type—with whom duty—in all matters—is always a business and never a pleasure."[48] The observation continued with a compliment, however, which hints at the opposition faced by the missionary: "the truth is that a less cold & determined set of people would be badgered almost to death & driven away."[49]

Given the early history of local white resistance to the mission, it is surprising that there is no record of a direct attack on or conspiracy against Shaw University for the remainder of the nineteenth century. This, however, did not mean that the 1880s and 1890s were hospitable to African Americans— and especially educated African Americans—in North Carolina. Although the Ku Klux Klan terror campaign of the late 1860s and early 1870s had ended, its political and social consequences were lasting. Historian Stephen Kantrowitz writes, "By 1870, the terror had spread to every corner of the state and encompassed everything from veiled threats to political assassination. . . . In the end, the Reconstruction Republican experiment, rooted in a faith in democratic rules and institutions, could not counter the terrorist challenge."[50] White "redemption" of the state meant that those in control of the Democratic Party could pursue a policy of intimidation, violence, and peonage, designed to increase their fortunes through a dependent African American labor force.[51]

Although the formalization of the white supremacist state would not come until after a vituperative campaign by the Democratic Party and a bloody coup in 1898 and the subsequent passage of a series of comprehensive and systematic laws, the last decades of the nineteenth century in North Carolina were marked by racially aggressive, antagonistic, and oppressive practice and legislation. Despite the nominal freedom of African American North Carolinians, the chains of poverty still bound them to exploitative labor and farming arrangements, such as sharecropping and debt peonage. Historian Raymond Gavins estimates that only 4 to 5 percent of the state's freedmen owned land and observes that the dire conditions of poverty are illuminated in the migration of 2,500 to 3,000 blacks from North Carolina to Indiana in 1879.[52] Moreover, legislative action began strengthening the color line separating whites and blacks. The legislature had outlawed interracial marriage and created a separate department for "the colored" at the State School for the Blind and Deaf.[53] Although custom (and coercion) already dictated separate black and white sections on common carriers, legislators in 1892 proposed to segregate railway travel formally.[54] It was within this climate that Shaw's managers and students continued to develop the institution through a continued, though increasingly bounded, devotion to achievement and uplift.

The Farmers' Alliance spearheaded the most significant challenge to the Democratic regime, eventually growing into the People's Party (or Populists). In the mid-1890s, the Populists joined Republicans in a "Fusion" party marked by a biracial coalition. Astonishingly successful in 1894 and 1896, Fusionists held positions in all levels of government and elected black politicians to office. This success brought an even more vicious and calculated response by white supremacists in charge of the Democratic Party.[55]

In 1898, the Democrats used violence and coercion to overturn the Fusion government. This white supremacy campaign warned of "negro domination" and intimidated voters with armed militia called "Red Shirts" or "White Leagues."[56] Orchestrated by Democratic Party leader Furnifold M. Simmons and supported by most of the state's newspapers, including Raleigh's *News and Observer*, edited by Josephus Daniels, the campaign achieved an electoral victory on November 8, 1898. Its effect went well beyond the polls, however. In Wilmington, where elections were not contested and Populists and Republicans still governed, the white supremacy campaign reached its real crescendo in a fit of brutality two days later. This race riot began with an attack on Alexander Manly's newspaper, but quickly grew, targeting black men and Fusion leaders. Stephen Kantrowitz writes, "The official death toll came to seven black men, but even [Alfred] Waddell [white leader of the riot] acknowledged the actual total to be three times higher."[57] The coup d'état in Wilmington signaled the triumph of white supremacy in the state.[58] As Democrats took office throughout North Carolina the following year, Simmons and other leaders "claimed . . . that the overwhelming victory for white supremacy required black disfranchisement."[59]

Henry Martin Tupper did not live to experience this most stunning display of white supremacy in North Carolina. He died on November 12, 1893, and he was briefly succeeded by N. F. Roberts, an African American graduate of Shaw. Roberts's tenure as the school's head lasted only five months, and it is unclear precisely why he was replaced by Charles Meserve, a white native of Maine and the former president of the Haskell Institute in Lawrence, Kansas. In the worsening racial climate of the state, a black president, though most likely welcomed by the students and other African American leaders, would have been too controversial for the ABHMS, Shaw's trustees, and, especially, local whites.[60] Meserve's term as principal would last until 1919 and was characterized by serious fiscal retrenchment.[61]

Tupper's final decade as the head of Shaw reflected, though somewhat obliquely, the increasing pressure placed on black North Carolinians and their institutions. The national movement which began to undercut broadly conceived, liberal arts education for blacks first manifested itself in 1882. That year, the school received its first pledge from the John G. Slater Fund for industrial education.[62] Tupper's administration—supported by student enrollment—maintained its commitment to liberal arts, theological education, and professional education, establishing a medical school 1882, a law school in 1885, and a school of pharmacy in 1891. Yet beginning with the initial grant from the Slater Fund, Shaw's budget reflected an increasing commitment to mechanical or industrial education. From 1883 to 1892, expenditures in this area had nearly doubled from roughly $2,980 to $5,889.90.[63]

It is impossible to characterize this increase in devotion to industrial education as either wholly negative or wholly positive. As Gavins observes, among black educators, "Theory on pedagogy varied from instruction in 'industrial pursuit' and 'that which best prepares for life' to that stressing development of the 'power of the mind.' But eclecticism and pragmatism about content or what to teach gave way to consensus on the transcendent value of black education."[64] Shaw and ABHMS supporters actively opposed the "Hampton model" of industrial education in favor of a classical liberal education.[65] Nevertheless, by the final decades of the nineteenth century, as Shaw sought to expand and scrambled to pay for its expansion, it was forced to go beyond its traditional means of support and look toward philanthropic organizations interested in providing industrial training to African Americans. Lamented Charles Meserve in 1898, "The fact must not be overlooked that as the years go by the North is taking less and less interest in this work in the South. The old friends have gone, or are fast going, and the younger generation are not imbued with the ideas and enthusiasm of the old anti-slaver, agitations, workers and friends."[66] Historian James D. Anderson has persuasively argued that white supremacy's racialist assumptions lay at the foundation of these philanthropic organizations' goals to provide a "second-class education to prepare blacks for subordinate roles in the southern economy"—the essence of black industrial training.[67] Although Shaw's administrators and students remained committed to a broad curriculum, this reliance on other funding shaped the institution.

In some ways, especially for white North Carolinians and an increasing number of white mission advocates, Charles Meserve was a logical choice to lead Shaw during the decade that Rayford Logan famously referred to as the "nadir" of American race relations. Not only was he willing to undertake the financial retrenchment desired by the Executive Board of the ABHMS, but he also seemed to echo the increasingly harsh racial assumptions of the day. While Henry Martin Tupper heeded his calling out of a deep appreciation for the abolitionist cause and sympathy, at least, for the egalitarian bent of evangelical Christianity, Meserve appears to have believed in the culturalist assumptions that buttressed late nineteenth-century understandings of racial difference. In assessing home mission work in the South, he expressed wonder at the great distance that needed to be traveled in order to accomplish civilizing uplift: "The negroes themselves were the crudest of raw material. Their ideas of morality were loose in the extreme. Their worship was a strange mixture of religious practices, superstitious rites, emotional utterances, and plantation melodies. Improper relations between the ignorant flock, or between the brethren and sisters themselves, intemperance and drunkenness, lying and stealing, were not bars to church membership and church fellowship."[68]

As the shadow of Jim Crow descended upon North Carolina, this perspective surely drew less negative attention to the mission school from local whites. Indeed, in the midst of the bloody riot in Wilmington, as African Americans throughout the state feared for their lives, Meserve reported no act directed toward Shaw's campus.[69] But Meserve's leadership of Shaw underscored just how far the evangelical hopes of the mission project and the freedom dreams of black students had been compromised by the vicious reassertion of white supremacy. In the volatile environment after Wilmington, any transgression of the newly reinforced color line could be deadly. If the statements of Shaw's students, teachers, and supporters had been deliberate before, after 1898, they would need to make doubly certain not to offend.

In Portland, the larger currents of white supremacy had less of an effect on the Chinese Mission School. The buffer of elite sponsorship helped to prevent direct attacks on the mission school, and the soothing words of prominent members of the community could insulate the school and its students from the pervasive anti-immigrant agitation that marked the last quarter of the nineteenth century. Indeed, the moderating pronouncements of white leaders preempted most complaints even within an environment marked by hostility toward the Chinese.

The opposition to immigrants, though perhaps less virulent in Oregon than in California or Washington Territory, nonetheless appears to have been pervasive.[70] The 1874 establishment of the evangelical project in Portland had been preceded by a flurry of anti-Chinese activity. After the mission's founding, periodic hostility surfaced, usually surrounding the employment of immigrant labor. In the spring of 1879, for instance, the *Spokane Times* reported that mass "workingmen's" meetings were being held in Portland and that a movement was afoot to run the Chinese out of town.[71]

In 1885–86, a wave of violence spread throughout the West. On September 5, 1885, white workers in Rock Springs, Wyoming, murdered twenty-eight Chinese and laid waste to the village where hundreds of others lived. As historian Robert Wynne has observed, Rock Springs "became the signal for other outrages in the Pacific Northwest within six months."[72] He has documented the murder of three Chinese in the Issaquah Valley of the Washington Territory on September 7, and that incident was followed by a more well-known race riot in Tacoma on September 11.[73] In Seattle, a movement to expel the Chinese began in late September, subsided in November, gained new life in January 1886, and culminated with a full-scale riot in February.[74]

While Portland's contribution to this unhappy record was modest, it does suggest that the city was influenced by the larger trend of extralegal violence throughout the region. In February 1886 an organization called the "East Portland Encampment No. 4 of the Merchants' and Laboring Men's Anti-Coolie League" came into existence, inspired by the arrival of California agitator Burnette G. Haskell.[75] The group's first (and seemingly only) act was to attack thirty Chinese workers employed by the Oregon City Woolen Mill.[76] While a parade honoring George Washington's birthday degenerated into an anti-Chinese demonstration, little violence occurred.[77]

In the meantime, Portland's newspaper, though accused of sympathizing with the Chinese, continued to carry items about anti-immigrant activities in California. This constant barrage of information most certainly contributed to the city's generally unfriendly atmosphere for its Chinese residents. Moreover, the legislative results of these extralegal actions began to bear fruit and culminated with the Chinese Exclusion Act of 1882.[78] Interestingly, neither the extant records of the Chinese Mission School nor those of First Baptist Church mention the new law's effect on its mission. For its part, the ABHMS issued a strongly worded statement in which it denounced the restriction as inconsistent with "the fundamental principles of our free government and opposed to the spirit of the Christian religion," and the result of "an unchristian race-prejudice."[79]

Although it is difficult to discern the practical effect of such opposition on the everyday workings of the mission, it is possible to detect a more moderate position in the rhetoric of the school's managers and supporters. As early as 1878, Rev. A. S. Coats of First Baptist Church distanced the Portland project from the claim by ABHMS officials that the goal of missions was to make the Chinese citizens.[80] Coats assured white residents of Portland that classes at the school were not intended to facilitate or encourage assimilation or settlement.[81] In fact, Coats proclaimed that "we neither know nor care" whether the Chinese "could be Americanized" and that the mission school was merely "a base of operations" to return Christian converts to China.[82]

Yet the workings of the mission seem to suggest that Coats's statements were merely meant to appease potentially antagonistic Portlanders. Indeed, in the fall of 1879, the mission completed and dedicated a "beautiful and commodious chapel."[83] This new building and the observation that the mission "was to so large an extent self-supporting" seems to indicate deeper roots than Coats let on.[84] Indeed, a number of Chinese members of the church had already begun to establish families and settle in the city. These individuals, such as Seid Back, were generally merchants who did not have to move from place to place in search of work. Although not yet as well established as he would soon be, Back by 1877 had already attended the mission school, married in First Baptist Church, and had a son.[85]

The mission school's founders were among Portland's most powerful men. They maintained a strong political and commercial hold on the city, and their desire to keep social stability, in addition to their evangelical zeal, fueled the mission to the Chinese. Indeed, from their perspective, evidence of disorder resulting from the immigrant presence in the city, state, and region was pervasive. The threat came as much—if not more—from white gangs as from the Chinese. Thus community leaders attempted to appease white residents by denying any desire to see the Chinese settle. At the same time, they not only affirmed the rationale for the school's existence by claiming the primacy of the gospel but supported and expanded the mission. Indeed, by the end of the century, the mission had become a stable and rooted institution, having baptized at least one second-generation Chinese member.[86]

The American Baptist missions in Raleigh and Portland were forged in a crucible of opposition. Conflict helped to define the contours of community by illuminating the social cost of belonging. The disagreements and disputes within groups of potential proselytes underscored the choices made by black and Chinese mission participants. In Raleigh, conflict between church members turned on issues of authority and leadership and resulted in a smaller congregation loyal to the ABHMS school with which it shared space. In Portland, attending the mission school often had dire consequences, for condemnation by non-Christian Chinese and the disavowal of traditional belief often placed immigrant students in the position of having to decide between mutually exclusive communities. In both cases, students defined themselves not only by affiliating with the ABHMS mission but also by choosing *not* to associate with other potential congregants or community members.

But in this choice, they exposed a fundamental tension in the development of new post-Emancipation and immigrant identities. As they acted on their individual aspirations and collective responsibilities, educated black and Chinese Baptists hoped to demonstrate the limitless capacity of their respective races to achieve while providing effective race leadership. Yet as they cast this ambition in the prescriptive terms set forth by the "assimilationist leanings" of white evangelical nationalism, they risked alienating the very people they hoped to lead.[87]

On a broader level, general antiblack and anti-Chinese sentiment also shaped both missions. But local contexts mattered greatly. The hostility of local whites in Raleigh and the brutality that resulted in the terror of the 1898 white supremacy campaign contrasted with the subtle mode of social control exercised by Portland's leading citizens. In North Carolina, without support from local elites, the mission retreated to accommodationist language and practice in order to survive. In Oregon, the local environment was less immediately hostile, and the city's leaders helped to protect the mission from any direct attacks. Although forced by anti-Chinese sentiment to appease protesters by claiming a limited vision for the mission, the elites who managed the Chinese Mission School seemed less willing in practice to compromise its role as a vital community institution. But the veil of white supremacy would descend on Chinese America, too, just as it was descending upon the South, and African Americans and Chinese immigrants would be left to their own devices—their traditions and institutions and beliefs—to imagine a different world.

CONCLUSION

Transformations

The stone which the builders rejected, The same was made the head
of the corner.
    Matthew 21:42 (ASV)

For our citizenship is in heaven.
    Philippians 3:20–21 (ASV)

IN JANUARY 1899, Charles Meserve, the white president of Shaw University
in Raleigh, North Carolina, presented his annual report to the ABHMS. A
single tragic event loomed large in Meserve's report. Just two months earlier,
the devastating race riot had ripped through Wilmington in the eastern part
of the state, the culminating event in the "white supremacy campaign" orchestrated by the Democratic Party, a carefully devised scheme to wrest power
from the state's Republicans, Populists, and Fusionists and to ensure that
blacks would not and could not participate in the political process.[1]

Meserve described the impact of the events on Shaw. He noted that the
first sign that something was awry occurred when the school received reports
"that bodies of men, armed and known as red-shirts . . . were intercepting
colored citizens and threatening to shoot them if they went to town and registered [to vote]." Black students "gathered in knots on the campus and in their
rooms." According to Meserve, many "had parents, others near relatives and
friends, and some of them property, in Wilmington," making an event that

was unquestionably an outrage to all African Americans in the state an even more intimate and painful affront to the Shaw community.[2]

The university president did not mince words as he described the students' shock and anger. He reported that as they "walked their rooms in anguish of soul . . . their indignation and sense of injustice were wrought up to the highest pitch." Yet in his account to the Executive Board, mission advocates, and supporters, Meserve emphasized the restraint demonstrated by black members of the community. Although he "counseled moderation and forbearance," he found that his concern was unwarranted, for the students "controlled themselves splendidly, and there was nothing that could be considered even bordering upon a disturbance." In an ironic but nonetheless revealing twist, Meserve even noted that Josephus Daniels, editor of Raleigh's News and Observer and, by Meserve's own account, "the leading factor in the 'white man, white metal' campaign," lived across the way from Shaw and heard not a sound from the over two hundred men and women living on campus. "I would not suppose there were forty [people living there]," Daniels reportedly commented, "every thing is so quiet and orderly."[3]

The white supremacy campaign of 1898 and its murderous result vividly demonstrated the disciplinary savagery that could be brought to bear on black southerners. The goal of such explosions of brutality was to underscore the threat of everyday violence that reinforced—and defined—the racial boundaries of late nineteenth-century citizenship. As historian Joel Williamson has so succinctly stated, "Once the riot had actually occurred in Wilmington, there was no need for it to happen elsewhere."[4]

Even in the immediate wake of Emancipation and as Reconstruction provided blacks in the South with rights and protections, white southerners had begun attempting to roll back what they perceived to be a radical transformation of the South's social and racial structure.[5] To be sure, the racial terror of the post-Reconstruction period differed in ferocity and specific cause from the violence of the immediate postwar period, but the underlying goal was still the same: to police the boundaries of civic participation.[6] Moreover, although less dramatic than the physical injury and threat of mob action and lynching, the structural arrangements—legal, economic, and political—that resulted in physical and nonphysical injury to all African Americans also characterized the "violence" of the white supremacist South.[7]

At the very same time, white supremacy imposed itself in no less violent fashion among Chinese living in the United States. Almost as soon as they had begun arriving in America, Chinese were subjected to physical abuse and intimidation. During the 1870s and 1880s, the Pacific Coast and Mountain West states and territories saw periodic, full-scale riots, usually culminating with attempts at driving terrorized Chinese from towns or cities. The string of uprisings peaked in 1885 with the deadly riot in Rock Springs, Wyoming, which left twenty-eight Chinese dead, and in 1886 with the purging of Chinese from Tacoma and Seattle in Washington Territory.

White evangelical Jesse Boardman Hartwell, the American Baptist head of Chinese missions on the Pacific Coast, expressed his horror at "the spirit of hatred and violence" aimed at those to whom he ministered. Referring to Rock Springs, Tacoma, and Seattle, Hartwell reported to the Executive Board of the ABHMS on the damage done by the rioters: "Outbreaks have occurred in which scores of Chinese have been massacred, their houses burned or otherwise demolished, and their property destroyed or scattered to the extent of many hundreds of thousands of dollars." In language that would be echoed by his fellow evangelical Charles Meserve some years later, despite a desire for "justice and right" to "avenge the wrongs" that resulted from "cruelty" and "race prejudice," Chinese, according to Hartwell, were notably restrained in their response to the violence. "With marvelous forbearance," he reported, "these strangers have refrained from forcible resistance, and have patiently awaited the operation of law."[8]

As in the South, the anti-Chinese riots of the 1870s and 1880s were only the most dramatic manifestations of boundary-making terror. These eruptions punctuated a steady flow of local, state, and national legislation that can be described as a type of violence, too.[9] From municipal and state statutes attacking the ability of Chinese miners to stake and maintain claims and restricting residential options to national acts that excluded specific "classes" of immigrants, these forms of legislative duress struck at the heart of Chinese economic, social, and political lives. They were aimed at discouraging settlement and keeping the migrant labor force "flexible" and therefore vulnerable. Historian Sucheng Chan, in fact, has described what she calls the "Era of Exclusion," foreshadowed by the 1875 Page Act that restricted the entry of Chinese women and ushered in by the 1882 Chinese Exclusion Act, as a "dark age . . . [of] immense suffering and deprivation."[10] The formal end of unrestricted immigration had a deleterious effect on the development of Chinese settlements in America. It staunched the flow of new immigrants and established barriers that prevented laborers already in the United States from moving back and forth across the Pacific.[11] These legal assaults worked in concert with extralegal violence, for the noncitizen status of most Chinese in America left them with limited legal recourse or protection.

Ubiquitous violence, then, was a fact of everyday life for blacks and Chinese during the late nineteenth century. That an upsurge in terror against both of these groups occurred roughly simultaneously is no coincidence. Black freedom and Chinese settlement—and both groups' hopes and struggles for equality—were perceived as direct attacks on the links between whiteness and American national identity. Increasingly, solutions to the Negro Problem and the Chinese Question relied on physical and structural violence to reinforce the racial bounds of citizenship.

While the broad patterns and goals appear quite similar, the differences are as instructive. The Fourteenth and Fifteenth Amendments provided blacks with hard-won citizenship rights, but when Reconstruction came to an end with the corrupt compromise of 1877 and the withdrawal of federal oversight and protection, these new citizens found themselves at the mercy of local and state governments hostile to their equal standing. State legislatures from Mississippi to North Carolina began legislative efforts at reversing the gains of Reconstruction, efforts buttressed by extralegal (though often tacitly sanctioned) violence. The "redeemer" white governments of the South did not invent the color line of segregation. However, the statutory regulations that legalized the second-class citizenship of southern blacks codified the hierarchy of Jim Crow, as did the Supreme Court's 1896 *Plessy v. Ferguson* decision that upheld the legality of "separate but equal" public accommodations. The legal contortions of the segregation-enabling "separate but equal" standard and the disfranchisement-facilitating measures like literacy tests and grandfather clauses effectively rendered blacks outside the bounds of the nation and attacked the foundations of the Reconstruction Amendments, yet the principle of equal citizenship nonetheless remained theoretically in place. This is the principle of which Justice John Marshall Harlan reminded the Court in his dissenting opinion in the *Plessy* case. Although he acknowledged the social realities of the Jim Crow regime, Harlan argued that "in view of the Constitution, in the eye of the law, there is in this country no superior, dominant, ruling class of citizens. There is no caste here. Our Constitution is color-blind, and neither knows nor tolerates classes among citizens. In respect of civil rights, all citizens are equal before the law."[12] Perhaps the existence of this principle helps explain the spectacular brutality and unrelenting intimidation that distinguished the white supremacy of the segregated South.

The 1790 Naturalization Act, in the meantime, continued to bar Chinese immigrants from becoming citizens. Outsiders by law, with limited legal recourse and little state protection, Chinese may have enjoyed certain rights and privileges that African Americans did not, but they nonetheless occupied a legal position beyond the bounds of the nation.[13] Significantly, Congress revised the naturalization law in 1870 to allow people of African nativity and descent to become citizens but maintained the barrier to Chinese.[14] Moreover, whereas those who sought to limit the rights of blacks in the South had to contend with a population that had grown from roughly 4 million at the time of Emancipation to almost 7.5 million by 1890, the movement to check the Chinese faced a population that had been slowed substantially by the Chinese Exclusion Act of 1882.[15] Immigration exclusion and the prohibition on naturalization were complemented by violence and intimidation, to be sure, but the work of the federal government largely accomplished the goal of delimiting Chinese membership in the nation. It is worth noting that within four years of the Supreme Court case that established that the Fourteenth Amendment's provision for *jus soli* applied to the Chinese, Congress extended immigration exclusion indefinitely.[16]

By the end of the nineteenth century, then, the American nation had indeed been transformed, but in a drastically different manner than African Americans, Chinese, and even white evangelicals had desired. The white missionaries who had heeded the call of the changing nation and the possibilities engendered by evangelical nationalist conversion found their project partially fulfilled. The institutions they had helped establish did sustain interracial interaction. Yet the tepid reaction of white evangelicals to the violence directed toward blacks and Chinese suggests that the institutional growth and achievements of the American Baptist Home Mission Society outstripped the broader national conversion—spiritual and social—they had envisioned. Acts of racial terror limited the radical hopes of the home mission project and frustrated the attempts of evangelicals, blacks, and Chinese to fashion an inclusive nation through such interracial enterprises. Threatened, harassed, and attacked for their positions on the Chinese Question and the Negro Problem, American Baptists found safe refuge in the strain of evangelical nationalism that emphasized orderly hierarchy and stability over redemptive equality and democracy.

But even as the African Americans and Chinese affiliated with Baptist home missions watched the nation they had so faithfully hoped to transform move not toward broader freedoms and equality and justice but rather into violence and oppression and separation, they continued to fight for the transformation *they* desired. These strivings reveal not only the depth and strength of their aspirations but also the creativity of their solutions to the problem not of difference but of white supremacy. Their faith in the egalitarian promise of evangelical Christianity sustained their engagement with mission projects, and they used mission resources to position themselves in the larger battle over their place in the civic order. Their actions illuminate responses to boundary-making racial violence, subverting the goals of that violence and serving as the foundation for alternate imaginings of national—and transnational—belonging.

In the South, as the specter of violence haunted American Baptist missions and encouraged missionaries like Charles Meserve to counsel caution, black participants wove together an intricate array of institutions that endeavored to salvage the hope of Emancipation. The ABHMS fought attempts by African Americans to run missions throughout the late nineteenth century. In fact, even as the North Carolina mission was reeling from the Wilmington riot, the Executive Board of the ABHMS found itself embroiled in a dispute over black desires for control over Baptist institutions in Richmond, Virginia.[17] Nonetheless, Shaw-educated men and women established themselves as religious, educational, and political leaders beyond the confines of the mission institution. They represented a positive assertion of black identity in an increasingly hostile environment as they provided models of aspiration and accomplishment. They also created a broad network of institutions and informal associations that had a lasting impact. The autonomous space carved out by Shaw graduates, educators, and evangelicals, as well as other black Baptists who took part in ABHMS endeavors throughout the South, not only provided shelter from the constant threat of violence but also ultimately served as a crucial infrastructure for later battles for freedom and equality.

African Americans laid the groundwork for more opportune moments of protest and struggle, especially as the reign of white supremacist terror descended throughout the Jim Crow South. But this foundation meant more than merely institutional space for organizing. The black church, with its theological emphasis on liberation and justice, provided a critical angle of vision on the white supremacist nation that meshed neatly with the ethos of aspiration and leadership at the center of mission educational aims. More than merely "bequeath a significant legacy of hope to the next generation," as historian Raymond Gavins argues, Shaw graduates drew from the traditions of emancipatory Christianity, the hopes and aspirations of postslavery freedom, and the rhetoric of evangelical equality to craft enduring institutions and bonds of fellowship that would enable future generations to continue the long, hard struggle for equality.[18]

Yet even before the end of the nineteenth century, as the worst fears of

African Americans who still remembered the hopeful days of Emancipation and Reconstruction were being realized and the window of hope was being slammed shut, black Baptists began pushing their white brethren to take a public stand against the most dramatic manifestation of the post-Reconstruction period: lynching.[19] In fact, Evelyn Brooks Higginbotham has argued that black southern women were ultimately responsible for the 1899 Woman's American Baptist Home Mission Society (WABHMS) resolution condemning the growing violence in the South.[20] As she notes, the women's organization did not "temper their words" as they protested that "a man made in the image of God, destined for eternal life or death, is mutilated, partly burned at the stake, then cut up, and pieces of flesh and bones sold for souvenirs, while a part of the heart is sent in triumph to the Governor of the State."[21]

On the Pacific Coast, Chinese also used mission programs to launch autonomous and semiautonomous institutions and networks that hoped to uphold the promise of migration and Gold Mountain in the face of growing hostility and increasing restriction. Some Chinese converts provided models of aspiration and achievement in a society that seemed determined to limit their life chances, while others acted as brokers, hoping to maintain the protection of elite paternalism that shielded them from the worst abuses of anti-immigrant white supremacy. Other Chinese Baptists, following a different trajectory, created a loose web of transnational Christian institutions that modeled alternate visions of belonging that emphasized fellowship and congregation more than the nation.

Systematically excluded from formal citizenship by law, Chinese converts, through their trans-Pacific network of churches, missions, meetings, and informal association, articulated a version of "community" in which the boundaries of the nation mattered less than religious fellowship and congregation. This cosmopolitan vision of belonging enabled Chinese Christians in America to focus on two different goals simultaneously. On one hand, they continued to put their money and energy into sustaining institutions throughout the U.S. Pacific Coast and in China, modeling their ideas of cosmopolitan Christianity.

On the other hand, they acted upon their belief in the egalitarian underpinnings of evangelical Christianity by voicing periodic protests against discrimination. In 1882, for example, just after the Chinese Exclusion Act became law, Portland missionary and transnational Christian Fung Chak chastised Congress for its actions. Holding America to the inclusive promise of evangelical nationalism, he took the "nominally Christian nation" to task for its disregard of "principle." Fung understood the devastating effect the law would have on the Chinese in America, and he hoped for the triumph of "righteousness" as he explicitly advocated for the quick reversal of the act.[22]

Portland mission school alumnus Sam Song Bo also decried the Exclusion Act. In a letter to the *New York Sun* reprinted in the *American Missionary*, Sam explained that "a paper was presented to me . . . for subscription among my countrymen toward the Pedestal Fund of the Bartholdi Statue of Liberty." With barely controlled indignation, the Chinese Baptist alerted readers that "the word liberty makes me think of the fact that this country is the land of liberty for men of all nations except the Chinese." He continued, "I consider it as an insult to call on us to contribute toward building in this land a pedestal for a statue of Liberty. That statue represents Liberty holding a torch which lights the passage of those of all nations who come into this country. But are the Chinese allowed to come? As for the Chinese who are here, are they allowed to enjoy liberty as men of all other nationalities enjoy it? Are they allowed to go about everywhere free from the insults, abuse, assaults, wrongs, and injuries from which men of other nationalities are free?" Sam concluded by challenging the United States: "Whether this statute against the Chinese or the statue to Liberty will be the more lasting monument to tell future ages of the liberty and greatness of this country, will be known only to future generations."[23]

The ABHMS, too, appeared to allude to the inclusive tradition of evangelical nationalism when its Committee on Chinese Missions, in May 1882, stated, "We earnestly deprecate such discrimination in our immigration laws as contrary to the fundamental principles of our free government and opposed to the spirit of the Christian religion." The Society's objections, though, rested less on the injustice perpetrated against the Chinese than on the corrupt reasoning on which the law was based. While in part decrying the "unchristian race-prejudice" that brought about the legislation, the ABHMS was equally incensed by "the rivalry of political parties ambitious for power" that had resulted in the law.[24] Moreover, the home mission organization's actions belied the urgency that Fung and Sam had signaled. While Fung, for example, would remain outspoken in his criticism of the immigration legislation, the response of the ABHMS, beyond rhetoric, was surprisingly restrained. Perhaps it was modeling its preferred behavior for Chinese proselytes.

It would take another decade for the Society to act to try to put an end to immigration legislation. Although a direct causal link is impossible to establish, ABHMS corresponding secretary Henry L. Morehouse must have relied on the experiences of Chinese under the exclusion regime to form his critique when he organized a multidenominational and multiorganizational campaign to repeal the 1892 Geary Act, which had renewed exclusion for another ten years. In the fall of that year, Morehouse began recruiting representatives of mission organizations to a conference to plan a broad-based, evangelical objection to the law. He found many groups eager to join him, including the Methodist Episcopal Church, the Domestic and Foreign Missionary Society of the Protestant Episcopal Church, the Board of Foreign Missions of the Presbyterian Church, and the American Missionary Association, among others.[25]

However, the objections of Edward W. Gilman, corresponding secretary of the American Bible Society, are instructive. Gilman replied to Morehouse's invitation by expressing his dissatisfaction with the Geary Act, but added that it was not "clear to our mind that it would be advisable to take action aiming at its modification or repeal." In fact, explained Gilman, "we are not informed that it has yet exerted any disastrous influence upon any work the American Bible Society is doing in this country or in China."[26] The extant record provides no evidence of the deliberations involved in the crafting of the statement produced by the "Conference on Repeal of the Anti-Chinese Legislation" held on January 26, 1893, but the minutes of the meeting indicate that Morehouse spent much time answering Gilman's doubts. He held forth on "the course of the legislation on the exclusion of the Chinese, and particularly dwelt upon the passage of the several bills, giving the pith of the arguments, pro and con, in both Houses of Congress, as drawn from the Congressional record." Yet before he concluded his remarks, Morehouse turned his attention away from legalities and toward the experiences of those who lived under the exclusion legislation; he "called attention to the oppressive character of the regulations."[27]

It was a discussion that clearly relied on the accounts from the field by those most harmed by the law. In a twist on missionary ethnology, these accounts may have been forwarded by white evangelicals, but they also may have been gleaned from the dispatches of Chinese converts like Sam Song Bo or Chinese missionaries like Fung Chak. Whatever the conduit, the experiences and views of the Chinese who suffered under exclusion legislation found their way into the final statement of the conference. In fact, whereas the Society's objections a decade earlier had dwelled on the legalities of exclusion, the statement authored by Morehouse, Joshua Kimber of the Episcopal Church, and F. F. Ellinwood of the Presbyterian Board of Foreign Missions privileged the plight of the Chinese. Enumerating the "grave objections" to the Geary Act, the conference focused on the excessive regulations ("it tags a man like a dog"), the vulnerability of immigrants ("it subjects a man at any time, or anywhere, to arrest at the discretion of a horde of officers"), and the undue costs ("it imposes heavy expense and much trouble to many"), as well as what it deemed to be the reversal of "all principles of justice." Even as the evangelicals concluded that the law represented "the lamentable spectacle of a Christian nation breaking its treaty with a people whom we are endeavoring to win the acceptance of the Gospel," they emphasized not Sino-U.S. relations or the damage the law would do to mission efforts in China but rather the effects of the law on the lives of those to whom they ministered.[28]

When missionary superintendent Jesse Hartwell tempered his indignation about the violence perpetrated against Chinese on the Pacific Coast and in the Mountain West with an emphasis on "marvelous forbearance" and the avoidance of "forcible resistance" in favor of "the operation of law," he effectively retreated from the democratic possibility engendered by the most radical strain of evangelical nationalism. His position, in fact, reinforced the subordination and deference hoped for by white intimidation. The evidence was fairly clear by the mid-1880s that the law was not, in fact, on the side of the Chinese. To be sure, an evangelical, egalitarian understanding of the nation provided the foundation for well-intentioned and committed missionaries and officials like Hartwell and Henry Lyman Morehouse to imagine and even to try to build a Christian democracy, but it was the vision, desire, and activity of Chinese that most ardently pushed white evangelicals toward that goal.

Within a year of the failed attempt by Morehouse and other leaders to loosen the constraints of the Geary Act, Hartwell's successor as superintendent of Chinese missions on the Pacific Coast provided a hint that the Society would be happy merely to reap souls through a narrower focus on spiritual conversion while letting the fields that sustained the broader social conversions of evangelical nationalism lie fallow. H. F. Norris bolstered the message of accommodation that signaled the evangelical retreat in language that was as proscriptive as it was prescriptive. As he praised the "decision [by Chinese in the United States] to no longer resist the enforcement of the recent laws regarding registration," Norris revealed his hope as much as he described a social reality. Indeed, it was with a palpable sense of anticipated relief that Norris concluded that the dampening of Chinese protest against the Geary Act would allow them to reconcile their status in America and allow them to concentrate on the spiritual lessons of conversion: "They are now adjusting themselves to the situation and taking more interest in the schools."[29]

Similarly, in counseling "moderation" and celebrating black restraint, Shaw University's Charles Meserve exemplified the accommodationist strategy desired by white supremacist violence. His anecdote recounting Josephus Daniels's praise of black students at Shaw during the Wilmington riot is telling. Daniels was one of the most vituperative public white supremacists in North Carolina and a proud chief architect of the 1898 campaign. When Meserve chose to boast about Daniels's compliment, he signaled the triumph of "respectability" as the elusive standard of white toleration of black civic participation.[30] The activism of black Baptist women may have driven the WABHMS toward their 1899 antilynching resolution, and the ABHMS itself may have, in the fall of that year, finally been moved by black outrage to decry the "lawlessness" and "evil" of "the brutalities of white people."[31] However, Baptist evangelicals who feared that southern violence would undo the significant institutional gains of the home mission project found safe haven in the strain of their ideology that emphasized order and stability as the ultimate aim.[32] Even as an editorial in the Society's official publication chastised white southerners for their violence, it also offered a rebuke of "short-sighted Negroes appealing to race passions and seeking to stir up antagonism between their people and the white people."[33] A follow-up editorial underscored this desire for accommodation as it outlined the key principles of ABHMS policy in the South. White northern missionaries, almost thirty-five years after the end of the Civil War, still had a place in the former Confederacy to provide a counterweight to "hot-headed Negroes" and to encourage friendly relations between black and white southerners.[34] By recasting themselves as mediators and conciliators between blacks and whites in the South, ABHMS officials, at the close of the peak decade of black lynching in the region, made explicit their turn away from the broadly transformative evangelical nationalism of the post-Emancipation period.

Nonetheless, black Baptists who publicly protested lynching and Chinese converts who decried immigration restrictions were silenced neither by the violence to which they were subjected nor by the declining support of their white evangelical brethren. In part, that these particular voices can be heard more than a century later may be due as much to the institutional legacies of Baptist missions as to the uniqueness of the act of speaking out itself. The continuing missionary society, its enduring schools and churches, and the preservation of institutional records surely account for the ability of twenty-first-century researchers to hear the WABHMS or Sam Song Bo. As historians unearth more records and as oral traditions continue within black and Chinese families, churches, and communities, surely the echoes of other voices will be audible to those who listen attentively.

Yet that the intimidation of white supremacist violence and the gospel of accommodation preached by northern missionaries failed to completely quiet protest is significant. Black Baptists could rely both on the institutional infrastructure built during the years of hope following Emancipation and on the long history of endurance and struggle that suffused Afro-Christianity. While white American Baptist evangelicals coped with the shattering of their hope for a nation transformed by egalitarian Christianity by taking solace in a kind of proselytizing that relied on a more narrow accounting of progress—the number of souls converted and the number of institutions claimed—African Americans continued to be sustained by the bonds of fellowship they had begun nurturing decades earlier, and they continued to remember the lessons of resistance and fortitude that reached back to their parents' and grandparents' time in bondage. A similar tradition of emancipatory Christianity among Chinese in the United States is not discernible. Nevertheless, the institutional framework of the mission project—as well as the evangelical emphasis on egalitarian brotherhood—provided Chinese Christians a way to model an alternate idea of belonging. Their focus on linking institutions along the Pacific Coast and across the ocean to China was a way for them to create space to protect themselves psychologically and, often, physically from the abuses of a nation that made clear its desire to keep them alienated subjects. Rather than merely focus on the loss of possibility, transnational, cosmopolitan Chinese converts forged a new way of understanding Christian belonging that sought to minimize the role of the nation and the state.

During the 1860s and 1870s, as American Baptist home missionaries began their work in earnest among newly emancipated blacks and Chinese arrivals to the United States, they hoped to convert these potential proselyte populations and the nation as a whole. At stake was nothing less than the Christian conversion and subsequent social transformation of America. Indeed, American Baptist evangelicals hoped to alter the very standard of national belonging from an overtly racial measure to one in which Christianity would serve as the primary marker. By the close of the nineteenth century, a transformation had indeed occurred in the relationship between race and nation. But rather than pursuing the opening created by Emancipation, immigration, and the egalitarian possibilities of evangelical Christianity, the nation turned its back on this democratic promise and plowed full bore toward the exclusions and oppressions of white supremacy. The ABHMS reactions to lynching and immigration restriction not only reveal the degree to which the insistent and ferocious movement to ensconce the white nation constrained the inclusiveness of the evangelical nationalist project. They also shed light on the ways in which this liberal Christian tradition's internal tensions limited the actions of and perhaps even implicated often well-meaning evangelicals. In the battle against lynching and the campaign against exclusion, it was blacks and Chinese themselves, not white missionaries, who drove the engine to transform the ABHMS and the nation as a whole. These late nineteenth-century efforts not only foreshadowed later, similar engagements; they also laid the groundwork for future confrontations. It would be those cast off by the white supremacist nation whose hope and faith and striving would fortify them as the cornerstone of the next century's struggles for a more egalitarian and democratic nation.[35]

Notes

Introduction

1. Excerpt of letter reprinted in *Baptist Home Mission Monthly* 4:10 (October 1882), 285.

2. H. M. Tupper, "Shaw University: Annual Report of President H. M. Tupper," reprinted in *Baptist Home Mission Monthly* 5:5 (May 1883), 102. Emphasis in the original.

3. For more on the Chinese Exclusion Act and its effect on the Chinese in the United States, see Erika Lee, *At America's Gates: Chinese Immigration During the Exclusion Era, 1882–1943* (Chapel Hill: University of North Carolina Press, 2003).

4. William J. Simmons, *Men of Mark: Eminent, Progressive and Rising* (Cleveland, 1887), 206–207.

5. E. G. Robinson, "Race and Religion on the American Continent," *Baptist Home Mission Monthly* 5:3 (March 1883), 49–53.

6. Ibid., 49, 52–53.

7. I use "American Baptist" here and throughout the book to indicate the organizational affiliation of the evangelicals, not to specify their nationality. "American Baptists" thus refers to those individuals associated with the New York-based, northern-dominated American Baptist Home Mission Society. The group's counterpart is Southern Baptists, which refers to evangelicals affiliated with the Southern Baptist Convention. When I use the lower-case variation ("southern Baptist" or "northern Baptist"), I am referring to geographic location. Members of the ABHMS helped found the American Baptist Anti-Slavery Convention (ABASC) in 1840. ABASC agitation, especially its opposition to the appointment of slaveholding missionaries, precipitated the split of northern and southern Baptists in 1845. For more on the ABASC, see Elon Galusha, "Address to Southern Baptists, delivered 30 April 1840," reproduced in A. F. Foss and E. Mathews, *Facts for Baptist Churches* (Utica, N.Y., 1850), 46; Nathaniel Colver, *A Review of the Doings of the Baptist Board of Foreign Missions, and of the Triennial Convention, at Baltimore, April, 1841* (n.p., 1841), 46; Henry Yu, *Thinking Orientals: Migration, Contact, and Exoticism in Modern America* (New York: Oxford University Press, 2001), 21.

8. Robinson, "Race and Religion," 49.

9. This approach builds upon scholarship in colonial and postcolonial studies that ex-

amines the limits of liberal, inclusive colonial policies. See especially Frederick Cooper and Ann Laura Stoler, "Between Metropole and Colony: Rethinking a Research Agenda," in *Tensions of Empire: Colonial Cultures in a Bourgeois World*, ed. Cooper and Stoler (Berkeley: University of California Press, 1997), 1–56; Ann Laura Stoler, "Tense and Tender Ties: The Politics of Comparison in North American History and (Post) Colonial Studies," *Journal of American History* 88:3 (December 2001), 829–65. Yet as Mary A. Renda perhaps most concisely articulated in a *Journal of American History* "roundtable" response to an article by Stoler on colonial and postcolonial studies in North American history, such analytical frameworks tend to privilege processes of domination. I share Renda's concerns. My approach in this book is to balance an analysis of the subtleties of racial domination as engendered by the home mission project with an understanding of, to use Renda again, "the cultural histories" that blacks and Chinese "brought to bear on their experience of domination." Mary A. Renda, "'Sentiments of a Private Nature': A Comment on Ann Laura Stoler's 'Tense and Tender Ties,'" *Journal of American History* 88:3 (December 2001), 886.

10. Robinson, "Race and Religion," 51–52.

11. Lemuel Moss, "Results of Home Mission Work," *Baptist Home Mission Monthly* 5:5 (May 1883), 101. My framework of analysis for the late nineteenth-century home mission movement extends Laurie F. Maffly-Kipp's excellent work on home missions in the American West. Maffly-Kipp's examination of California during the antebellum years presents a masterful examination of home mission ideology, but it neglects the experiences and ideas of blacks and, especially, Chinese. Laurie F. Maffly-Kipp, *Religion and Society in Frontier California* (New Haven, Conn.: Yale University Press, 1994). See also idem, "Assembling Bodies and Souls: Missionary Practices on the Pacific Frontier," in *Practicing Protestants: Histories of Christian Life in America, 1630–1965*, ed. Maffly-Kipp, Leigh E. Schmidt, and Mark Valeri (Baltimore: Johns Hopkins University Press, 2006), 51–76.

12. The scholarship that explores white-led, northern home missions to African Americans in the aftermath of the Civil War is particularly rich. See especially Willie Lee Rose, *Rehearsal for Reconstruction: The Port Royal Experiment* (1964; New York: Oxford University Press, 1976); David M. Reimers, *White Protestantism and the Negro* (New York: Oxford University Press, 1965); James M. McPherson, *The Abolitionist Legacy: From Reconstruction to the NAACP* (Princeton, N.J.: Princeton University Press, 1975); Jacqueline Jones, *Soldiers of Light and Love: Northern Teachers and Georgia Blacks, 1865–1873* (Athens: University of Georgia Press, 1980); Joe M. Richardson, *Christian Reconstruction: The American Missionary Association and Southern Blacks, 1861–1890* (Athens: University of Georgia Press, 1986); Evelyn Brooks Higginbotham, *Righteous Discontent: The Women's Movement in the Black Baptist Church, 1880–1920* (Cambridge, Mass.: Harvard University Press, 1993); William E. Montgomery, *Under Their Own Vine and Fig Tree: The African-American Church in the South, 1865–1900* (Baton Rouge: Louisiana State University Press, 1993); Paul Harvey, *Redeeming the South: Religious Cultures and Racial Identities Among Southern Baptists, 1865–1925* (Chapel Hill: University of North Carolina Press, 1997); Daniel W. Stowell, *Rebuilding Zion: The Religious Reconstruction of the South, 1863–1877* (New York: Oxford University Press, 1998); Sally G. McMillen, *To Raise Up the South: Sunday Schools in Black and White*

Churches, 1865–1915 (Baton Rouge: Louisiana State University Press, 2001); Edward J. Blum, *Reforging the White Republic: Race, Religion, and American Nationalism, 1865–1898* (Baton Rouge: Louisiana State University Press, 2005). Higginbotham and Harvey, in particular, include extended examinations of the work of the ABHMS. The two most focused studies on the ABHMS project in Raleigh are Wilmoth A. Carter, *Shaw's Universe: A Monument to Educational Innovation* (Rockville, Md.: D. C. National Publishing, 1973), and an unpublished dissertation, Archie Doyster Logan, Jr., "Henry Martin Tupper and His Adult Education Activities Among African-Americans, 1865–1893" (Ed.D. diss., North Carolina State University, 1993). For an excellent study that links the post-Reconstruction South and religion, see James B. Bennett, *Religion and the Rise of Jim Crow in New Orleans* (Princeton, N.J.: Princeton University Press, 2005). Although Bennett's work focuses not on missionaries but on the local religious landscape of New Orleans, this persuasive book is instructive, for it charts the movement from interracial congregation within Methodist and Catholic churches to the triumph of "religious segregation."

13. The scholarly work on Chinese in the United States and home missions is thinner, but some of it is quite good. See Peggy Pascoe's work on women and home missions in *Relations of Rescue: The Search for Female Moral Authority in the American West, 1874–1939* (New York: Oxford University Press, 1990), and Wesley S. Woo, "Chinese Protestants in the San Francisco Bay Area," in *Entry Denied: Exclusion and the Chinese Community in America, 1882–1943*, ed. Sucheng Chan (Philadelphia: Temple University Press, 1991), 213–45. Woo's essay is a distillation of his very useful unpublished dissertation, "Protestant Work Among the Chinese in San Francisco Bay Area" (Ph.D. diss., Graduate Theological Union, 1984). In addition to Pascoe and Woo, Judy Tzu-Chun Wu provides a thoughtful assessment of mission work among the Chinese in "'The Ministering Angel of Chinatown': Missionary Uplift, Modern Medicine, and Asian American Women's Strategies of Liminality," in *Asian/Pacific Islander American Women: A Historical Anthology*, ed. Shirley Hune and Gail Nomura (New York: New York University Press, 2003), 155–71, drawn from her broader project on the life of Margaret Chung. See idem, *Doctor "Mom" Chung of the Fair-Haired Bastards: The Life of a Wartime Celebrity* (Berkeley: University of California Press, 2005). Mary Ting Yi Lui explores the dynamics of white female missionaries who ministered to Chinese men in her excellent *The Chinatown Trunk Mystery: Murder, Miscegenation, and Other Dangerous Encounters in Turn-of-the-Century New York City* (Princeton, N.J.: Princeton University Press, 2005); and Nayan Shah examines the role of missionaries in creating discourses of respectability in San Francisco's Chinatown in his thought-provoking *Contagious Divides: Epidemics and Race in San Francisco's Chinatown* (Berkeley: University of California Press, 2001). In addition, Brian Masaru Hayashi's work on Japanese American Christianity provides a thoughtful exploration of questions of Christian conversion and assimilation. *"For the Sake of Our Japanese Brethren": Assimilation, Nationalism, and Protestantism Among the Japanese of Los Angeles, 1895–1942* (Stanford, Calif.: Stanford University Press, 1995).

14. This approach, which seeks to integrate cultural and intellectual history with social history, takes up the challenge that Thomas C. Holt made to historians in the mid-1990s

to explore the "subtle interaction between various levels of terrain and human experience" at the heart of race and race making. Thomas C. Holt, "Marking: Race, Race-making, and the Writing of History," *American Historical Review* 100:1 (February 1995), 6. Asian American historians, in particular, have produced nuanced and inspiring examples of this sort of undertaking. See especially John Kuo Wei Tchen, *New York Before Chinatown: Orientalism and the Shaping of American Culture, 1776–1882* (Baltimore: Johns Hopkins University Press, 1999); Lee, *At America's Gates*; Eiichiro Azuma, *Between Two Empires: Race, History, and Transnationalism in Japanese America* (New York: Oxford University Press, 2005); Moon-Ho Jung, *Coolies and Cane: Race, Labor, and Sugar in the Age of Emancipation* (Baltimore: Johns Hopkins University Press, 2006). My multitiered approach is also inspired by work in microhistory and specifically the linking of microhistorical and macrohistorical levels of inquiry. See especially Carlo Ginzburg, "Microhistory: Two or Three Things That I Know About It," trans. John and Anne C. Tedeschi, *Critical Inquiry* 20:1 (Autumn 1993), 10–35. See also Paul K. Eiss, "To Write Liberation: Time, History, and Hope in Yucatán," in *Small Worlds: Method, Meaning, and Narrative in Microhistory*, ed. James F. Brooks, Christopher R. N. DeCorse, and John Walton (Santa Fe, N.M.: School for Advanced Research Press, 2008), 53–76.

15. Michael Omi and Howard Winant have explored the process of racial formation in the United States as "the sociohistorical process by which racial categories are created, inhabited, transformed, and destroyed." In their analysis, they understand racial rearticulation as the process by which the established (in this case racist) social order is rearticulated through a careful redefinition of racist discourse. This process "produces new subjectivity by making use of information and knowledge already present in the subject's mind" and can become a powerful antiracist tool. *Racial Formation in the United States: From the 1960s to the 1990s*, 2nd ed. (New York: Routledge, 1994): 55–56, 60–61, 99–101.

16. Robinson, "Race and Religion," 50, 53. For an exploration of normative whiteness, see Ross Chambers, "The Unexamined," in *Whiteness: A Critical Reader*, ed. Mike Hill (New York: New York University Press, 1997), 187–203.

17. My understanding of the critical role of the nation in defining difference is influenced by the work of Amy Kaplan. Kaplan writes that "a sense of the foreign is necessary to erect the boundaries that enclose the nation as home. Domesticity, furthermore, refers not to a static condition, but to a process of domestication, which entails conquering and taming the wild, the natural, the alien. 'Domestic' in this sense is related to the imperial project of civilizing, and the conditions of domesticity often become markers that distinguish civilization from savagery. Domestication implies that the home contains within itself those wild or foreign elements that must be tamed; domesticity monitors the borders between the civilized and the savage as it regulates the traces of savagery within its purview." *The Anarchy of Empire in the Making of U.S. Culture* (Cambridge, Mass.: Harvard University Press, 2002), 25–26. See also idem, "Manifest Domesticity," *American Literature* 70:3 (1998), 581–606; idem, "'Left Alone with America': The Absence of Empire in the Study of American Culture," in *Cultures of United States Imperialism*, ed. Kaplan and Donald E. Pease (Durham, N.C.: Duke University Press, 1993), 3–21; Etienne Balibar, "Racism

and Nationalism," in *Race, Nation, Class: Ambiguous Identities*, ed. Balibar and Immanuel Wallerstein (1988; London: Verso, 1991), 37–67.

18. Robinson, "Race and Religion," 51–52.

19. My argument here elaborates upon scholarship in Asian American Studies that locates the foundations of Asian American racial formation not in biology but in "institutionalized legal definitions of race and national origins." Lisa Lowe, *Immigrant Acts: On Asian American Cultural Politics* (Durham, N.C.: Duke University Press, 1996), 10–12. Or, as Claire Jean Kim has argued, Asian Americans have been racially positioned through an "insider-outsider" model. Claire Jean Kim, "The Racial Triangulation of Asian Americans," *Politics and Society* 37 (1999), 105–38. See also Angelo Ancheta, *Race, Rights, and the Asian American Experience* (New Brunswick, N.J.: Rutgers University Press, 1998). However, while Kim and Ancheta, in particular, contrast Asian American racialization along this insider-outsider axis with the racialization of African Americans primarily along a "superior-inferior" axis, I argue that both forms of differentiation played a critical role in black and Chinese racial formation and that the specific regional and local histories and discourses explain the differential racialization of each group.

20. Historian Edward J. Blum has also made the case for understanding the relationships among race, nation, and evangelical Protestantism in late nineteenth-century America. In his thought-provoking and ambitious work, Blum quite perceptively probes the role of religion in constructing a national vision of whiteness among reformers, evangelicals, and politicians. Blum argues that this vision of white racial unity was *the* crucial foundation upon which sectional reconciliation was built. Significantly, although Blum and I both explore the same general themes, our books traverse different terrain. Whereas Blum is interested mostly in the interplay of religious ideology, cultural politics, and sectional relations, I focus on the links among religious and nationalist ideology, evangelical practice, and the lived experiences of racial domination and resistance. Whereas Blum's assessment of race focuses exclusively on black-white relations, mine triangulates black-Chinese-white relations. Whereas Blum's focus requires him to dwell solely in the South, my book integrates the Far West into my analysis. Whereas Blum's book deals primarily with the religious enterprise from the perspective of leaders, my study offers an analysis both of evangelizing efforts of well-known missionaries and theorists and responses by local, everyday, and heretofore unknown blacks and Chinese. This last difference, especially, leads us to different conclusions about the racial implications of white missionary work among blacks in the South. Blum, writing mostly from the perspective of white missionaries in the immediate aftermath of the Civil War, finds their self-perception altered to be more accepting of blacks while former slaves praised the efforts of these northern evangelicals. My argument pays closer attention to black desires for autonomy and places evangelical actions and interactions within a process of racial formation that accounts not just for the construction and maintenance of racial hierarchy but also for how subjugated groups sought to transform racial structures and meanings. Moreover, the main thrust of Blum's argument—that northern white evangelical leaders sacrificed their support of black rights and racial egalitarianism to a reunited white nation—is a crucial contribution to the work on post-Reconstruction America and is

an important complement to works such as David W. Blight's *Race and Reunion: The Civil War in American Memory* (Cambridge, Mass.: Harvard University Press, Belknap Press, 2001). But because ordinary blacks (and Chinese) who were subject to the maneuverings of evangelical leaders are not the focus of his study, Blum is not able to do justice to the ways in which these ordinary folk lived under, struggled with, and did their best to reshape America's white supremacist legacy. My study attempts to rework this part of Blum's story to account for a particular and historicized kind of agency within black and Chinese communities. Blum, *Reforging the White Republic*. For a useful discussion of agency, see Walter Johnson, "On Agency," *Journal of Social History* 37:1 (Fall 2003), 113–24. For a more focused discussion of the role of religion during the contested period following Reconstruction and the institution of segregation in the South, see Bennett, *Religion and the Rise of Jim Crow*. Bennett's examination of New Orleans means that the scale of his study is fundamentally different from Blum's; it is a local and regional rather than a national framework. As such, it enables Bennett to provide a greater sense of contestation and black agency than Blum. Nevertheless, like Blum, Bennett's interest in the rise of white supremacy in the late nineteenth and early twentieth centuries lies solely in the South.

21. Paul Gilroy, *"There Ain't No Black in the Union Jack": The Cultural Politics of Race and Nation* (1987; Chicago: University of Chicago Press, 1997), 43, 59–60. See also Etienne Balibar, "Is There a 'Neo-Racism'?" in Balibar and Wallerstein, *Race, Nation, Class*, 17–28; Stuart Hall, "New Ethnicities," in *"Race," Culture and Difference*, ed. James Donald and Ali Rattansi (London: Sage, 1992), 252–59. Ann Laura Stoler, especially, has questioned the "newness" of Gilroy's "new racism," and my understanding of cultural racism in historical perspective draws on her argument that "physiological attributes only signal the nonvisual and more salient distinctions of exclusion on which racism rests" and that cultural constructions of difference, especially when used in conjunction with defining the nation, "provide the observable conduits, the indexes of psychological propensities and moral susceptibilities seen to shape which individuals are suitable for inclusion in the national community and whether those of ambiguous racial membership are to be classified as subjects or citizens within it." Ann Laura Stoler, "Sexual Affronts and Racial Frontiers: European Identities and the Cultural Politics of Exclusion in Colonial Southeast Asia," in Cooper and Stoler, *Tensions of Empire*, 203, 214. See also Ann Laura Stoler, *Carnal Knowledge and Imperial Power: Race and the Intimate in Colonial Rule* (Berkeley: University of California Press, 2002), 84, 97. For an analysis of the way in which Asian Americans have historically been cast as culturally foreign and thus subject to "civic ostracism," see Kim, "The Racial Triangulation of Asian Americans." For a particularly careful—and insightful—discussion of the relationships among race, ethnicity, biology, and culture, see Viranjini Munasinghe, *Calloloo or Tossed Salad? East Indians and the Cultural Politics of Identity in Trinidad* (Ithaca, N.Y.: Cornell University Press, 2001), 8–16.

22. Pascoe, *Relations of Rescue*, 143–44.

23. My argument here, in addition to drawing on Gilroy, Balibar, and Stoler, is inspired by anthropologist Viranjini Munasinghe's discussion of the relationship between "ethnicity" and "race" in her study of East Indians in Trinidad. She argues, in part, that

"ethnicity, like race, is indelibly linked to external processes of exclusion." Munasinghe, *Tossed Salad*, 10. Within Asian American history, Stuart Creighton Miller most famously explored the influence of missionaries in espousing notions of racial difference. *The Unwelcome Immigrant: The American Image of the Chinese, 1785–1882* (Berkeley: University of California Press, 1969). More recently, Henry Yu has explored the links between missionaries among the Chinese abroad and in the United States and the racialized notions of "Orientals" embedded within the Chicago School of Sociology in his excellent intellectual history, *Thinking Orientals.*

24. This cosmopolitan Christianity represented what historian Jessica Harland-Jacobs has called a "supranational identity." According to Harland-Jacobs, "a supranational identity results when people define a community of belonging that extends beyond their place of origin." Jessica L. Harland-Jacobs, *Builders of Empire: Freemasons and British Imperialism, 1717–1927* (Chapel Hill: University of North Carolina Press, 2007), 12.

25. Raymond Gavins, "Fear, Hope, and Struggle: Recasting Black North Carolina in the Age of Jim Crow," in *Democracy Betrayed: The Wilmington Race Riot of 1898 and Its Legacy*, ed. David S. Cecelski and Timothy B. Tyson (Chapel Hill: University of North Carolina Press, 1998), 201–2.

26. W. E. B. Du Bois, *The Souls of Black Folk* (1903; New York: W. W. Norton, 1999), 1, 5. Du Bois first used his sentence about the color line and the twentieth century in July 1900 in an address entitled "To the Nations of the World" that he gave before the first pan-African conference in London. He repeats the statement in *Souls* at the end of ch. 2.

27. For scholarship that links the experiences of African Americans and Asian Americans under white supremacy, see Gary Y. Okihiro, *Margins and Mainstreams: Asians in American History and Culture* (Seattle: University of Washington Press, 1994); Tomás Almaguer, *Racial Fault Lines: The Historical Origins of White Supremacy in California* (Berkeley: University of California Press, 1994); Najia Aarim-Heriot, *Chinese Immigrants, African Americans, and Racial Anxiety in the United States, 1848–82* (Urbana: University of Illinois Press, 2003); Jung, *Coolies and Cane.* Some recent scholarship has argued against the comparability of African American and Asian American experiences. Lon Kurashige, for instance, in his otherwise insightful study of Japanese Americans in twentieth-century Los Angeles, argues for the differentiation between the racial context in which Asian Americans on the West Coast lived and the Jim Crow South. At first glance, this is sensible advice. But a closer look at Kurashige's assertion reveals that he bases his admonition on a belief that Japanese immigrants and their children "operated in racial situations in which they had a range of cultural, economic, and political resources at hand to contest and deflect domination" while intimating that African Americans did not have such resources. Lon Kurashige, *Japanese American Celebration and Conflict: A History of Ethnic Identity and Festival in Los Angeles, 1934–1990* (Berkeley: University of California Press, 2002), 2. Recent African American scholarship belies this assessment, pointing to the myriad sources of black agency, community, and dignity even within the dehumanizing conditions of the segregated South. See especially Robin D. G. Kelley, *Hammer and Hoe: Alabama Communists During the Great Depression* (Chapel Hill: University of North Carolina Press, 1990); idem,

Race Rebels: Culture, Politics, and the Black Working Class (New York: Free Press, 1994); Earl Lewis, *In Their Own Interests: Race, Class, and Power in Twentieth-Century Norfolk, Virginia* (Berkeley: University of California Press, 1991); Higginbotham, *Righteous Discontent*; Glenda E. Gilmore, *Gender and Jim Crow: Women and the Politics of White Supremacy in North Carolina, 1896–1920* (Chapel Hill: University of North Carolina Press, 1996); Gavins, "Fear, Hope, and Struggle," 185–206; William H. Chafe, Raymond Gavins, and Robert Korstad, eds., *Remembering Jim Crow: African Americans Tell About Life in the Segregated South* (New York: New Press, 2001); Steven Hahn, *A Nation Under Our Feet: Black Political Struggles in the Rural South from Slavery to the Great Migration* (Cambridge, Mass.: Harvard University Press, Belknap Press, 2003); Paul Ortiz, *Emancipation Betrayed: The Hidden History of Black Organizing and White Violence in Florida from Reconstruction to the Bloody Election of 1920* (Berkeley: University of California Press, 2006).

28. See Vicki L. Ruiz, "Dead Ends or Gold Mines? Using Missionary Records in Mexican American Women's History," in *Unequal Sisters: A Multicultural Reader in U.S. Women's History*, 2nd ed., ed. Ruiz and Ellen Carol DuBois (New York: Routledge, 1994), 312.

29. Ibid.

30. Historians such as James D. Anderson, Evelyn Brooks Higginbotham, Glenda E. Gilmore, James B. Bennett, Paul Harvey, Judy Tz-Chun Wu, and Mary Ting Yi Lui have explored the interactions between white missionaries and black or Chinese proselytes, but they have also shifted their focus to a broader realm. Anderson, Higginbotham, and Gilmore explore the world of autonomous black organizations while Harvey examines the relationships between white and black Baptists in the South and Bennett explores the relationships between white and black Methodists and Catholics. And Wu and Lui have demonstrated the effect of mission relationships beyond the boundaries of home mission projects. James D. Anderson, *The Education of Blacks in the South, 1860–1935* (Chapel Hill: University of North Carolina Press, 1988); Higginbotham, *Righteous Discontent*; Gilmore, *Gender and Jim Crow*; Harvey, *Redeeming the South*; Bennett, *Religion and the Rise of Jim Crow*; Wu, *Dr. "Mom" Chung*; Lui, *The Chinatown Trunk Mystery*. For more on autonomous black institutions, see especially some of the excellent work on the black church in the South: Montgomery, *Under Their Own Vine and Fig Tree*; James Melvin Washington, *Frustrated Fellowship: The Black Quest for Social Power* (Macon, Ga.: Mercer University Press, 2004); James T. Campbell, *Songs of Zion: The African Methodist Episcopal Church in the United States and South Africa* (1995; Chapel Hill: University of North Carolina Press, 1998); Clarence E. Walker, *Rock in a Weary Land: The African Methodist Episcopal Church During the Civil War and Reconstruction* (Baton Rouge: Louisiana State University Press, 1981).

31. My work thus follows the example of James Scott's examination of subordinate groups. See James C. Scott, *Domination and the Arts of Resistance: Hidden Transcripts* (New Haven, Conn.: Yale University Press, 1990). My broader understanding of "agency" and its constraints and the relationship between culture and oppression follows on the critical engagement of Walter Johnson's work on slavery. See especially Johnson, "On Agency."

For a particularly powerful discussion of the intersection of cultural change, agency, and politics, which "calls attention to people's strategies for using cultural practices to fulfill a variety of pressing needs in difficult and dangerous circumstances," see Vincent Brown, *The Reaper's Garden: Death and Power in the World of Atlantic Slavery* (Cambridge, Mass.: Harvard University Press, 2008), 7–8.

32. Lewis, *In Their Own Interests*, 91. Lewis's broader understanding of congregation as an idea that informed and sustained black community formation under Jim Crow is significantly more expansive than the narrower, more formal definition usually applied within social scientific studies of American religion. For the use of "congregation" within the sociology of religion, see especially R. Stephen Warner, "The Place of the Congregation in the American Religious Configuration," in *American Congregations*, vol. 2, ed. James P. Wind and James W. Lewis (Chicago: University of Chicago Press, 1994). 54–99; Fenggang Yang and Helen Rose Ebaugh, "Transformations in New Immigrant Religions and Their Global Implications," *American Sociological Review* 66 (2001), 269–88. For a penetrating critique of the social scientific literature, see Manuel A. Vasquez, "Historicizing and Materializing the Study of Religion: The Contribution of Migration Studies," in *Immigrant Faiths: Transforming Religious Life in American*, ed. Karen I. Leonard, Alex Stepick, Manuel A. Vasquez, and Jennifer Holdaway (Lanham, Md.: Altamira, 2005), 219–42. See also Nancy Ammerman, *Congregation and Community* (New Brunswick, N.J.: Rutgers University Press, 1997); Penny Edgell Becker, *Congregations in Conflict: Cultural Modes of Local Religious Life* (Cambridge: Cambridge University Press, 1999). This broader perspective also enables me to take advantage of a handful of excellent local studies in my examinations of Raleigh and Portland. On Raleigh, I have found Roberta Sue Alexander's study of North Carolina during presidential Reconstruction and Wilmoth A. Carter's study of Shaw University to be indispensable starting points. The unpublished dissertation by Archie Doyster Logan, Jr., about the mission work of Henry Martin Tupper has also been invaluable. Roberta Sue Alexander, *North Carolina Faces the Freedmen: Race Relations During Presidential Reconstruction, 1865–67* (Durham, N.C.: Duke University Press, 1985); Carter, *Shaw's Universe*; Logan, "Henry Martin Tupper." For Portland, I found Marie Rose Wong's exploration of the development of Portland's Chinese ethnic enclaves to be critical in my understanding, especially, of the spatial dimensions of Chinese-white relations in the city. Marie Rose Wong, *Sweet Cakes, Long Journey: The Chinatowns of Portland, Oregon* (Seattle: University of Washington Press, 2004). See also Lee Bessie Ying, "Perpetuation of the Primary Group Patterns Among the Chinese in Portland, Oregon" (Ph.D. diss., University of Oregon, 1938).

33. Gilmore, *Gender and Jim Crow*, 5. Historian Sucheng Chan has argued for special attention to be paid to the lives of Chinese Americans during the period of exclusion, bracketed by the Chinese Exclusion Act of 1882 and 1943, when Congress repealed exclusion and granted Chinese the right of naturalization. She has described this period as a "dark age . . . [of] immense suffering and deprivation." Sucheng Chan, preface to *Entry Denied*, x.

Chapter 1. "A Grand and Awful Time"

1. Executive Board of the ABHMS, *Thirtieth Annual Report of the American Baptist Home Mission Society* (New York, 1862), 25.

2. See Executive Board of the ABHMS, *Twenty-eighth Annual Report of the American Baptist Home Mission Society* (New York, 1860), 43; Executive Board of the ABHMS, *Thirty-first Annual Report of the ABHMS* (New York, 1863), 59.

3. Executive Board, *Thirty-first Annual Report*, 18. The hymn, "We Are Living, We Are Dwelling," was written by Episcopal minister Arthur Cleveland Coxe in 1840.

4. Ibid.

5. See John Stanford Holme, "The Freedmen of the United States—Who They Are and What They Are," *Baptist Home Mission Monthly* 8:1 (February 1879), 116–17.

6. The Central Pacific Railroad began employing Chinese workers in 1865. By the end of the year some three thousand Chinese men toiled for the company. At its peak, the corporation employed about ten thousand workers of Chinese origin. Sucheng Chan, *Asian Americans: An Interpretative History* (Boston: Twayne, 1991), 30–31.

7. Executive Board, *Thirty-first Annual Report*, 18–19.

8. For the 1873 operating budget and contributions, see Executive Board of the ABHMS, *Forty-first Annual Report* (New York, 1873), 56–57, 73.

9. U.S. Bureau of the Census, *Population of the United States in 1860; Compiled from the Original Returns of the Eighth Census* (Washington, D.C., 1864); idem, *Ninth Census,*vol. 1, *The Statistics of the Population of the United States* (Washington, D.C., 1872); idem, *Statistics of the Population of the United States at the Tenth Census* (Washington, D.C., 1883).

10. For more on America's "manifest destiny," see Frederick Merk, *Manifest Destiny and Mission in American History* (Cambridge, Mass.: Harvard University Press, 1963); Reginald Horsman, *Race and Manifest Destiny: The Origins of American Racial Anglo-Saxonism* (Cambridge, Mass.: Harvard University Press, 1981); Thomas R. Hietala, *Manifest Design: American Exceptionalism and Empire*, rev. ed. (Ithaca, N.Y.: Cornell University Press, 1985).

11. Executive Board of the ABHMS, *Thirty-third Annual Report of the American Baptist Home Mission Society* (New York, 1865), 9.

12. Ibid., 9–10.

13. Ibid., 10.

14. Ibid.

15. Executive Board of the ABHMS, *Thirty-seventh Annual Report of the American Baptist Home Mission Society* (New York, 1869), 20.

16. Quote from H. M. King's "Report of the Committee on Chinese Missions," published in Executive Board of the ABHMS, *Fiftieth Annual Report of the American Baptist Home Mission Society* (New York, 1882), 16. For more on Baptist home missionaries' criticisms of the anti-Chinese movement, see, for example, "The Chinese in California," *Home and Foreign Journal* 2:3 (September 1852), 2; John Loud, "Thirty Thousand Chinese in California," *Home and Foreign Journal* 2:5 (November 1852), 2; "Glad to Hear It," *Home*

and Foreign Journal 8:9 (March 1859), 1; "Chinese Immigration," *Home and Foreign Journal* 2:4 (August 1869), 4; Henry Ward Beecher, "The American Christian's Duty to America," *Baptist Home Mission Monthly* 1:12 (June 1879), 182–85.

17. Executive Board, *Thirty-third Annual Report*, 10.

18. See especially Perry Miller, *The Life of the Mind in America: From the Revolution to the Civil War* (New York: Harcourt, Brace and World, 1965), 36–72; Laurie F. Maffly-Kipp, *Religion and Society in Frontier California* (New Haven, Conn.: Yale University Press, 1994), 3, 35. Maffly-Kipp's extraordinary book is the best treatment available of the ideology and practice of antebellum home missions.

19. As a centralized Baptist body, the ABHMS was not without precedent. In the late eighteenth and early nineteenth centuries, Baptists had supported missions through contributions to local and state associations and to organizations run by other denominations, particularly the Congregationalists' American Board of Foreign Missions. In 1814, local, state, and regional Baptist associations formed the General Missionary Convention of the Baptist Denomination in the United States for Foreign Missions. This body, commonly referred to as the Triennial Convention because it held general meetings every three years, allowed for the centralized collection and distribution of funds for evangelical work. Originally, domestic missions to the North American territories west of the Appalachian Mountains were also supervised by the Triennial Convention. For more on the Triennial Convention and the establishment of the ABHMS, see especially Robert G. Torbet, *A History of the Baptists*, 3rd ed., rev. (Valley Forge, Pa.: Judson Press, 1963), 248–49, 358–61; H. L. Morehouse, "Historical Sketch of the ABHMS for Fifty Years," in *Baptist Home Missions in North America; Including a Full Report of the Proceedings and Addresses of the Jubilee Meeting, and a Historical Sketch of the ABHMS, Historical Tables, Etc., 1832–1882* (New York, 1883), 302–6, 313–22; Rufus Babcock, *Memoir of John Mason Peck, D.D.* (Philadelphia, 1864), 166, 219–20, 234–43.

20. Morehouse, "Historical Sketch," 300.

21. Going quoted in ibid., 317–18. For Going's tour of the Mississippi Valley and John Mason Peck's influence, see Babcock, *Memoir*, 186, 234–44; Torbet, *A History of Baptists*, 360.

22. Maffly-Kipp, *Religion and Society*, 26. Representatives of the four major Protestant denominations—with the lion's share of support coming from Presbyterians and Congregationalists—cooperated to established the American Home Mission Society (AHMS) in 1826. By the end of the 1840s, Northern Methodists, Episcopalians, and Old School Presbyterians had joined the AHMS and the ABHMS with home mission societies of their own. See especially Colin Brummitt Goodykoontz, *Home Missions on the American Frontier, with Particular Reference to the American Home Mission Society* (Caldwell, Idaho: Caxton Printers, 1939).

23. Quoted in Morehouse, "Historical Sketch," 324.

24. Steven Chapin, "A Discourse before the ABHMS, Delivered at Their Annual Meeting, Held in Calvert-Street Baptist Church, in the City of Baltimore, April 27, 1841," in *The Southern Baptist Preacher; or, Sermons by Living Baptist Ministers in the South*, no. 12, ed. William H. Stokes, (Penfield, Ga., 1841), 166.

25. Martin E. Marty argues that American evangelicals, especially between 1776 and 1877, "set out consciously to create an *empire*. They set out to attract the allegiance of all the people, develop a spiritual kingdom, and to shape the nation's ethos, mores, manners, and often its laws." *Righteous Empire: The Protestant Experience in America* (New York: Dial Press, 1970), 1.

26. Lemuel Moss, "Results of Home Mission Work," *Baptist Home Mission Monthly* 5:5 (May 1883), 101.

27. Maffly-Kipp, *Religion and Society*, 17. Maffly-Kipp relies heavily on Daniel Walker Howe's insightful interpretation and explanation of beliefs of antebellum evangelicals linked to the Whig Party, and Howe (and Maffly-Kipp) explicitly contrasts Whig notions of territorial expansion with those advocated by the Democratic Party represented by Andrew Jackson. *The Political Culture of the American Whigs* (Chicago: University of Chicago Press, 1979), 150–80.

28. Susan Thorne, *Congregational Missions and the Making of an Imperial Culture in Nineteenth-Century England* (Stanford, Cal.: Stanford University Press, 1990), 147.

29. Mark A. Noll, *A History of Christianity in the United States and Canada* (Grand Rapids, Mich.: William B. Eerdmans, 1992), 178. For more on the voluntary principle and revivalism, see especially Paul E. Johnson, *A Shopkeeper's Millennium: Society and Revivalism in Rochester, New York, 1815–1837* (New York: Hill and Wang, 1978).

30. For more on the ABASC, see Elon Galusha, "Address to Southern Baptists, delivered 30 April 1840," reproduced in A. F. Foss and E. Mathews, *Facts for Baptist Churches* (Utica, N.Y., 1850), 45–47. See also Nathaniel Colver, *A Review of the Doings of the Baptist Board of Foreign Missions, and of the Triennial Convention, at Baltimore, April, 1841* (n.p., 1841).

31. Maffly-Kipp, *Religion and Society*, 20–23.

32. Moss, "Results of Home Mission Work," *Baptist Home Mission Monthly* 5:5 (May 1883), 101.

33. Maffly-Kipp, *Religion and Society*, 25. As Maffly-Kipp herself acknowledges, this narrow spectrum limits the focus of her book, which does not examine in any depth the experiences of blacks or Chinese. Ibid., 8. For more on Anglo-Saxonism and westward expansion, see Horsman, *Race and Manifest Destiny.*

34. Committee on the State of the Country report reproduced in Executive Board, *Thirty-third Annual Report*, 43.

35. "Burning of Churches in Petersburg," *Harper's Weekly*, May 19, 1866, 317. For Smith's account, see Executive Board of the ABHMS, *Thirty-fourth Annual Report of the American Baptist Home Mission Society* (New York, 1866), 27–28.

36. Executive Board, *Thirty-third Annual Report*, 44.

37. H. C. Fish, "Report to the Executive Board of the ABHMS," reproduced in Morehouse, "Historical Sketch," 398.

38. For an excellent study of Adoniram Judson, his family, and his mission, see Joan Jacobs Brumberg, *Mission for Life: The Story of the Family of Adoniram Judson, the Dramatic Events of the First American Foreign Mission, and the Course of Evangelical Religion in the Nineteenth Century* (New York: Free Press, 1980).

39. Editorial, *American Baptist Missionary Magazine* 14 (March 1834), 94–95.

40. "China and Oregon," *Religious Herald* (Richmond, Va.), March 26, 1846, p. 2, col. 2.

41. "Board of Domestic Missions: Operations of the Board," *Home and Foreign Journal* 2:4 (October 1852), 1.

42. "Address of the San Francisco Baptist Association," *Home and Foreign Journal* 2:6 (December 1852), 1–2.

43. It is possible that the October 1852 SBC report that a domestic missionary had been appointed to work among the Chinese was referring to Shuck. In fact, at the time of the report, he was sailing from Guangdong to the United States aboard the *White Squall,* hoping to regroup with his family after the death of his second wife and desiring to remove his surviving children from the dangers of climate and disease that had also claimed his first wife, three other children, and at least one colleague. However, Shuck would not resign his Foreign Mission Board commission for another ten months. See "China Mission," *Home and Foreign Journal* 2:9 (March 1853), 2; "Resignation of Rev. J. L. Shuck," *Home and Foreign Journal* 3:2 (August 1853), 2.

44. See "Missionary Table," in Executive Board of the ABHMS, *Thirty-eighth Annual Report of the American Baptist Home Mission Society* (New York, 1870), 48. The Southern Baptist Convention would appoint its first postbellum missionary to the Chinese in America in 1879.

45. Executive Board, *Thirty-eighth Annual Report*, 18.

46. "California—Chinese," *Religious Herald* (Richmond, Va.), May 12, 1853, p. 2, col. 4.

47. Articles by A. W. Loomis in *Overland Monthly* include "Chinese in California: Their Sign-Board Literature," 1:2 (August 1868), 152–56; "The Chinese Six Companies," 1:3 (September 1868), 221–27; "The Old East in the New West," 1:4 (October 1868), 360–67; "Our Heathen Temples," 1:5 (November 1868), 453–61; "What Our Chinamen Read," 1:6 (December 1868), 525–30; "Holiday in the Chinese Quarter," 2:2 (February 1869), 144–53; "How Our Chinamen Are Employed," 2:3 (March 1869), 231–40; "Chinese Women in California," 2:4 (April 1869), 344–51; "Medical Art in the Chinese Quarter," 2:6 (June 1869), 496–506; "Chinese 'Funeral Baked Meats,'" 3:1 (July 1869), 21–29; "The Chinese as Agriculturalists," 4:6 (June 1870), 526–32; and "Occult Science in the Chinese Quarter," 3:2 (August 1869), 160–69.

48. For more on the sacralization of the colonial American landscape, see Jon Butler, *Awash in a Sea of Faith: Christianizing the American People* (Cambridge, Mass.: Harvard University Press, 1990), 106–16.

49. Loomis, "Our Heathen Temples," 453.

50. Ibid., 461.

51. "Chinese Immigration," *Home and Foreign Journal* 2:4 (August 1869), 4.

52. For more on this expanded definition of violence, see Peter Iadicola and Anson Shupe, *Violence, Inequality, and Human Freedom* (Lanham, Md.: Rowman and Littlefield, 2003), 23.

53. "The Chinese in California," *Home and Foreign Journal* 2:3 (September 1852), 1; "Glad to Hear It," *Home and Foreign Journal* 8:9 (March 1859), 1.

54. Executive Board of the ABHMS, *Fiftieth Annual Report of the American Baptist Home Mission Society* (New York, 1882), 16.

55. Morehouse, "Historical Sketch," 490.

56. David W. Blight, *Race and Reunion: The Civil War in American Memory* (Cambridge, Mass.: Harvard University Press, Belknap Press, 2001), 364.

57. Quoted in ibid., 360.

58. See Moon-Ho Jung, *Coolies and Cane: Race, Labor, and Sugar in the Age of Emancipation* (Baltimore: Johns Hopkins University Press, 2006); Najia Aarim-Heriot, *Chinese Immigrants, African Americans, and Racial Anxiety in the United States, 1848–82* (Urbana: University of Illinois Press, 2003), 37; Henry Yu, *Thinking Orientals: Migration, Contact, and Exoticism in Modern America* (New York: Oxford University Press, 2002), 7; Linda Frost, *Never One Nation: Freaks, Savages, and Whiteness in U.S. Popular Culture, 1850–1877* (Minneapolis: University of Minnesota Press, 2005), 139–64; Robert G. Lee, *Oriental: Asian Americans in Popular Culture* (Philadelphia: Temple University Press, 1999), 51–82; Andrew Gyory, *Closing the Gate: Race, Politics, and the Chinese Exclusion Act* (Chapel Hill: University of North Carolina Press, 1998); Lisa Lowe, *Immigrant Acts: On Asian American Cultural Politics* (Durham, N.C.: Duke University Press, 1996); Gary Y. Okihiro, *Margins and Mainstreams: Asians in American History and Culture* (Seattle: University of Washington Press, 1994), 31–63, 118–47.

59. "The Chinese Again," *Harper's Weekly,* October 18, 1879, 822.

60. "Editorial Notes," *Baptist Home Mission Monthly* 5:1 (January 1883), 10.

61. Executive Board of the ABHMS, *Forty-eighth Annual Report of the American Baptist Home Mission Society* (New York, 1880), 37.

62. Executive Board of the ABHMS, *Thirty-ninth Annual Report of the American Baptist Home Mission Society* (New York, 1871), 20–21.

CHAPTER 2. FAITH AND HOPE

1. For details of this initial meeting, see Tupper's own account in Henry Martin Tupper, "Shaw University—A Brief History," n.d., Henry Martin Tupper Manuscript Collection (hereinafter cited as HMT MSS), box 1, James E. Cheek Learning Resource Center, Special Collections and Archives, Shaw University, Raleigh, N.C. Unless otherwise noted, all diaries, letters, and similar manuscript documents are in the respective authors' own hands.

2. For details of this meeting, see Chinese Mission School, Portland, Oreg., 1873–85, Baptist Church Records, MSS 1560, Oregon Historical Society, Portland (hereinafter cited as OHS); First Baptist Church, Portland, Oreg., Minutes, 1854–1906, Baptist Church Records.

3. Notable recent exceptions include Linda Frost, *Never One Nation: Freaks, Savages, and Whiteness in U.S. Popular Culture, 1850–1877* (Minneapolis: University of Minnesota

Press, 2005), 139–64; Najia Aarim-Heriot, *Chinese Immigrants, African Americans, and Racial Anxiety in the United States, 1848–82* (Urbana: University of Illinois Press, 2003); Elliott West, "Reconstructing Race," *Western Historical Quarterly* 34 (Spring 2003), 7–26; Ronald Takaki, *Iron Cages: Race and Culture in Nineteenth-Century America* (1979; New York: Oxford University Press, 1990;). Other works that, often problematically, seek to place blacks and Chinese immigrants into a liberal, multicultural context include David M. Reimers, *Other Immigrants: The Global Origins of the American People* (New York: New York University Press, 2005); Desmond King, *Making Americans: Immigration, Race, and the Origins of the Diverse Democracy* (Cambridge, Mass.: Harvard University Press, 2000); Ronald Takaki, *A Different Mirror: A History of Multicultural America* (Boston: Little, Brown, 1993); Lawrence H. Fuchs, *The American Kaleidoscope: Race, Ethnicity, and the Civic Culture* (Middletown, Conn.: Wesleyan University Press, 1990).

4. Lo Hsiang-lin, comp., *Yuedongzhifeng* (Taipei: Orient Cultural Service, 1947), 268; quoted in Yong Chen, *Chinese San Francisco, 1850–1943: A Trans-Pacific Community* (Stanford, Calif.: Stanford University Press, 2000), 40.

5. See Michael Omi and Howard Winant's definition of "racial formation" in n. 15 to the Introduction.

6. Howard N. Rabinowitz, *Race Relations in the Urban South, 1865–1890* (1978; Athens: University of Georgia Press, 1996), 8–9; Guion Griffis Johnson, *Ante-Bellum North Carolina: A Social History* (Chapel Hill: University of North Carolina Press, 1937), 116.

7. In 1860, Raleigh's population stood at 4,780 while Wilmington, the state's largest city, had a population of 9,522. U.S. Census Office, "Table No. 3—Population of Cities, Towns, &c.," *Population of the United States in 1860; Compiled from the Original Returns of the Eighth Census* (Washington, D.C., 1864), 359.

8. Rabinowitz, *Race Relations*, 9–10.

9. Carlos Arnaldo Schwantes, *The Pacific Northwest: An Interpretative History*, rev. ed. (Lincoln: University of Nebraska Press, 1996), 236.

10. Karin L. Zipf, "'The White Shall Rule the Land or Die': Gender, Race, and Class in North Carolina Reconstruction Politics," *Journal of Southern History* 65:3 (August 1999), 503–5.

11. Ministers, theologians, and professionals from the Northeast ran the ABHMS. In 1870, for example, twenty-one of the twenty-two officers and managers (excluding the three field secretaries) hailed from New York (13), New Jersey (4), Massachusetts (3), and Pennsylvania (1). The remaining individual lived in Missouri. And sources of revenue reinforced this geographic distribution of power: Contributions from individuals from New York, Massachusetts, Rhode Island, Pennsylvania, and New Jersey constituted nearly 75 percent of the $179,689.32 donated in 1870. Executive Board of the ABHMS, *Thirty-eighth Annual Report of the American Baptist Home Mission Society* (New York, 1870), 3, 43. For an articulation of the ABHMS perspective on the South and the Far West, see especially ABHMS president M. B. Anderson's address in Executive Board of the ABHMS, *Thirty-third Annual Report of the American Baptist Home Mission Society* (New York, 1865), 9–11. For the desire of home missionaries, theorists, and advocates to create Christian communities in

the Far West that mimicked the moral, social, and cultural order of the eastern seaboard, see especially Laurie F. Maffly-Kipp, *Religion and Society in Frontier California* (New Haven, Conn.: Yale University Press, 1994), 35.

12. Of course, the percentage increase in the number of Chinese may be a bit misleading. The 1870 federal census had recorded a mere 456 souls from China living in Portland, and the 1880 count enumerated 1,668. U.S. Bureau of the Census, *Ninth Census*, vol. 1, *The Statistics of the Population of the United States* (Washington, D.C., 1872), 225; idem, *Statistics of the Population of the United States at the Tenth Census* (Washington, D.C., 1883), 423. The number of whites living in Portland, as enumerated in the 1870 census, was 7,660. That number rose to 15,707 ten years later. Ibid.

13. See David Roediger, *The Wages of Whiteness: Race and the Making of the American Working Class* (London: Verso, 1991), 36.

14. U.S. Congress, House of Representatives, "An Act to Establish an Uniform Rule of Naturalization," in *The Public Statutes at Large of the United States of America*, vol. 1 (Boston, 1848), 103; *Statutes at Large* 16 (1870), 254.

15. See especially Dan Caldwell, "The Negroization of the Chinese Stereotype in California," *Southern California Quarterly* 53 (June 1971), 123–31; Tomás Almaguer, *Racial Fault Lines: The Historical Origins of White Supremacy in California* (Berkeley: University of California Press, 1994), 153–82; Moon-Ho Jung, *Coolies and Cane: Race, Labor, and Sugar in the Age of Emancipation* (Baltimore: Johns Hopkins University Press, 2006). See also Aarim-Heriot, *Chinese Immigrants*; Frost, *Never One Nation*, 139–64; Robert G. Lee, *Oriental: Asian Americans in Popular Culture* (Philadelphia: Temple University Press, 1999), 51–82; Andrew Gyory, *Closing the Gate: Race, Politics, and the Chinese Exclusion Act* (Chapel Hill: University of North Carolina Press, 1998); Lisa Lowe, *Immigrant Acts: On Asian American Cultural Politics* (Durham, N.C.: Duke University Press, 1996); Gary Y. Okihiro, *Margins and Mainstreams: Asians in American History and Culture* (Seattle: University of Washington Press, 1994), 31–63, 118–47.

16. George M. Fredrickson, *White Supremacy: A Comparative Study in American and South African History* (New York: Oxford University Press, 1981), xi. It is important to note, however, that Fredrickson's understanding of "race," in this context, hinges "primarily, if not exclusively, on physical characteristics and ancestry." Ibid.

17. Larry E. Tise, "Confronting the Issue of Slavery," in *The North Carolina Experience*, ed. Lindley S. Butler and Alan D. Watson (Chapel Hill: University of North Carolina Press, 1984), 196; Jeffrey J. Crow, Paul D. Escott, and Flora J. Hatley, *A History of African Americans in North Carolina* (Raleigh: Division of Archives and History, N.C. Department of Cultural Resources, 1992), 48–49; John Hope Franklin, *The Free Negro in North Carolina, 1790–1860* (Chapel Hill: University of North Carolina Press, 1995), 63.

18. Roberta Sue Alexander, following the observations of John Dennett, a northern journalist in post-Emancipation North Carolina, argues that the full force of white supremacist legislation may have been dampened by the desire of state legislators for a speedy readmission to the Union and the removal of federal troops—both of which depended on the passage of moderate laws that allowed for some modicum of judicial liberties for

blacks. However, the state Black Codes enacted in 1865 and 1866 occurred prior to the establishment of the more demanding "radical" congressional Reconstruction program. Roberta Sue Alexander, *North Carolina Faces the Freedmen: Race Relations During Presidential Reconstruction, 1865–67* (Durham, N.C.: Duke University Press, 1985), 41; John Richard Dennett, *The South as It Is: 1865–1866*, ed. Henry M. Christman (New York: Viking Press, 1965), 148–49.

19. John Hope Franklin, *Reconstruction After the Civil War* (Chicago: University of Chicago Press, 1961), 48–49. See also Alexander, *North Carolina Faces the Freedmen*, 44–47; Eric Foner, *Reconstruction: America's Unfinished Revolution, 1863–1877* (New York: Harper and Row, 1988), 198–99.

20. Raymond Gavins, "Fear, Hope, and Struggle: Recasting Black North Carolina in the Age of Jim Crow," in *Democracy Betrayed: The Wilmington Race Riot of 1898 and Its Legacy*, ed. David S. Cecelski and Timothy B. Tyson (Chapel Hill: University of North Carolina Press, 1998), 187. See also James B. Browning, "The North Carolina Black Code," *Journal of Negro History* 15:4 (October 1930), 461–73.

21. Joint Committee on Reconstruction, *Report of the Joint Committee on Reconstruction*, part 2, 39th Cong., 1st sess., 1866 (Washington, D.C., 1866), 182.

22. Gavins, "Fear, Hope, and Struggle," 187; Alexander, *North Carolina Faces the Freedmen*, 3; Joint Committee on Reconstruction, *Report*, 188.

23. "City and State Items," *Daily Standard* (Raleigh, N.C.), August 26, 1865, p. 3, col. 1.

24. Schwantes, *The Pacific Northwest*, 154.

25. Charles Henry Carey, ed., *The Oregon Constitution and Proceedings and Debates of the Constitutional Convention of 1857* (Salem, Oreg.: State Printing Department, 1926), 27.

26. The published federal census lists no Chinese residing in Oregon, but an examination of the manuscript schedules reveals that the Census Bureau failed to publish what census takers in the state reported. In fact, in Multnomah County, enumerators ignored the three options under "Color"—"white, black or mulatto"—and marked "chin." where appropriate. In Josephine County, the census taker recorded individuals who listed their place of birth as China with an "m" for mulatto. U.S. Bureau of the Census, *Manuscript Schedules of the Federal Census*, 1860, Multnomah County, Oreg., series M653, roll 1056, pp. 476–509; U.S. Bureau of the Census, *Manuscript Schedules of the Federal Census,* 1860, Josephine County, Oreg., series M653, roll 1055, pp. 207–27.

27. U.S. Bureau of the Census, *Manuscript Schedules of the Federal Census*, 1860, Multnomah County, Oreg., series M653, roll 1056, pp. 476–509; U.S. Bureau of the Census, *Manuscript Schedules of the Federal Census,* 1860, Josephine County, Oreg., series M653, roll 1055, pp. 207–27; U.S. Bureau of the Census, *The Seventh Census of the United States: 1850*, vol. 1 (Washington, D.C., 1853), 982; idem, *Population of the United States in 1860, Compiled from the Original Returns of the Eighth Census* (Washington, D.C., 1864), 28.

28. Carey, *The Oregon Constitution*, 318. In fact, at the Oregon Constitutional Convention, delegates L. F. Grover and William H. Farrar referred to the *Dred Scott* decision

in discussions over the citizenship status of blacks. Ibid. For an insightful analysis of the Supreme Court decision and its racial and constitutional consequences, see Don E. Fehrenbacher, *Slavery, Law, and Politics: The Dred Scott Case in Historical Perspective* (New York: Oxford University Press, 1981).

29. Carey, *Oregon Constitution*, 320–21. For the text of the final draft see article 2, section 6 in ibid., 405.

30. Ibid., 318.

31. *Oregonian* (Portland), September 16, 1865, p. 3, col. 1.

32. See, for example, *Oregonian* issues of November 19, 1863, p. 3, col. 1; August 30, 1866, p. 3, col. 1; December 12, 1867, p. 3, col. 1; February 26, 1868, p. 3, col. 1; February 28, 1868, p. 3, col. 1.

33. *Oregonian*, June 3, 1873, p. 3, col. 1.

34. *Oregonian*, June 28, 1873, p. 3, col. 1.

35. *Oregonian* issues of "Protest Against Chinese Labor to Oregon Iron Company by Citizens of Oswego," April 10, 1867, p. 2, col. 1; "Chinese Cheap Labor. Indignation Meeting," April 10, 1867, p. 3, col. 1; "Anti-Chinese Movements at Oregon City," January 18, 1869, p. 3, col. 1; January 21, 1869, p. 3, col. 1; "Formation of Anti-Chinese Alliance," June 6, 1873, p. 3, col. 1; "Organization of 'Protectors of American Industry'—Anti-Chinese Secret Society," June 13, 1873, p. 3, col. 1; "Meeting of Anti-Chinese Association," June 13, 1873, p. 3, cols. 1–2.

36. "The Freedmen's Convention: Official Proceedings," *Journal of Freedom*, October 17, 1865, p. 1, col. 2.

37. Alexander, *North Carolina Faces the Freedmen*, 17. Alexander's account of the Freedmen's Convention remains the most complete—or at least the most focused—scholarly treatment of the gathering and the movement leading to it. See also Leon F. Litwack, *Been in the Storm So Long: The Aftermath of Slavery* (New York: Vintage Books, 1979), 502–7; Sidney Andrews, *The South Since the War: As Shown by Fourteen Weeks of Travel and Observation in Georgia and the Carolinas* (Boston, 1866), 120–31; Dennett, *The South as It Is*, 148–54.

38. Quoted in Alexander, *North Carolina Faces the Freedmen*, 17.

39. Excerpted in Andrews, *The South Since the War*, 122, 129, 127, 130.

40. See especially Litwack, *Been in the Storm So Long*, 336–449; Foner, *Reconstruction*, 102–75; Julie Saville, *The Work of Reconstruction: From Slave to Wage Laborer in South Carolina, 1860–1870* (New York: Cambridge University Press, 1996); Amy Dru Stanley, *From Bondage to Contract: Wage Labor, Marriage, and the Market in the Age of Slave Emancipation* (New York: Cambridge University Press, 1998).

41. See especially James D. Anderson, *The Education of Blacks in the South, 1860–1935* (Chapel Hill: University of North Carolina Press, 1988), 4. See also Foner, *Reconstruction*, 77–123; Litwack, *Been in the Storm So Long*, 450–501; Jacqueline Jones, *Soldiers of Light and Love: Northern Teachers and Georgia Blacks, 1865–1873* (Athens: University of Georgia Press, 1980), 49–84.

42. Robin D. G. Kelley, *Freedom Dreams: The Black Radical Imagination* (Boston: Beacon Press, 2002).

43. See Foner, *Reconstruction*, 78; William E. Montgomery, *Under Their Own Vine and Fig Tree: The African-American Church in the South, 1865–1900* (Baton Rouge: Louisiana State University Press, 1993), 42, 46–56, 99.

44. See Foner, *Reconstruction*, 77–123.

45. Raleigh *Weekly Progress*, September 26, 1867. Quoted in Rabinowitz, *Race Relations*, 21–22. See also Litwack, *Been in the Storm So Long*, 310–16; Foner, *Reconstruction*, 81.

46. Daniel W. Stowell, *Rebuilding Zion: The Religious Reconstruction of the South, 1863–1877* (New York: Oxford University Press, 1998).

47. The black members of Raleigh's First Baptist Church, acting in 1865, may well have been among the "vanguard" of ex-slaves in the post–Civil War South, for, as Daniel W. Stowell observes, "the exodus would not reach its peak until several years after the war." Stowell, *Rebuilding Zion*, 70. William E. Montgomery notes that, although there is little "reliable data" to confirm the number of ex-slaves who left white-controlled churches, the evidence nonetheless demonstrates "clearly that a massive black withdrawal took place." Montgomery, *Under Their Own Vine and Fig Tree*, 98–99. See also Litwack, *Been in the Storm So Long*, 466–69; Foner, *Reconstruction*, 92.

48. Stowell, *Rebuilding Zion*, 66.

49. Albert J. Raboteau, *Slave Religion: The "Invisible Institution" in the Antebellum South* (New York: Oxford University Press, 1978), 318.

50. Sterling Stuckey, *Slave Culture: Nationalist Theory and the Foundations of Black America* (New York: Oxford University Press, 1987), 33.

51. Montgomery, *Under Their Own Vine and Fig Tree*, 55, 54; Stowell, *Rebuilding Zion*, 66. For a fascinating discussion of the role of religion, especially the Book of Exodus, in the formation of black nationalism in the antebellum North, see Eddie S. Glaude, Jr., *Exodus! Religion, Race, and Nation in Early Nineteenth-Century Black America* (Chicago: University of Chicago Press, 2000).

52. Montgomery, *Under Their Own Vine and Fig Tree*, 92.

53. Eric Foner, *Nothing but Freedom: Emancipation and Its Legacy* (Baton Rouge: Louisiana State University Press, 1983).

54. Tupper, "Shaw University—A Brief History."

55. J. S. Backus to H. M. Tupper, February 13, 1866. Quoted in Archie Doyster Logan, Jr., "Henry Martin Tupper and His Adult Education Activities Among African Americans, 1865–1893" (Ed.D. diss., North Carolina State University, 1993), 94.

56. Anderson, *The Education of Blacks in the South;* Foner, *Reconstruction*, 78, 96–98. William E. Montgomery, in his otherwise excellent work on the development of the black church in the post–Civil War South, suggests that, in many instances, northern missionaries presented freedpeople with a difficult choice between funding either education or religious institutions. Yet he provides only one example—from Natchez, Mississippi—of such a case. Undoubtedly, given the limited resources available and the proclivities of northern missionaries, freedpeople confronted such dilemmas often. However, the emphasis on instances of such "either-or" quandaries ignores the degree to which northern missionaries of the ABHMS (as well as other groups, such as the Congregationalists' American Missionary

Association) viewed their project as more encompassing, hoping to provide *both* spiritual and educational aid. Montgomery, *Under Their Own Vine and Fig Tree*, 93.

57. *New York Tribune*, February 3, 1866. Quoted in Logan, *Henry Martin Tupper*, 88–89.

58. Stowell, *Religious Reconstruction*, 7, 65–66. See also Montgomery, *Under Their Own Vine and Fig Tree*, 84.

59. See Elizabeth Reid Murray, *Wake: Capital County of North Carolina*, vol. *I, Prehistory through Centennial* (Raleigh, N.C.: Capital County Publishing, 1983), 642–47; Linda Simmons-Henry and Linda Harris Edmisten, *Culture Town: Life in Raleigh's African American Communities* (Raleigh, N.C.: Raleigh Historic Districts Commission, 1995), 1–36. For Tupper's activities in and around Raleigh in 1865, see Henry Martin Tupper, diary for 1865, HMT MSS, box 1.

60. Simmons-Henry and Edmisten, *Culture Town*, 52.

61. Catherine Devereux Edmonston, *Journal of a Secesh Lady: The Diary of Catherine Ann Devereux Edmonston, 1860–66*, ed. Beth G. Crabtree and James W. Patton (Raleigh, N.C.: Division of Archives and History, Department of Cultural Resources, 1979), 707. For the antebellum history of the Guion Hotel (originally called the Eagle), see Murray, *Wake*, 159, 221, 352.

62. Murray, *Wake*, 610.

63. Ibid.

64. Simmons-Henry and Edmisten, *Culture Town*, 116–17.

65. H. M. Tupper, "Received of the A.B.H. Mission Society to Assist in Building a House for a Church and Schools," March 1867, HMT MSS, box 1.

66. C. W. Foster, assistant adjutant-general, to David Tod, governor of Ohio, January 11, 1864, in U.S. Department of War, *The War of the Rebellion: A Compilation of the Official Records of the Union and Confederate Armies*, series 3, vol. 4 (Washington, D.C.: Government Printing Office, 1900), 25; "General Summary of Casualties in the Union Forces Operating Against Richmond, Virginia, July 1–31, 1864, Including Deep Bottom (27th–29th), 'The Crater' (30th), and Along the Line," in U.S. Department of War, *The War of the Rebellion*, series 1, vol. 47, part 1 (1895), 260; and also in U.S. Department of War, *The War of the Rebellion*, the following: series 1, vol. 46, part 1 (1894), 399, 405; U.S. Department of War, *The War of the Rebellion: A Compilation of the Official Records of the Union and Confederate Armies*, series 1, vol. 47, part 1 (1895), 57; series 1, vol. 47, part 2 (1895), 625; series 1, vol. 47, part 3 (1895): 253.

67. See, for example, Litwack, *Been in the Storm So Long*, 71–72; Ira Berlin, Joseph P. Reidy, and Leslie S. Rowlands, eds, *Freedom: A Documentary History of Emancipation, 1861–1867*, series 2, *The Black Military Experience* (Cambridge: Cambridge University Press, 1982), 519.

68. In 1863, for example, a mass meeting to recruit troops and raise support for the 27th concluded with this declaration: "We stand as ever on the side of the Government, and pledge to it 'our lives, our property, and our sacred honor,' in its efforts to subdue the rebellion of the slave oligarchy of the country, in its determination to emancipate the slaves

of all rebels . . . to recognize the citizenship of native-born colored Americans, and to protect the colored soldiers, who, taking the American musket and bayonet, have gone forth at the call of their country to *do* and *die* for the Government and the Union." *Liberator*, September 4, 1863.

69. See especially Berlin et al., *Freedom*, 27.

70. Leviticus 25:10 (ASV).

71. Genesis 28:12–17 (ASV).

72. June Mei, "Socioeconomic Origins of Emigration, Guangdong to California, 1850–1882," *Modern China* 5:4 (October 1979), 463–501.

73. Takaki, *Strangers from a Different Shore*, 32.

74. The federal census for 1860 did not enumerate the Chinese for Oregon. This figure is from a local census for the year. Rose Marie Wong, *Sweet Cakes, Long Journey: The Chinatowns of Portland, Oregon* (Seattle: University of Washington Press, 2004), 158; U.S. Bureau of the Census, "Table 14.—Chinese, Japanese, and Civilized Indian Population, by States and Territories: 1860 to 1890," *Report on the Population of the United States at the Eleventh Census: 1890*, part 2 (Washington, D.C., 1897), 401.

75. *Oregonian*, December 6, 1851, p. 3, col. 4.

76. U.S. Bureau of the Census, *Manuscript Schedules of the Federal Census*, 1860, Multnomah County, Oreg., series M653, roll 1056, pp. 476–509; "The Chinese," *Oregonian*, February 16, 1865, p. 3, col. 1.; U.S. Bureau of the Census, *Manuscript Schedules of the Federal Census*, 1870, series M593, roll 1287, pp. 172–276.

77. See n. 47 in Chapter 1 for a list of Loomis's articles on Chinese in San Francisco. See Chapter 3 for a discussion of this ethnographic production.

78. *Oregonian*, March 14, 1857, p. 1, col. 2.

79. *Oregonian* issues of February 28, 1862, p. 2, col. 2; March 24, 1864, p. 3, col. 1; July 21, 1864, p. 3, col. 2.

80. *Oregonian*, May 5, 1866, p. 3, col. 1; *Oregonian*, "The Chinese Menace," December 12, 1866, p. 3, col. 1.

81. For examples of coverage of brothels and bawdy houses, see *Oregonian* issues of February 7, 1861, p. 3, col. 1; September 17, 1861, p. 3, col. 1; January 27, 1862, p. 3, col. 1; November 19, 1863, p. 3, col. 1; August 30, 1866, p. 3, col. 1. For examples of coverage of Chinese fistfights and "gang" activity, see *Oregonian* issues of May 2, 1861, p. 3, col. 2; October 11, 1861, p. 3, col. 1; December 8, 1861, p. 3, col. 1; May 10, 1862, p. 3, col. 1; October 9, 1863, p. 3, col. 1; April 13, 1864, p. 3, col. 1; November 30, 1864, p. 3, col. 1.

82. For the best account of the two Chinatowns, see Wong, *Sweet Cakes, Long Journey*, 204–62. Wong notes that Chinese workers were contracted in 1873 to build a culvert to prevent further flooding of a section near B Street; by 1879, Sanborn Fire Insurance Company surveyors would mention the rural settlement in the surrounding Tanner Creek gulch by its new name, the Chinese Vegetable Gardens community. In her well-researched book, Wong follows the ebb and flow of the "boundaries" surrounding the urban enclave while tracking the development and establishing, quite definitively, the existence and location of the Chinese Vegetable Gardens community.

83. See "Portland's Old Chinatown, 1873," in Wong, *Sweet Cakes, Long Journey*, 246.

84. "The Chinese Menace," *Oregonian*, December 12, 1866, p. 3, col. 1.

85. Wong, *Sweet Cakes, Long Journey*, 208.

86. See *Oregonian* issues of "Protest against Chinese Labor to Oregon Iron Company by Citizens of Oswego," April 10, 1867, p. 2, col. 3; April 17, 1867, p. 3, col. 1; April 16, 1868, p. 3, col. 1; April 3, 1869, p. 3, col. 1.

87. *Oregonian* issues of February 22, 1862, p. 3, col. 1; July 8, 1864, p. 3, col. 1; May 12, 1863, p. 3, col. 1; December 21, 1864, p. 3, col. 1.

88. *Oregonian*, January 26, 1865, p. 3, col. 2; *Oregonian*, February 13, 1866, p. 3, col. 2.

89. *Oregonian*, July 7, 1867, p. 3, col. 1; *Oregonian*, September 24, 1867, p. 3, col. 1. By 1872, the only "joss house" listed in the city directory was on Second Avenue, between Stark and Oak Streets. S. J. McCormick, *Portland City Directory for 1872* (Portland, Oreg., 1872), 55. By 1886, the city directory listed another joss house. See *Oregon, Washington and Idaho Gazetteer and Business Directory*, vol. 2, 1886–87 (Portland, Oreg., 1886), 295, 314.

90. The first mention of a Chinese "bawdy house" in the *Oregonian* occurs on August 13, 1859, p. 2, col. 1. In addition, the 1860 manuscript schedule of the U.S. census lists a "bawdy" house in which three of the five Chinese women in all of Portland resided. U.S. Bureau of the Census, *Manuscript Schedules of the Federal Census*, 1860, Multnomah County, Oreg., series M653, roll 1056, p. 504.

91. *Oregonian* issues of November 11, 1872, p. 3, col. 3; January 23, 1873, p. 3, col. 1; February 11, 1873, p. 3, col. 1.

92. Takaki, *Strangers from a Different Shore*, 127.

93. *Oregonian*, June 15, 1869, p. 3, col. 1; *Oregon, Washington and Idaho Gazetteer*, 361

94. Hugh Clark, *Portland's Chinese: The Early Years* (Portland, Oreg.: Center for Urban Education, 1978), 6.

95. Lee Bessie Ying, "Perpetuation of the Primary Group Patterns Among the Chinese in Portland, Oregon" (Ph.D. diss., University of Oregon, 1938), 69.

96. Sucheng Chan, *Asian Americans: An Interpretive History* (Boston: Twayne, 1991), 65–66.

97. Ibid., 63.

98. Ibid., 64.

99. Ibid., 65.

100. Wong, *Sweet Cakes, Long Journey*, 27. Even before the establishment of the Jung Wah Association, the Portland-based and very influential labor contractor Wa Kee and Co., stepped forward to represent interests of Chinese workers. *Oregonian*, October 1, 1869, p. 3, col. 1. They were soon joined by other merchants who came together to hire a white attorney, J. F. McCoy, to protest the unfair assessment of the poll tax and mining licenses. *Oregonian* issues of February 7, 1870, p. 3, col. 1; March 29, 1870, p. 2, col. 4; June 6, 1870, p. 3, col. 2.

101. Chan, *Asian Americans*, 66.

102. *Oregonian*, August 11, 1876, p. 2, cols. 1–2.

103. Chan, *Asian Americans*, 67; Takaki, *Strangers*, 118; Clark, *Portland's Chinese*, 6.

104. Chinese Mission School Records. See entries for August 1873; October 8, 1874; and November 11, 1874.

105. Ibid. See entry for April 2, 1878.

106. Ibid. See entry for August 7, 1877.

107. Even less obviously stratified social spaces, such as Chinese stores, were not immune from a hierarchy that many immigrants may have felt stifling. In fact, by the mid-1880s, at least two Chinese general stores, the Wing On Co. and the Wing Sing Co., also functioned as labor contractors, thus exacerbating class tensions also evident in district associations. *Oregon, Washington and Idaho Gazetteer*, 361. Historian Chris Friday has demonstrated both the power of labor contractors among Chinese in Oregon and the class fault lines within the Chinese population. See Chris Friday, *Organizing Asian American Labor: The Pacific Coast Canned-Salmon Industry, 1870–1942* (Philadelphia: Temple University Press, 1994), 38, 70–75.

108. See especially A. W. Loomis, "Our Heathen Temples," *Overland Monthly* 1:5 (November 1868), 453–61; California Senate Special Committee on Chinese Immigration, *Chinese Immigration: The Social, Moral, and Political Effect of Chinese Immigration; Testimony Taken Before a Committee of the Senate of the State of California (appointed April 3, 1876)* (Sacramento, Calif, 1876), 98, 149, 152; Harry L. Wells, "A Night in Chinatown," *West Shore* 12:10 (October 1886), 293.

109. See, for example, First Baptist Church, Minutes. See record for October 22, 1875; copy of certificate of residence for Wong King, dated May 3, 1894; no. 55690, Chinese Ethnology Files, MSS 1521, OHS.

110. *Oregonian*, November 25, 1878, p. 3, col. 2.

111. *The Oregonian's Handbook of the Pacific Northwest* (Portland, Oreg., 1894), 119.

112. Ibid., 119–20.

113. Ibid., 119.

114. Wong, *Sweet Cakes, Long Journey*, 122.

115. *Oregonian*, June 23, 1875, p. 3, col. 2; First Baptist Church, Minutes. See entry for June 22, 1875.

116. Ibid. See entry for June 3, 1875.

117. Edmonston, *Journal of a Secesh Lady*, 707.

118. Stowell, *Rebuilding Zion*, 7.

119. For coverage of the fire of August 3, 1873, see *Oregonian* issues of "Second Big Fire in Portland," August 4, 1873, p. 3, cols. 2–6; "The Portland Fire and the Anti-Chinese Movement," August 9, 1873, p. 1, col. 3; "The Ku Klux Klan Letters and the Fire," August 11, 1873, p. 2, col. 1; August 14, 1873, p. 3., col. 3. For coverage of the December 1872 fire, see "Big Fire in Portland," *Oregonian*, December 23, 1872, p. 3, cols. 1–3; *Oregonian*, January 6, 1873, p. 3, col. 3.

120. Karen Sawislak, in her analysis of Chicago's Great Fire of 1871, writes, "In the face of an urban catastrophe, the fears of urban dwellers were raised to the fore, anxieties that were to some degree structured by the notion of the city as a place that always verged on some sort of disruption . . . It is important to recognize that the experience of conflagra-

tion not only brought the people of Chicago face-to-face with the elemental force of fire. It also, to a most unusual degree, brought them face-to-face with each other, offering a blunt reminder of the social differences that were part of every great city." Karen Sawislak, *Smoldering City: Chicagoans and the Great Fire, 1871–1874* (Chicago: University of Chicago Press, 1995), 23–24.

121. For fascinating discussions of the links between the slave South and western expansion, see Frost, *Never One Nation*; West, "Reconstructing Race." For the connections between the racialization of blacks and Chinese, see Aarim-Heriot, *Chinese Immigrants, African Americans, and Racial Anxiety*; Jung, *Coolies and Cane*; Okihiro, *Margins and Mainstreams*, 31–63, 118–47.

122. Historian David W. Blight has perhaps put it most concisely: "The great challenge of Reconstruction was to determine just how defeated the South really was, and to establish how free the emancipated slaves really were." David W. Blight, *Race and Reunion: The Civil War in American Memory* (Cambridge, Mass.: Harvard University Press, Belknap Press, 2001), 44.

123. See n. 15 in the Introduction on Michael Omi and Howard Winant's discussion of racial rearticulation.

124. James Oliver Horton, *Free People of Color: Inside the African American Community* (Washington, D.C.: Smithsonian Institution Press, 1993), 146.

125. "The Chinese Again," *Harper's Weekly*, October 18, 1879, 822.

CHAPTER 3. CALLINGS

1. Henry L. Morehouse, *H. M. Tupper, D.D.: A Narrative of Twenty-five Years Work in the South, 1865–1890* (New York, 1890), 18. The document officially commissioning Tupper is in the Henry Martin Tupper Manuscript Collection (hereinafter cited as HMT MSS), box 1, James E. Cheek Learning Resource Center, Special Collections and Archives, Shaw University, Raleigh, N.C.

2. This account was elicited by a researcher named Jack Partain in an interview from 1989 with William H. Fuller, a former student of Tupper's. It is part of the oral tradition that relates the founding of Shaw University. William H. Fuller, interview by Jack Partain, February 23, 1989, notes, HMT MSS, box 1. It is important to note that this account differs from the narratives offered by the two most in-depth studies of Shaw's early history. Wilmoth A. Carter simply states, "Tupper asked to be permitted to preach . . . but Dr. Skinner denied the request." Wilmoth A. Carter, *Shaw's Universe: A Monument to Educational Innovation* (Rockville, Md.: D. C. National Publishing, 1973), 2. Archie Logan, without citing any evidence, asserts in his dissertation that "Reverend Skinner did give the Tuppers a warm welcome." And he suggests that "apparently, Reverend Skinner felt that Tupper needed time to adjust to the southern attitudes of Raleigh, North Carolina." Archie Doyster Logan, Jr., "Henry Martin Tupper and His Adult Education Activities Among African-Americans, 1865–1893" (Ed.D. diss., North Carolina State University, 1993), 74.

In Tupper's own account, the missionary claimed that although the initial meeting was "gentlemanly," Skinner "gave me no encouragement" and that, subsequently, Skinner refused Tupper "with a great deal of warmth and took the ground that there was no field for me in Raleigh." Henry Martin Tupper, "Some Facts Connected with the Lawsuit," n. d., HMT MSS, box 1. Logan's version appears to hinge on a misinterpretation of "a great deal of warmth," which he takes to mean "kindly," but which, given the context, most likely means "heatedly."

3. Chinese Mission School Records, Portland, Oreg., 1873–85, Baptist Church Records, MSS 1560, Oregon Historical Society, Portland (hereinafter cited as OHS). See entry for November 13, 1875. As discussed later in the chapter, other important figures in Portland business and politics joined Failing and Corbett in donating to the mission school.

4. For the twelve months ending March 31, 1866, for example, 33.97 percent of all ABHMS funds disbursed for salaries went to evangelicals laboring in the states of the former Confederacy, Tennessee, Kentucky, and Washington, D.C. The following year, the percentage had risen to 41.55 percent. For both years, the ABHMS committed between 27 and 28 percent of its missionaries, missionary assistants, and teachers to the region. Figures compiled by author from Executive Board of the ABHMS, *Thirty-fourth Annual Report of the American Baptist Home Mission Society* (New York, 1866), 40–48, 56–57; Executive Board of the ABHMS, *Thirty-fifth Annual Report of the American Baptist Home Mission Society* (New York, 1867), 33–42, 46–47.

5. "Loud and Earnest Appeal from the Baptist State Convention of California," in Executive Board of the ABHMS, *Thirty-ninth Annual Report of the American Baptist Home Mission Society* (New York, 1871), 13.

6. Executive Board of the ABHMS, "Report of the Committee on Occupation of the Southern Fields," *Thirtieth Annual Report of the American Baptist Home Mission Society* (New York, 1862), 50.

7. Paul Harvey, *Redeeming the South: Religious Cultures and Racial Identities Among Southern Baptists, 1865–1925* (Chapel Hill: University of North Carolina Press, 1997), 23. See also Daniel W. Stowell, *Rebuilding Zion: The Religious Reconstruction of the South, 1863–1877* (New York: Oxford University Press, 1998), 133–35.

8. William R. Hutchison, *Errand to the World: American Protestant Thought and Foreign Mission* (Chicago: University of Chicago Press, 1987), 91–124; David J. Bosch, *Transforming Mission: Paradigm Shifts in Theology of Mission* (Maryknoll, N.Y.: Orbis Books, 1991), 301.

9. Hutchison, *Errand to the World,* 95.

10. Michael Omi and Howard Winant, *Racial Formation in the United States: From the 1960s to the 1990s,* 2nd ed. (New York: Routledge, 1994), 55–56. According to Omi and Winant, "A racial project is simultaneously an interpretation, representation, or explanation of racial dynamics, and an effort to reorganize and redistribute resources along particular racial lines."

11. Ibid., 56.

12. Executive Board, *Thirty-fourth Annual Report,* 16.

13. Executive Board of the ABHMS, *Thirty-third Annual Report of the American Baptist Home Mission Society* (New York, 1865), 46.

14. Morehouse, *H. M. Tupper*, 5–6.

15. Ibid.

16. Logan, "Henry Martin Tupper," 55–56; adjutant general, comp. and ed., *Massachusetts Soldiers, Sailors, and Marines in the Civil War*, vol. 3 (Norwood, Mass.: Norwood Press, 1932), 734.

17. An undocumented (and hagiographic) account of Tupper's decision described his decision: "On a spring morning in 1861 two students, Henry S. Burrage and Henry M. Tupper, met upon the campus of the Theological Seminary, Newton Center, Mass., and discussed the progress of the Civil War. Union forces had met with some reverse, and the people in the North were disappointed; there was a growing feeling that the contest was to be long and sanguinary, instead of short and decisive, as had been generally supposed. After they had looked over the morning paper, Tupper remarked: 'Burrage, it's time we stopped studying and went to the front.' Both enlisted and served until the close of the war." W. M. Hartshorn, ed., *An Era of Progress and Promise, 1863–1910: The Religious, Moral, and Educational Development of the American Negro Since His Emancipation* (Boston: Priscilla Publishing, 1910), 87.

18. Henry Martin Tupper, diary of 1862–63, HMT MSS, box 1.

19. Tupper, "Some Facts."

20. Ibid.

21. J. S. Backus to H. M. Tupper, October 31, 1865. Quoted in Logan, "Henry Martin Tupper," 75.

22. Stowell, *Rebuilding Zion*, 7.

23. J. S. Backus to H. M. Tupper, October 19, 1865. Quoted in Logan, "Henry Martin Tupper," 74.

24. Tupper, however, did have at least one opportunity to preach to the church before the resolution of the Skinner complaint. See Henry Martin Tupper, diary of 1865, HMT MSS, box 1.

25. Executive Board of the ABHMS, *Fifty-fifth Annual Report of the American Baptist Home Mission Society* (New York, 1887), 68–69.

26. "Shaw University, Raleigh, N.C. Founded 1865," in Hartshorn, 88–89. This account is repeated in Logan, "Henry Martin Tupper," and in Carter, *Shaw's Universe*. It is also mentioned in Sydney Nathans, *The Quest for Progress: The Way We Lived in North Carolina, 1870–1920* (Chapel Hill: University of North Carolina Press, 1983). The Tuppers were not alone in the attention they received from the Klan. For more on the harassment of northern missionaries in the South, see Stowell, *Rebuilding Zion*, 133.

27. Tupper, diary of 1865.

28. Ibid.

29. Author's compilation from ibid.

30. Henry Martin Tupper, "Shaw University—A Brief History," n.d., HMT MSS, box 1.

31. As historian Daniel W. Stowell has observed, "Most southerners viewed northern missionaries and religious scalawags with suspicion and contempt." *Rebuilding Zion*, 133.

32. Henry Martin Tupper, "Received of the A.B.H. Mission Society to Assist in Building a House for a Church and Schools," March 1867, HMT MSS, box 1; idem. "Money Raised to Assist Building Second Baptist Church," March 31, 1867–March 31, 1868, HMT MSS, box 1.

33. Henry Martin Tupper, "Received of the A. B. H. Mission Society to Assist in Building a House for a Church and Schools," March 1867, HMT MSS, box 1; idem. "Money Raised to Assist Building Second Baptist Church," March 31, 1867–March 31, 1868, HMT MSS, box 1. The Massachusetts towns represented on the lists include Monson, where Tupper was raised and where he attended secondary school; Wales, where he was baptized and attended church; and South Wilbraham, where his wife's family lived.

34. Ibid. These contributors were Judson Leonard, Lavinia Tupper, and Mrs. Earl Tupper.

35. Ibid. Elijah Shaw, a woolens manufacturer, would be a frequent and generous supporter of the Raleigh mission, and the institution would soon bear his name. Andrew Porter was a professor at Mt. Holyoke Seminary.

36. Ibid.; Carter, *Shaw's Universe*, 3.

37. The struggle to gain equal treatment in the military, in particular, galvanized black troops. As noted in Chapter 2, their unequal treatment even in this army of liberation demonstrated that achieving certain rights might result not in equality but in second-class citizenship. See especially Ira Berlin, Joseph P. Reidy, and Leslie S. Rowlands, eds, *Freedom: A Documentary History of Emancipation, 1861–1867*, series 2, *The Black Military Experience* (Cambridge: Cambridge University Press, 1982), 27, 17. After much agitation and organization, black soldiers secured equal pay in June 1864, retroactive to January 1, 1864, and for those who had been free as of April 19, 1861, retroactive to the date of enlistment. In March 1865, Congress passed another act that granted retroactive equal pay to all black soldiers who had been promised equal pay when they enlisted. *An Act Making Appropriations for the Support of the Army for the Year Ending the Thirtieth June, Eighteen Hundred and Sixty-five, and for Other Purposes. Statutes at Large* 13 (1864–65), 129–30; *An Act to Amend the Several Acts Heretofore Passed to Provide for the Enrolling and Calling Out the National Forces, and for Other Purposes. Statutes at Large* 13 (1864–65), 488. Because equal pay was made retroactive to each soldier's date of enlistment, many active duty soldiers and veterans of the U.S. Colored Troops received lump sum payments. It is possible that these large payments were used by veterans and soldiers who otherwise had very little financial margin to help create community institutions, such as schools and churches. See Sharon Ann Holt, *Making Freedom Pay: North Carolina Freedpeople Working for Themselves, 1865–1900* (Athens: University of Georgia Press, 2000), 159 n. 9.

38. "The Situation in North Carolina," *Journal of Freedom*, October 7, 1865, p. 3, col. 3.

39. "Tina Johnson: Ex-Slave Story," in *The American Slave: A Composite Autobiography*, vol. 15, *North Carolina Narratives, Part 2*, ed. George P. Rawick (Westport, Conn.: Greenwood, 1941), 22.

40. "Narrative," in Rawick, *The American Slave*, vol. 15, 122.

41. Holt, *Making Freedom Pay*, xviii. Freedpeople also used this "discretionary income" to establish individual or family security. Ex-slave Mattie Curtis, for example, recounted how she managed to defy odds to become a landowner. "I done a heap of work at night too, all of my sewin' an' such an' de piece of land near de house over dar ain't never got no work 'cept at night. I finally paid fer de land." "Mattie Curtis: Before and After the War," in *The American Slave: A Composite Autobiography*, vol. 14, *North Carolina Narratives, Part 1*, ed. George P. Rawick (Westport, Conn.: Greenwood, 1941), 221.

42. Frank Freeman, "Testimony," in Rawick, *The American Slave*, vol. 14, 320–21.

43. Tupper, "Shaw University—A Brief History."

44. Ibid.

45. Ibid. For the debate about common school versus ministerial training, see Executive Board, *Thirty-fourth Annual Report*, 31–35. In the summer of 1867, in accordance with the decision to focus the national board's resources on ministerial education, Tupper distributed a circular announcing that his mission would increase its commitment to educating black ministers and recruiting students interested in ministerial labor from all parts of the state. Carter, *Shaw's Universe*, 3.

46. For an item on the Congregationalists' mission to the Chinese in Portland, see *Oregonian*, February 13, 1873, p. 3, col. 1.

47. Membership lists in First Baptist Church, Portland, Oreg., Minutes, 1854–1906, Baptist Church Records. See entries for August 31, 1861, and January 1, 1875. For the address of Douglas Williams's business, Williams and Myers, see S. J. McCormick, *Portland City Directory for 1872* (Portland, Oreg., 1872), 84. For a map of Chinatown's boundaries in 1873 and the extent of the August 1873 fire, see Marie Rose Wong, *Sweet Cakes, Long Journey: The Chinatowns of Portland, Oregon* (Seattle: University of Washington Press, 2004), 246.

48. First Baptist Church, Minutes. See entry for July 26, 1874; John F. Pope, "The First Baptist Church, San Francisco: A Historical Sketch," *Baptist Home Mission Monthly* 21:5 (May 1899), 187.

49. "Resignation of Rev. J. L. Shuck," *Home and Foreign Journal* 3:2 (August 1853), 2.

50. See the following articles in *Home and Foreign Journal*: "California," 4:6 (December 1854), 1; "Chinese Chapel at Sacramento City," 4:10 (April 1855), 1; "Rev. J. L. Shuck," 4:11 (May 1855), 2; "Shuck in California," 5:5 (November 1855), 1. For Shuck's activities throughout northern California, see these articles in *Home and Foreign Journal*: "Chinese Baptism," 5:7 (January 1856), 1; "A Chinese Wedding in America," 6:6 (December 1856), 2; "Sacramento," 6:12 (June 1857), 2; "California," 7:9 (March 1858), 1–2; "Visit to San Ramon Valley," 8:9 (March 1859), 1.

51. "Narrow Escape of Bro. Shuck," *Home and Foreign Journal* 9:2 (August 1859), 1–2.

52. Executive Board of the ABHMS, *Thirty-eighth Annual Report of the American Baptist Home Mission Society* (New York, 1870), 8.

53. First Baptist Church, Minutes.

54. Rom 8:38–39 (ASV).

55. First Baptist Church, Minutes. See entry for August 1873.

56. Ibid.

57. First Baptist Church, Portland, Oregon, *Manual and Directory of First Baptist Church, The White Hall Temple, Portland, Oregon* (Portland, Oreg.: F. W. Baltes and Co., Printers, 1906), 15–16.

58. Chinese Mission School. See entry for October 8, 1874.

59. The 1870 manuscript census for Albany County, Wyoming, lists only two native Chinese. U.S. Bureau of the Census, *Manuscript Schedules of the Federal Census*, 1870, Albany County, Wyoming, series M593, roll 1748, pp. 357–89.

60. Chinese Mission School. See entry for August 2, 1874.

61. Mal. 1:11 (ASV).

62. Chinese Mission School. See entries for October 8, 1874, and October 15, 1874. After one week, G. W. Traver resigned from the committee, and Douglas Williams replaced him. Ibid. See entry for October 22, 1874.

63. Ibid.

64. Carlos Arnaldo Schwantes, *The Pacific Northwest: An Interpretative History*, rev. ed. (Lincoln: University of Nebraska Press, 1996), 237.

65. For the best treatment of the ideological and cultural impulses behind the home mission movement in regard to western settlement, see Laurie F. Maffly-Kipp, *Religion and Society in Frontier California* (New Haven, Conn.: Yale University Press, 1994).

66. First Baptist Church, Minutes. See entry for October 26, 1854.

67. Membership list in ibid. See entry for January 1, 1875.

68. On August 31, 1860, the original covenant for First Baptist Church was voided, and the church was reconstituted under the same name with twelve new members joining Josiah, Henrietta, and Elizabeth Failing (the only remaining founding members of the original congregation). Ibid. See the entry for August 31, 1861, for the reorganization and new agreement, and the entry for May 5, 1855, for the original "covenant" among congregants.

69. That both men worshipped at the church is clear from their various roles as trustee, collection agent, and missionary committee chair. Moreover, a letter of "dismission," or transfer, for Henry from New York's Sixteenth Baptist Church dated September 2, 1854, appears in the Henry Failing Papers, box 1, folder 2, business correspondence, 1851–1870, OHS, MSS 650. This document recommends him to "church fellowship at the First Baptist Church, Portland, OR." For evidence of Henry's interest in church financial affairs, see, for example, a letter from him to Josiah and Henrietta Failing, November 10, 1874, Henry Failing Papers.

70. See, for example, First Baptist Church, Minutes. See entry for January 1, 1873. For Josiah Failing's participation on the first board of directors for the Chinese Mission School, see Chinese Mission School Records. For Henry Failing's election to the board, see Chinese Mission School Records, entry for September 15, 1877. For James F. Failing's service as Missionary Committee chairman, see First Baptist Church, *Manual and Directory*, 38.

71. Harvey W. Scott, *History of Portland, Oregon: With Illustrations and Biographical Sketches of Prominent Citizens and Pioneers* (Syracuse, N.Y., 1890), 523.

72. Ibid., 523; undated *Oregonian* obituary in Henry Failing Papers.

73. Scott, *History of Portland,* 521–23.

74. Ibid.

75. Peter J. Lewty, *To the Columbia Gateway: The Oregon Railway and the Northern Pacific, 1879–1884* (Pullman: Washington State University Press, 1987), 43; S. J. McCormick, *The Portland Director for the Year Commencing January, 1868* (Portland, Oreg., 1868), 21.

76. Lewty, *To the Columbia Gateway,* 71.

77. Henry W. Corbett was elected to the U.S. Senate as a Republican; Henry Failing joined the Republican Party (and later joined the Union Party that carried Oregon in 1862 and endorsed the Lincoln administration); and Josiah Failing served as a delegate to the Republican National Conventions of 1864 and 1868.

78. Scott, *History of Portland,* 487, 523.

79. Chinese Mission School Records. See entry for November 13, 1875.

80. Ibid.; McCormick, *Portland City Directory for 1872,* 3, 53, 77.

81. The Good Templar's Hall Building remained the Chinese Mission School's home for nine months. Chinese Mission School Records, Portland, 1873–1885, Baptist Church Records, MSS 1560, OHS. See entries for October 29, 1874, and June 7, 1875.

82. Henry Failing Papers, box 1, business papers, 1869–1875, receipts for payment, MSS 650, OHS.

83. Chinese Mission School Records. See entries for August 1873; October 8, 1874; and November 11, 1874.

84. Ibid. For an example of early mission activities, see the first monthly report, dated October 15, 1874.

85. "Baptist Chinese Mission School, Portland, Oregon," circular, dated November 15, 1876, in ibid.

86. Executive Board of the ABHMS, *Forty-sixth Annual Report of the American Baptist Home Mission Society* (New York, 1878), 46.

87. "Missionary Table," in ibid., 95.

88. Executive Board of the ABHMS, *Forty-eighth Annual Report of the American Baptist Home Mission Society* (New York, 1880), 60.

89. Southern Baptist Convention, Home Mission Board Minutes, entry for January 29, 1884, Southern Baptist Library and Archives, Nashville, Tennessee; Executive Board of the ABHMS, *Fifty-second Annual Report of the American Baptist Home Mission Society* (New York, 1884), 19–20.

90. Executive Board of the ABHMS, *Fifty-third Annual Report of the American Baptist Home Mission Society* (New York, 1885), 107–9.

91. Executive Board, *Thirty-third Annual Report,* 16.

92. Ibid.

93. Executive Board, *Thirty-eighth Annual Report,* 21, 24–26.

94. Elijah C. Branch, "Quarterly Report," in Executive Board of the ABHMS, "Report of the Executive Board," *Thirty-second Annual Report of the American Baptist Home Mission Society* (New York, 1864), 22–23.

95. Susan Thorne, *Congregational Missions and the Making of an Imperial Culture in Nineteenth-Century England* (Stanford, Calif.: Stanford University Press, 1999), 147.

96. Brumberg's analysis of "missionary ethnology" is based on a study of the letters and reports of American women foreign missionaries during the late nineteenth and early twentieth centuries. She focuses specifically on the distinctions drawn by American missionary women between themselves and proselyte women. Joan Jacobs Brumberg, "The Ethnological Mirror: American Evangelical Women and Their Heathen Sisters, 1870–1910," in *Women and the Structure of Society: Selected Research from the Fifth Berkshire Conference on the History of Women*, ed. Jo Ann K. McNamara and Barbara J. Harris (Durham, N.C.: Duke University Press, 1984), 108–28.

97. James C. Thomson, Jr., Peter W. Stanley, and John Curtis Perry, *Sentimental Imperialists: The American Experience in East Asia* (New York: Harper and Row, 1981), 45. For more on this theme, see Henry Yu, *Thinking Orientals: Migration, Contact, and Exoticism in Modern America* (New York: Oxford University Press, 2001); John K. Fairbank, ed., *The Missionary Enterprise in China and America* (Cambridge, Mass.: Harvard University Press, 1974); and Stuart Creighton Miller, *The Unwelcome Immigrant: The Image of the Chinese, 1875–1882* (Berkeley: University of California Press, 1969), 57.

98. Evangelicals' accounts of black southerners were complemented by secular literature produced by northerners who traveled south in the aftermath of the Civil War. See, for example, Whitelaw Reid, *After the War: A Southern Tour* (New York, 1866); J. T. Trowbridge, *The South: A Tour of Its Battlefields and Ruined Cities* (Hartford, Conn., 1866); Sidney Andrews, *The South Since the War: As Shown by Fourteen Weeks of Travel and Observation in Georgia and the Carolinas* (1868; Boston: Houghton Mifflin, 1971); and Linda Warfel Slaughter, *The Freedmen of the South* (Cincinnati, Ohio, 1869).

99. Quoted in Jacqueline Jones, *Soldiers of Light and Love: Northern Teachers and Georgia Blacks, 1865–1875* (1980; Athens: University of Georgia Press, 1992), 154.

100. Elizabeth Ware Pearson, ed., *Letters from Port Royal Written at the Time of the Civil War* (Boston: W. B. Clarke, 1906), 36.

101. "The Seven Freedmen Schools," in Executive Board of the ABHMS, *Forty-fourth Annual Report of the American Baptist Home Mission Society* (New York, 1876), 30.

102. Ibid.

103. E. G. Trask, "Quarterly Report," reproduced in Executive Board, *Thirty-third Annual Report*, 24.

104. See, for example, the 1868 and 1869 dispatches of Presbyterian missionary Augustus Ward Loomis in the *Overland Monthly* listed in n. 47 in Chapter 1.

105. A. W. Loomis, "Our Heathen Temples," *Overland Monthly* 1:5 (November 1868), 453, 461.

106. Carl T. Jackson, *The Oriental Religions and American Thought: Nineteenth-Century Explorations* (Westport, Conn.: Greenwood, 1981), 97.

107. Ibid.

108. Henrietta Shuck, *Sketches in China; or, Sketches of the Country, Religion, and Customs of the Chinese* (Philadelphia, 1852), 30. For more on Henrietta Shuck, see Louis B.

Gimelli, "'Borne Upon the Wings of Faith': The Chinese Odyssey of Henrietta Hall Shuck, 1835–1844," *Journal of the Early Republic* 14:2 (Summer 1994), 221–45.

109. E. G. Robinson, "Race and Religion on the American Continent," *Baptist Home Mission Monthly* 5:3 (March 1883), 49–53.

110. Joseph Le Conte, *The Race Problem in the South* (1892; Miami: Mnemosyne, 1969), 359–67.

111. Ibid., 361.

112. Ibid., 362.

113. Executive Board, *Forty-sixth Annual Report*, 33–34.

114. Quoted in Wendy J. Deichmann, "Domesticity with a Difference: Woman's Sphere, Women's Leadership, and the Founding of the Baptist Missionary Training School in Chicago, 1881," *American Baptist Quarterly* 9:3 (September 1990), 145–46.

115. Executive Board of the ABHMS, *Forty-fifth Annual Report of the American Baptist Home Mission Society* (New York, 1877), 25.

116. Joanna P. Moore, *"In Christ's Stead": Autobiographical Sketches* (Chicago: Women's Baptist Home Mission Society, 1902), 45.

117. See ibid., 55–56, 127, 128, 147, 152, 256, 262, 266.

118. Ibid., 23.

119. Executive Board of the ABHMS, *Fifty-seventh Annual Report of the American Baptist Home Mission Society* (New York, 1889), 59, 128; Kathryn Choy-Wong, "Sallie Stein: Two Continents, Two Conventions, One Mission," *American Baptist Quarterly* 14:4 (December 1995), 361.

120. Choy-Wong, "Sallie Stein," 357.

121. *The Home Mission Echo* (November 1888), 6. Quoted in Choy, "Sallie Stein," 361.

122. See Martha J. Ames, "The Chinese Work in Northern and Central California," *Baptist Home Mission Monthly* 21:5 (May 1899), 193–94. For background on Simmons's original commission to China and San Francisco, see E. Z. Simmons, Kossuth, Mississippi, to J. B. Taylor, Richmond, Virginia, April 5, 1870, Foreign Mission Board Missionary Correspondence (hereinafter cited as FMB Correspondence), box 54, E. Z. Simmons folder 1, Southern Baptist Historical Library and Archives, Nashville, Tennessee (hereinafter cited as SBHLA); E. Z. Simmons, Oakland, California, to H. A. Tupper, Richmond, Virginia, June 15, 1874, FMB Correspondence, box 54, E. Z. Simmons folder 2, 1869–1881.

123. Nellie Edwards Hartwell, San Francisco, California, to Henry A. Tupper, Richmond, Virginia, November 2, 1887, Nellie Edwards Hartwell Papers, SBHLA.

124. Executive Board of the ABHMS, *Sixtieth Annual Report of the American Baptist Home Mission Society* (New York, 1892), 75.

125. Henry L. Morehouse, "Historical Sketch of the American Baptist Home Mission Society for Fifty Years," in *Baptist Home Missions in North America* (New York, 1883), 417. In his text, Morehouse reproduced the exact language of the Society's annual report from 1880. See Executive Board, *Forty-eighth Annual Report*, 41.

126. Woman's American Baptist Home Mission Society (hereinafter cited as

WABHMS), *Sixth Annual Report of the Woman's American Baptist Home Mission Society, 1884* (Boston, 1884), 10–12.

127. Between 1842 and 1882, rates of return migration among Chinese stood roughly at 47 percent. See Sucheng Chan, "European and Asian Immigration into the United States in Comparative Perspective, 1820s to 1920s," in *Immigration Reconsidered: History, Sociology, and Politics*, ed. Virginia Yans-McLaughlin (New York: Oxford University Press, 1990), 38. For accounts of the obstacles to domestic evangelizing presented by the anti-Chinese movement, see Executive Board *Forty-sixth Annual Report*, 38; idem, *Forty-seventh Annual Report of the American Baptist Home Mission Society* (New York, 1879), 33; idem, *Forty-eighth Annual Report*, 37.

128. Executive Board of the ABHMS, *Forty-third Annual Report of the American Baptist Home Mission Society* (New York, 1875), 11.

129. Chan, "European and Asian Immigration," 38–39.

130. See Gary Y. Okihiro, *The Columbia Guide to Asian American History* (New York: Columbia University Press, 2001), 88–90. See also Chan, "European and Asian Immigration," 38.

131. For a provocative—and compelling—discussion of the relationship between racialization, American Orientalism, and representations of Chinese contract labor prior to the 1882 Chinese Exclusion Act, see John Kuo Wei Tchen, *New York Before Chinatown: Orientalism and the Shaping of American Culture, 1772–1882* (Baltimore: Johns Hopkins University Press, 1999), 167–95. See also Najia Aarim-Heriot, *Chinese Immigrants, African Americans, and Racial Anxiety in the United States, 1848–1882* (Urbana: University of Illinois Press, 2003). Erika Lee, in her excellent study of immigration during the Exclusion Era, argues persuasively that the sense of Chinese as foreigners was intensified by American immigration policy that focused on what she calls "gatekeeping." Erika Lee, *At America's Gates: Chinese Immigration During the Exclusion Era, 1882–1943* (Chapel Hill: University of North Carolina Press, 2003).

132. This argument is drawn from Lisa Lowe, *Immigrant Acts: On Asian American Cultural Politics* (Durham, N.C.: Duke University Press, 1996), 10–12.

133. Executive Board, *Forty-eighth Annual Report*, 50–51.

134. Executive Board, *Fifty-sixth Annual Report*, 128–29.

135. See especially Peggy Pascoe, *Relations of Rescue: The Search for Female Moral Authority in the American West, 1874–1939* (New York: Oxford University Press, 1990), xix, 33; Susan Yohn, *A Contest of Faiths: Missionary Women and Pluralism in the American Southwest* (Ithaca, N.Y.: Cornell University Press, 1995), 36, 101. See also Patricia Hill, *The World Their Household: The American Woman's Foreign Mission Movement and Cultural Transformation, 1870–1920* (Ann Arbor: University of Michigan Press, 1985), 23–60.

136. Quoted in Executive Board, *Forty-fifth Annual Report*, 24; from the constitution of the WABHMS, reproduced in "Women's Work," *Baptist Home Mission Monthly* 1:1 (May 1875), 11.

137. This argument echoes the one made by Susan Yohn. See *A Contest of Faiths*, 7. It should also be noted that, as Peggy Pascoe argues, the women's home mission movement

in the late nineteenth century not only provided an avenue for women to contribute to national discourses but also served to undermine male authority in and out of homes. *Relations of Rescue*, 36–40.

138. Moore, *"In Christ's Stead,"* 132.

139. Ibid., 60, 136, 150.

140. See especially Evelyn Brooks Higginbotham, *Righteous Discontent: The Women's Movement in the Black Baptist Church, 1880–1920* (Cambridge, Mass.: Harvard University Press, 1993), 33.

141. The earliest extant detailed description of Shaw's curriculum shows a pledge of eight hundred dollars from the Slater Fund for the school's "mechanical" department in addition to its normal, theological, and college departments and the newly named Leonard Medical School. Shaw Universsity Annual Report, December 25, 1883, Henry L. Morehouse Files, group 4, box 8, Archival Collection, Board of National Ministries (hereinafter BNM), American Baptist Historical Society, Valley Forge, Pa. The best work on the debates and tensions within black educational institutions during this period remains James D. Anderson, *The Education of Blacks in the South, 1860–1935* (Chapel Hill: University of North Carolina Press, 1988).

142. For the best work on rescue missions, see Pascoe, *Relations of Rescue*. See also Wesley S. Woo, "Protestant Work Among the Chinese in the San Francisco Bay Area" (Ph. D. diss., Graduate Theological Union, 1984), 154–66.

143. Peggy Pascoe, "Gender Systems in Conflict: The Marriages of Mission-Educated Chinese American Women, 1874–1939," in *Unequal Sisters: A Multicultural Reader in U.S. Women's History*, 2nd ed., ed. Vicki L. Ruiz and Ellen Carol DuBois (New York: Routledge, 1994), 144.

144. Between 1860 and 1900, women never exceeded 9 percent of the total Chinese population in the United States.

145. Him Mark Lai has calculated that, in 1870, only 1 percent of the Chinese population in the United States was American born, but, by 1900, about 10 percent of the population had been born in the United States. "Chinese," in *Harvard Encylcopedia of American Ethnic Groups*, ed. Stephen Thernstrom, Ann Orlov, and Oscar Handlin (Cambridge, Mass.: Harvard University Press, Belknap Press, 1980), 225. For Baptist classes for Chinese women, see, for example, Martha J. Ames to Mary G. Burdette, October 1, 1898, Martha J. Ames Files, Archival Collection, BNM.

146. J. B. Hartwell, "Missions to the Chinese in America," *Baptist Home Mission Monthly* 7:4 (April 1885), 94.

147. See Pascoe, "Gender Systems in Conflict," 143–44.

148. Chinese Mission School Records. See entry for February 18, 1875.

149. "Woman's American Baptist Home Mission Society," *Baptist Home Mission Monthly* 8:3 (March 1886), 65.

150. Pascoe argues that rescue missions were mechanisms through which fallen women might reestablish their piety and purity with the ultimate aim of marrying "kindly Protestant husbands." Pascoe, "Gender Systems in Conflict," 144. Historian Nayan Shah has

made the persuasive argument that "female prostitution and concubinage supposedly demonstrated the Chinese male disregard for marriage and respectable womanhood." *Contagious Divides: Epidemics and Race in San Francisco's Chinatown* (Berkeley: University of California Press, 2001), 79.

151. For the best discussion of Baptist-trained female African American leadership, see Higginbotham, *Righteous Discontent.*

152. Morehouse, "Historical Sketch," 145.

153. Raymond Gavins, "Fear, Hope, and Struggle: Recasting Black North Carolina in the Age of Jim Crow," in *Democracy Betrayed: The Wilmington Race Riot of 1898 and Its Legacy,* ed. David S. Cecelski and Timothy B. Tyson (Chapel Hill: University of North Carolina Press, 1998), 201–2.

154. Pascoe, *Relations of Rescue,* 157–65.

155. Higginbotham, *Righteous Discontent,* 102.

156. Pascoe, *Relations of Rescue,* 137–38.

157. Shah, *Contagious Divides,* 79.

158. George Anthony Pfeffer, *If They Don't Bring Their Women Here: Chinese Female Immigration Before Exclusion* (Urbana: University of Illinois Press, 1999), 86. See also Madeline Y. Hsu, *Dreaming of Gold, Dreaming of Home: Transnationalism and Migration Between the United States and South China, 1882–1943* (Stanford, Calif.: Stanford University Press, 2000), 93–95.

159. For a compelling analysis of turn-of-the-century discourses of manliness, see Gail Bederman, *Manliness and Civilization: A Cultural History of Gender and Race in the United States, 1880–1917* (Chicago: University of Chicago Press, 1996).

160. WABHMS, *One of His Jewels: A Story for Workers Among the Chinese* (Boston: WABHMS, 1896).

161. Ibid., 4.

162. The links between gender, interracial contact, and missionaries became more fraught at the turn of the century, and after an infamous murder case in New York City, the practice of commissioning white, female missionaries to minister to Chinese men came under intense scrutiny. See Mary Ting Yi Lui, *The Chinatown Trunk Mystery: Murder, Miscegenation, and Other Dangerous Encounters in Turn-of-the-Century New York City* (Princeton, N.J.: Princeton University Press, 2005), 111–42. For more on the relationship among restraint, aggression, and manliness, see Bederman, *Manliness and Civilization.*

163. Moore, *"In Christ's Stead,"* 87, 153.

164. "Women's Work," *Baptist Home Mission Monthly* 1:8 (February 1879), 126. See also in *Baptist Home Mission Monthly* "Women's Work," 1:9 (March 1879), 142–43; "Women's Work," 1:10 (April 1879), 158–59; "Women's Work," 1:13 (July 1879), 206; "From the Field," 2:1 (January 1880), 16.

165. "Women's Work," *Baptist Home Mission Monthly* 1:8 (February 1879), 126.

166. See especially Tera W. Hunter's discussion of tuberculosis and race, *To 'Joy My Freedom: Southern Black Women's Lives and Labors After the Civil War* (Cambridge, Mass.: Harvard University Press, 1997), 187–218. Significantly, a similar discourse of dirt, disease,

202 NOTES TO PAGES 97–101

and difference framed discussions of Chinese in San Francisco during the late nineteenth century. See Shah, *Contagious Divides.*

167. Amy Kaplan, "Manifest Domesticity," *American Literature* 70:3 (September 1998), 582.

168. Ibid.

169. Morehouse, "Historical Sketch," 46.

CHAPTER 4. CONGREGATION

1. H. M. Tupper, "Received of the A.B.H. Mission Society to Assist in Building a House for a Church and Schools," March 1867, Henry Martin Tupper Collection (hereinafter HMT MSS), box 1, James E. Cheek Learning Resources Center, Special Collections and Archives, Shaw University, Raleigh, N.C.

2. Chinese Mission School Records, Portland, Oreg., 1873–85, Baptist Church Records, MSS 1560, Oregon Historical Society, Portland (hereinafter OHS). See entry for April 13, 1875. "Program for Chinese Concert at the Baptist Church, Monday Eve'g. April 26, 1875," Chinese Baptist Church Records, Portland, box 2, MSS 1560, OHS.

3. In the South, the practice of performing concerts to support mission institutions would soon become relatively common. In 1873 the North Carolina Jubilee Singers, comprising in large part Shaw students and teachers, toured New England and Canada "in the interests of Shaw University. . . . From its entertainments eight thousand dollars or ten thousand dollars were realized for the institution." William J. Simmons, *Men of Mark: Eminent, Progressive, and Rising* (Cleveland, 1887), 960. The most famous example of this type of activity remains the Fisk Jubilee Singers. "The Jubilees" raised over $150,000 for the American Missionary Association's Fisk Free Colored School in Nashville, Tennessee, during three tours, including one trip to Great Britain, from the late 1860s through the mid-1870s. For a detailed account of the Jubilees, see Andrew Ward, *Dark Midnight When I Rise: The Story of the Jubilee Singers Who Introduced the World to the Music of Black America* (New York: Farrar, Straus and Giroux, 2000). See also W. E. B. Du Bois's rumination on "sorrow songs" and the Fisk Jubilee Singers in *The Souls of Black Folk* (1903; New York: Penguin Books, 1983).

4. "Chinese Concert," *Oregonian* (Portland), n.d. Chinese Baptist Church Records.

5. See, especially, Sylvia R. Frey and Betty Wood, *Come Shouting to Zion: African American Protestantism in the American South and British Caribbean to 1830* (Chapel Hill: University of North Carolina Press, 1998); Albert J. Raboteau, *Slave Religion: The "Invisible Institution" in the Antebellum South* (New York: Oxford University Press, 1978), 151–210; Donald G. Mathews, *Religion in the Old South* (Chicago: University of Chicago Press, 1977), 136–250.

6. Numerous scholars of African American religion have commented on the consonance between Christmas and the John Kunering festival, remarking, in particular, on the shared emphases on family gathering, worship, and gift exchange. Sterling Stuckey, for

instance, notes, "Considering the place of religion in West Africa, where dance and song are means of relating to ancestral spirits and to God, the Christmas season was conducive to Africans in America continuing to attach sacred value to John Kunering." He posits that New World practices bore striking similarities to the Egun masquerade among the Yoruba people. More recently, Sylvia Frey and Betty Wood have noted that, by the mid-eighteenth century, the celebration that coincided with the time off from work at Christmas "was an adaptation of West and West Central African yam festivals" that became known variously in the New World plantation colonies as John Canoe, John Cornu, or Jonkonnu." Sterling Stuckey, *Slave Culture: Nationalist Theory and the Foundations of Black America* (New York: Oxford University Press, 1987), 106, 68–70; Frey and Wood, *Come Shouting to Zion*, 54. See also Hubert H. S. Ames, "African Institutions in America," *Journal of American Folk-Lore* 18 (1905), 15–32; Dougald MacMillan, "John Kuners," *Journal of American Folk-Lore* 39 (1926), 56; Ira De A. Reid, "The John Canoe Festival: A New World Africanism," *Phylon* 3:4 (1942), 349–70; Kenneth M. Bilby, "Gumbay, Myal, and the Great House: New Evidence on the Religious Background of Jonkonnu in Jamaica," *African-Caribbean Institute of Jamaica Research Review* 4 (1991), 47–70. For more on the general link between the Christmas holiday, patterns of plantation life during slavery, and African traditions, see especially Roger D. Abrahams, *Singing the Master: The Emergence of African-American Culture in the Plantation South* (New York: Penguin Books, 1992).

7. For a discussion of the role of hymn singing in Sunday school education in the post–Civil War South, see Sally G. McMillen, *To Raise Up the South: Sunday Schools in Black and White Churches, 1865–1915* (Baton Rouge: Louisiana State University Press, 2001), 152–55. See also Paul Harvey, *Redeeming the South: Religious Cultures and Racial Identities Among Southern Baptists, 1865–1925* (Chapel Hill: University of North Carolina Press, 1997), 97–102, 127–32.

8. As early as 1862, whites published accounts of slaves' songs, and, after Emancipation, numerous northern missionaries took note of this African American cultural form. The most extensive and influential compilation from the period just following the war was published by Thomas Wentworth Higginson. Cited by subsequent scholars from James Weldon Johnson to Sterling Stuckey, Higginson's rendering of slave spirituals has been one of the cornerstones of modern scholarship. Thomas Wentworth Higginson, *Army Life in a Black Regiment* (1869; Boston: Beacon Press, 1962). For early northern publications of slave spirituals, see J. McKim, "Negro Songs," *Dwight's Journal of Music* (August 9, 1862), 148–49; Linda Warfel Slaughter, *Freedmen of the South* (1869; New York: Kraus Reprint Co., 1969), 134–37. For the links between spirituals and the ring shout, see Raboteau, *Slave Religion*, 68–75, 243–45; Stuckey, *Slave Culture*, 10–17, 5–37, 84–97. For the communal aspects of spirituals and their focus on hope, see Lawrence W. Levine, *Black Culture and Black Consciousness: Afro-American Folk Thought from Slavery to Freedom* (New York: Oxford University Press, 1977), 29–34; Du Bois, *The Souls of Black Folk*, 211–14; Raboteau, *Slave Religion*, 265. For more on African American spirituals, see James Weldon Johnson and J. Rosamond Johnson, *The Books of American Negro Spirituals, Including the Book of American Negro Spirituals and the Second Book of American Negro Spirituals* (1925–1926;

New York: Da Capo Press, 1962). It is important to note that the concert need not have directly mentioned John Kunering or similar rituals nor would students have had to sing spirituals for the event to have had a cultural resonance for the population of Raleigh's freedpeople who did not participate in the exhibition. As anthropologists Sidney W. Mintz and Richard Price have argued, "People ordinarily do not long for a lost 'cultural heritage' in the abstract, but for the immediately experienced personal relationships, developed in a specific cultural and institutional setting, that any trauma such as war or enslavement may destroy." Sidney W. Mintz and Richard Price, *The Birth of African-American Culture: An Anthropological Perspective* (Boston: Beacon Press, 1992), 47.

9. James C. Scott uses the term *hidden transcript* "to characterize discourse that takes place 'offstage,' beyond direct observation by powerholders. The hidden transcript is thus derivative in the sense that it consists of those offstage speeches, gestures, and practices that confirm, contradict or inflect what appears in the public transcript." In the case of the Raleigh and Portland concerts, the contradictory discourses of ex-slaves and Chinese, respectively, occurred quite literally "onstage." Nevertheless, the embedded themes and messages of community expressed by the participants differ considerably from the "open confrontation" of what Scott refers to as "the first public declaration of the hidden transcript." James C. Scott, *Domination and the Arts of Resistance: Hidden Transcripts* (New Haven, Conn.: Yale University Press, 1990), 4–5, 202–3.

10. See especially Dan T. Carter, "The Anatomy of Fear: The Christmas Day Insurrection Scare of 1865," *Journal of Southern History* 42:3 (August 1976), 345–64.

11. For more on the immediate post–Civil War position of African Americans in North Carolina, see Roberta Sue Alexander, *North Carolina Face the Freedmen: Race Relations During Presidential Reconstruction, 1865–67* (Durham, N.C.: Duke University Press, 1985); Karin L. Zipf, "'The Whites Shall Rule the Land or Die': Gender, Race, and Class in North Carolina Reconstruction Politics," *Journal of Southern History* 65:3 (August 1999), 499–534. Anti-Chinese riots on the Pacific Coast took place in Los Angeles in 1871, in Chico, California, in 1873, and in Waterville, California, in 1874. For more on the anti-Chinese movement in California, see Alexander Saxton, *The Indispensable Enemy: Labor and the Anti-Chinese Movement in California* (Berkeley: University of California Press, 1971). For more on the anti-Chinese agitation in Portland, see Chapter 2.

12. Earl Lewis, *In Their Own Interests: Race, Class, and Power in Twentieth-Century Norfolk, Virginia* (Berkeley: University of California Press, 1991), 92.

13. Laurie F. Maffly-Kipp, *Religion and Society in Frontier California* (New Haven, Conn.: Yale University Press, 1994), 26.

14. For more on interracial congregations, see especially James B. Bennett, *Religion and the Rise of Jim Crow in New Orleans* (Princeton, N.J.: Princeton University Press, 2005).

15. Raboteau, *Slave Religion*, 212. Sterling Stuckey, while not explicitly overturning Raboteau's findings, claims that "the great bulk of the slaves were scarcely touched by Christianity, their religious practices being vastly more African than Christian." Stuckey, *Slave Culture*, 37.

16. Historian William Montgomery has noted the difficulty of trying to ascertain

exactly how many African Americans counted themselves as Baptists in the two or three decades after the Civil War. He writes, "Black church records are too sparse to draw any solid figures from them." Nonetheless, he provides some evidence to support his contention that about half of all African American southerners who worshipped in exclusively black churches were Baptists. William E. Montgomery, *Under Their Own Fine and Fig Tree: The African-American Church in the South, 1865–1900* (Baton Rouge: Louisiana State University Press, 1993), 107.

17. Melville J. Herskovits, *The Myth of the Negro Past* (New York: Harper and Brothers, 1941), 232–35; Raboteau, *Slave Religion*, 178; Montgomery, *Under Their Own Vine and Fig Tree*, 107–8.

18. Herskovits, *Myth of the Negro Past*, 227–32; Raboteau, *Slave Religion*, 61–64.

19. Eugene D. Genovese, *Roll, Jordan, Roll: The World the Slaves Made* (1972; New York: Vintage Books, 1976), 255–79; Levine, *Black Culture*, 47–49.

20. Executive Board of the ABHMS, *Thirty-third Annual Report of the American Baptist Home Mission Society* (New York, 1865), 27.

21. Executive Board of the ABHMS, *Thirty-second Annual Report of the American Baptist Home Mission Society* (New York, 1864), 21.

22. Henry Martin Tupper, diary for 1865, HMT MSS, box 1. See entries for November 23, 26, 29, 1865, and December 2, 1865.

23. Leon F. Litwack, *Been in the Storm So Long: The Aftermath of Slavery* (New York: Vintage Books, 1980), 240.

24. Laura F. Edwards, *Gendered Strife and Confusion: The Political Culture of Reconstruction* (Urbana: University of Illinois Press, 1997), 45–47.

25. N.C. General Assembly, *Public Laws of the State of North Carolina, Passed by the General Assembly at the Session of 1865–66* (Raleigh, N.C., 1866), 99; Herbert G. Gutman, *The Black Family in Slavery and Freedom, 1750–1925* (New York: Vintage Books, 1976), 414–18.

26. See especially Raboteau, *Slave Religion*. Other important accounts of African American slave religion include Theophus H. Smith, *Conjuring Culture: Biblical Formations of Black America* (New York: Oxford University Press, 1994); Michael Mullin, *Africa in America: Slave Acculturation and Resistance in the American South and the British Caribbean, 1736–1831* (Urbana: University of Illinois Press, 1992); Margaret Washington Creel, *"A Peculiar People": Slave Religion and Community-Culture Among the Gullahs* (New York: New York University Press, 1998); Levine, *Black Culture*, 3–135; Stuckey, *Slave Culture*; Genovese, *Roll, Jordan, Roll*; Levine, *Black Culture and Consciousness*; John W. Blassingame, *The Slave Community: Plantation Life in the Ante-Bellum South*, rev. and enlarged ed. (New York: Oxford University Press, 1979). Raboteau, Smith, Stuckey, Genovese, and Blassingame all emphasize the ways in which slave religion developed as a separate institution, beyond the gaze of whites. John B. Boles has emphasized the ways in which antebellum black and white Christians worshipped together, arguing "that nowhere else in southern society were [blacks] treated so nearly as equals." John B. Boles, Introduction to *Masters and Slaves in the House of the Lord: Race and Religion in the American South, 1740–1870*, ed. Boles (Lexington: University of Kentucky Press, 1988), 9.

27. See Scott, *Domination and the Arts of Resistance*, 115–17.

28. Albert Raboteau has argued, quite persuasively, that the celebration of important life events, such as baptisms, weddings, and funerals, was an essential element of religious life in the slave community. Raboteau, *Slave Religion*, 227. Laura Edwards has also contrasted the prohibition on marriage during slavery with the desire of freedpeople to marry as an assertion of freedom. See Edwards, *Gendered Strife and Confusion*, 47.

29. Ibid., 35–38.

30. H. M. Tupper to J. S. Backus, October 31, 1865. Quoted in Archie Doyster Logan, Jr., "Henry Martin Tupper and His Adult Education Activities Among African-Americans, 1865–1893" (Ed.D. diss., North Carolina State University, 1993).

31. Henry Martin Tupper, "Shaw University—A Brief History," n.d., HMT MSS.

32. Logan, "Henry Martin Tupper," 40. Jett is referred to as a layman in J. A. Whitted, *A History of the Negro Baptists of North Carolina* (Raleigh: Edwards and Broughton Printing Co., 1908), 12.

33. Despite these numerous accounts, however, arriving at a specific number or percentage is difficult. Historian William Montgomery has noted that "not enough reliable data exist to show accurately and in complete detail the extent of the black exodus from white-controlled churches." Montgomery, *Under Their Own Vine and Fig Tree*, 98–99. Nevertheless, state association statistics illustrate, if only broadly, the scale of this flight from white authority. Daniel Stowell, for instance, has calculated that black membership in white-led churches in Georgia declined 61.1 percent between 1860 and 1876. Daniel W. Stowell, *Rebuilding Zion: The Religious Reconstruction of the South, 1863–1877* (New York: Oxford University Press, 1998), 80.

34. Chinese Mission School Records. See entries for October 15, 1874, and October 29, 1874. For payment of Dong's salary, see, for example, the entry for May 1, 1875.

35. Dong requested a salary almost equal to his European American counterparts laboring in the Society's principal field, the South. For the year 1868–69, for instance, the ABHMS paid Henry Martin Tupper $450 and directed his Second Baptist Church to pay him another $150. Although a dispute developed over the payment of his salary from the church, Tupper had been assigned a salary equal to $50 per month. Thus, through negotiation with First Baptist Church, Dong received ten dollars a month less than his white counterpart in Raleigh. Significantly, he was paid more than either of the two African American teachers who worked with Tupper. Wilmoth A. Carter, *Shaw's Universe: A Monument to Educational Innovation* (Rockville, Md.: D. C. National Publishing, 1973), 6; Henry Martin Tupper, Shaw University Annual Report, 1885–86, in Henry L. Morehouse Correspondence Files, box 8, folder 2, Archival Collection, Board of National Ministries, American Baptist Historical Society, Valley Forge, Pa.

36. Chinese Mission School Records. See entries for August 1873, October 8, 1874, November 11, 1874, February 21, 1875, and November 11, 1876.

37. Chinese Mission School Records. See entry for April 2, 1878.

38. First Baptist Church, Portland, Oreg., Minutes, 1854–1906, Baptist Church Re-

cords, MSS 1560, OHS. See entries for December 19, 1874, January 23, 1875, February 21, 1875, March 21, 1875, April 21, 1875, and April 25, 1875.

39. "Program for Chinese Concert," Chinese Baptist Church Records.

40. "Paganized Christianity," in *Proceedings of the Twenty-Third Session of the Southern Baptist Convention, Held with the First Baptist Church, Nashville, May 9–13, 1878* (Nashville, 1878), 53. Baptist leader E. G. Robinson also noticed this tendency when he observed, "The Mongol, with his Confucian ethics, will make, of the gospel, religion rather than piety." E. G. Robinson, "Race and Religion on the American Continent," *Baptist Home Mission Monthly* 5:3 (March 1883), 53. See also Chapter 3 for more on the racialization of the Chinese through religious discourse.

41. In some of the earliest records of the Chinese Mission School, observers commented upon the usefulness of hymn-based lessons. In the first monthly report of the school, Secretary Jennie S. Briggs noted, "They manifest a lively interest in singing the hymns and are learning rapidly, being led by Miss Mitchell with the organ at all the meetings, Thursday and Sunday included." Chinese Mission School Records. See entry for December 19, 1874. See also First Baptist Church, Minutes. See entries for November 22, 1874, and December 6, 1874. For more on the link between evangelical Christianity, hymn singing, and Sunday schools, see McMillen, *To Raise Up the South*, 152–54; Harvey, *Redeeming the South*, 97–102, 127–32.

42. *Oregonian*, November 25, 1878, p. 3, col. 2.

43. See also Bennett, *Religion and the Rise of Jim Crow*.

44. Executive Board of the ABHMS, *Thirty-fourth Annual Report of the American Baptist Home Mission Society* (New York, 1866), 17.

45. "My Summer Vacation," handwritten letter, 1879, Morehouse Correspondence Files, box 9. Historian Evelyn Brooks Higginbotham has written of the dilemma faced by black Baptist women, including those who attended the ABHMS school in Atlanta, Georgia, who encountered and eventually embraced the evangelical discourse of uplift. According to Higginbotham, these women practiced the "politics of respectability." In an effort to neutralize racist representations, educated black churchwomen adopted many white, middle-class ideals and practices, and these "converted" or "elevated" women, in turn, directed the same disapproving evangelical gaze toward "what they perceived to be negative practices among their own people." The result, argues Higginbotham, was a discourse that "disclosed class and status differentiation" among African Americans. Thus, even as black Baptist women modeled positive behavior that both won them respect from their white (and powerful) counterparts and "contested the plethora of negative stereotypes by introducing alternate images of black women," they also privileged self-improvement and self-regulation that cut across collective, community-based forms of identification. Evelyn Brooks Higginbotham, *Righteous Discontent: The Women's Movement in the Black Baptist Church, 1880–1920* (Cambridge, Mass.: Harvard University Press, 1993), 187, 191, 196. While not discounting the very real divisions within black communities, my argument differs from Higginbotham's in one fundamental way. In part, because my inquiry begins in the immediate aftermath of slavery, I am able to link mission-educated aspiring leaders

to the laboring and uneducated communities from which they hailed. My analysis thus focuses on the role of aspiration in the lives of upwardly striving children of black farmers and laborers. See, for example, Robin Kelley's analysis of black workers and sharecroppers who became members of the Communist Party during the 1930s. He locates many activists' roots in "respected, upwardly mobile, working-class families," and argues that, as late as the 1930s and in disputes as potentially contentious as those between black clergy and black communists, class differences among Alabama African Americans were often muted. "Intraracial class conflict was never clear-cut, and both sides exhibited ambivalence toward each other's ideas. Black Communists sometimes expressed aspirations that were more reflective of a bourgeois ethos and values than socialist ideology," writes Kelley. He continues: "Although class antagonism within the black community predated the Party's presence, in the past it had remained largely ambiguous, a grudging resentment combined with respect and admiration." Robin D. G. Kelley, *Hammer and Hoe: Alabama Communists During the Great Depression* (Chapel Hill: University of North Carolina Press, 1990), 113, 116.

46. U.S. Bureau of the Census, *Manuscript Schedules of the Federal Census*, 1870, Wake County, N.C., series M593, roll 1162, p. 235. Warrick's last name was spelled "Warick" by the census taker. Historian Sharon Ann Holt has documented the crucial role of household labor and production in ex-slaves' families. Sharon Ann Holt, *Making Freedom Pay: North Carolina Freedpeople Working for Themselves, 1865–1900* (Athens: University of Georgia Press, 2000).

47. U.S. Bureau of the Census, *Manuscript Schedules of the Federal Census*, 1870, Wake County, N.C., series M593, roll 1162, p. 301.

48. W. N. Hartshorn, ed., *An Era of Progress and Promise, 1863–1910: The Religious, Moral, and Educational Development of the American Negro Since His Emancipation* (Boston: Priscilla Publishing, 1910), 441.

49. U.S. Bureau of the Census, *Manuscript Schedules of the Federal Census*, 1880, Wake County, N.C., series T9, roll 984, p. 224; Whitted, *A History of Negro Baptists*, 34, 157; Shaw University, *General Catalogue of the Officers and Students of Shaw University, 1875–1882* (Raleigh, N.C., 1882), 4. For Caesar Johnson's ABHMS-commissioned work, see "Missionary Table" in Executive Board of the ABHMS, *Fortieth Annual Report of the American Baptist Home Mission Society* (New York, 1872), 119; idem, *Forty-first Annual Report of the American Baptist Home Mission Society* (New York, 1873), 66.

50. Kevin K. Gaines, *Uplifting the Race: Black Leadership, Politics, and Culture in the Twentieth Century* (Chapel Hill: University of North Carolina Press, 1996), 3.

51. For J. A. Kenney's career, see especially Hartshorn, *An Era of Progress and Promise*, 434, 441.

52. First Baptist Church, Minutes. See entries for April 22, 1875, and April 25, 1875. Chinese Mission School Records. See entries for June 7, 1875, September 2, 1875, and December 31, 1877.

53. "Program for Chinese Concert"; "Program for Chinese Anniversary Concert at the Baptist Church Auditorium, Monday Eve'g, Nov. 22, 1876," Chinese Ethnology Files, MSS 1521, OHS.

54. First Baptist Church, Minutes. See entries for June 3, 1875, and November 13, 1874.

55. "Chinese Concert," *Oregonian*, n.d.

56. Chinese Mission School Records. See entry for January 1876.

57. See especially Sue Fawn Chung and Priscilla Wegars, eds., *Chinese American Death Rituals: Respecting the Ancestors* (Lanham, Md.: Altamira Press, 2005), 3–7.

58. U.S. Bureau of the Census, *Manuscript Schedules of the Federal Census*, 1880, Multnomah County, Oreg., series T9, roll 1083, p. 410.

59. See, for example, *Oregonian* issues of November 17, 1877, p. 8, col. 1; November 23, 1877, p. 1, col. 6; January 25, 1879, p. 1, col. 5; "Annual Meeting of the Christian Church," November 8, 1879, p. 3, col. 1. See also Albert W. Wardin, Jr., *Baptists in Oregon* (Nashville: Curley Printing, 1969), 142–49.

60. "The Portland Chinese Mission," *Baptist Home Mission Monthly* 2:1 (January 1880), 15; "California," in Executive Board, *Forty-first Annual Report*, 25. Significantly, Graves would later become a home missionary to the Chinese in California; First Baptist Church, Portland, Oregon, *Manual and Directory of the First Baptist Church, The White Hall Temple, Portland, Oregon* (Portland, Oreg.: F. W. Baltes and Co., Printers, 1906), 15–16; Executive Board of the ABHMS, *Forty-ninth Annual Report of the American Baptist Home Mission Society* (New York, 1881), 46; "From the Field," *Baptist Home Mission Monthly* 3:3 (March 1881), 60.

61. Tong Tsin Cheung replaced Fung Chak in the mid-1880s. Tong did not begin his career in San Francisco, as had his predecessors, but he moved to northern California to work as a missionary after Fung's return to Oregon in 1887. When Fung retook his place at the Portland mission, he was joined by Lee Yon Chan, who was responsible for proselytizing in other parts of the state.

62. Other missionaries of Chinese origin included Fung Seung Nam, Ah Wing, Lee Key, Lum Chan, and Lee Yon Chan.

63. "From the Field," *Baptist Home Mission Monthly* 3:8 (August 1881), 172.

64. First Baptist Church, Minutes. See entry for December 23, 1875.

65. Wesley Woo, "Chinese Protestants in the San Francisco Bay Area," in *Entry Denied: Exclusion and the Chinese Community in America, 1882–1943* (Philadelphia: Temple University Press, 1991), 226. For Fung Seung Nam's ABHMS commission, see Executive Board, *Fortieth Annual Report*, 19, 99–100.

66. First Baptist Church, Minutes. See entry for October 22, 1875.

67. Copy of certificate of residence for Wong King, dated May 3, 1894. No. 55690. Chinese Ethnology Files, MSS 1521, OHS.

68. Hartshorn, *An Era of Progress and Promise*, 489.

69. August Shepard, George Perry, Joshua Perry, and Caesar Johnson were all among the earliest graduates of the Raleigh school, and each later received a commission from the ABHMS. See "Missionary Table," in Executive Board, *Fortieth Annual Report*, 14; "Missionary Table," in idem, *Forty-first Annual Report*, 66; Carter, *Shaw's Universe*, 3; Whitted, *A History of Negro Baptists*, 28–29.

70. Hartshorn, *An Era of Progress and Promise*, 509.

71. Higginbotham, *Righteous Discontent*, 7. Higginbotham is not the first scholar to have appreciated the multifaceted nature of black churches. See especially W. E. B. Du Bois, ed., *The Negro Church: Report of a Social Study Made Under the Direction of Atlanta University; Together with the Proceedings of the Eighth Conference for the Study of the Negro Problems, Held at Atlanta University, May 26th, 1903* (Atlanta: Atlanta University Press, 1903); E. Franklin Frazier, *The Negro Church in America* (1963; New York: Schocken Books, 1974).

72. "Waters Normal Institute, Winton, N.C.," typescript document, n.d., Morehouse Correspondence Files, box 9, folder 14; "Rev. C. S. Brown, D.D., Principal of the Waters Normal Institute, Winton, N.C.," in Hartshorn, *An Era of Progress and Promise*, 488.

73. Whitted, *A History of Negro Baptists*, 170.

74. "Waters Normal Institute."

75. Hartshorn, *An Era of Progress and Promise*, 497; Simmons, *Men of Mark*, 422–27; Whitted, *A History of Negro Baptists*, 160.

76. Hartshorn, *An Era of Progress and Promise*, 497. Whitted would later pastor the First Baptist Church, Colored, in Winston-Salem.

77. Simmons, *Men of Mark*, 422–27; Whitted, *A History of Negro Baptists*, 160.

78. Thomas O. Fuller, *Twenty Years in Public Life, 1890–1910, North Carolina—Tennessee* (Nashville: National Baptist Publishing Board, 1910).

79. Glenda E. Gilmore, *Gender and Jim Crow: Women and the Politics of White Supremacy in North Carolina, 1896–1920* (Chapel Hill: University of North Carolina Press, 1996), 62–63. See also Higginbotham, *Righteous Discontent*, 194–96.

80. Hartshorn, *An Era of Progress and Promise*, 489.

81. Executive Board, *Thirty-fourth Annual Report*, 34.

82. Whitted, *A History of Negro Baptists*, 53–55.

83. James T. Campbell has argued perhaps most forcefully for this perspective in his insightful comparative and connective study of the African Methodist Episcopal Church in the United States and South Africa. James T. Campbell, *Songs of Zion: The African Methodist Episcopal Church in the United States and South Africa* (1995; Chapel Hill: University of North Carolina Press, 1998), 97. See also idem, *Middle Passages: African American Journeys to Africa, 1787–2005* (New York: Penguin, 2006), 136–87; Donald F. Roth, "The 'Black Man's Burden': The Racial Background of Afro-American Missionaries and Africa," in *Black Americans and the Missionary Movement in Africa*, ed. Sylvia M. Jacobs (Westport, Conn.: Greenwood, 1982), 32; Gaines, *Uplifting the Race*, 39, 74.

84. Sylvia M. Jacobs, "The Historical Role of Afro-Americans in the American Missionary Efforts in Africa," in Jacobs, *Black Americans and the Missionary Movement*, 18. James T. Campbell explores the nuances of this tension in *Songs of Zion*. He also provides a remarkable case study of black Presbyterian missionary William Henry Sheppard and his "curious kind of ambivalence" in *Middle Passages*, 136–87.

85. Sandy Dwayne Martin, *Black Baptists and African Missions: The Origins of a Movement, 1880–1915* (Macon, Ga.: Mercer University Press, 1998), 22, 49.

86. Quoted in ibid., 49.

87. Ibid.

88. Campbell, *Songs of Zion*, xiii, 98.

89. Martin, *Black Baptists and African Missions*, 1. Martin argues, in fact, that black Baptists' interest in Africa stemmed in part from "the realization that blacks the world over faced similar oppressions and threats and that their separate paths all led to one destiny. In their encounters with Europeans, they observed that all peoples of African descent were placed at the periphery of significance in social and religious intercourse and at the very bottom of the economic and political pyramid." Ibid., 2.

90. I am sensitive here to James Campbell's assertion that "Africans and African Americans confronted one another as 'Others,' but in a context where the trope of race served not to distinguish but to render lines of similarity and difference immensely problematic. To put the matter more simply, people existed inside rather than outside history." Campbell, *Songs of Zion*, xiii.

91. For more examples of transnational Chinese Christians, see "The Chinese—Will They Carry Back the Gospel?" *Baptist Home Mission Monthly* 1:5 (November 1878), 72; J. B. Hartwell to H. L. Morehouse, April 6, 1891, Morehouse Correspondence Files.

92. Nayan Shah has quite perceptively examined how missionaries and government officials viewed this "queer domesticity" as a danger to respectable Christian morality and public health. Nayan Shah, *Contagious Divides: Epidemics and Race in San Francisco's Chinatown* (Berkeley: University of California Press, 2001), 77–104.

93. Madeline Y. Hsu, *Dreaming of Gold, Dreaming of Home: Transnationalism and Migration Between the United States and South China, 1882–1943* (Stanford, Calif.: Stanford University Press, 2000); idem, "Unwrapping Orientalist Constraints: Restoring Homosocial Normativity to Chinese American History," *Amerasia Journal* 29:2 (2003), 243.

94. Executive Board of the ABHMS, *Forty-second Annual Report of the American Baptist Home Mission Society* (New York, 1874), 34.

95. Higginbotham, *Righteous Discontent*, 186–88; Gilmore, *Gender and Jim Crow*, 18, 147–75.

96. Peggy Pascoe, *Relations of Rescue: The Search for Female Moral Authority in the American West, 1874–1939* (New York: Oxford University Press, 1990), 161–65.

97. Michael Omi and Howard Winant's formulation of racial rearticulation provides the foundation for this broader sense of creating a counterhegemonic discourse. *Racial Formation in the United States*, 55.

98. This is not, however, to argue that Chinese in the United States did not work exceedingly hard, especially through the legal system, to create legal standing in the United States. There is ample evidence that they, in fact, sought on various occasions to clarify the reach of the Fourteenth Amendment, pry open immigration restriction, and gain access to various constitutional protections. See especially Charles J. McClain, *In Search of Equality: The Chinese Struggle Against Discrimination in Nineteenth-Century America* (Berkeley: University of California Press, 1994); Lucy E. Salyer, *Laws Harsh as Tigers: Chinese Immigrants and the Shaping of Modern Immigration Law* (Chapel Hill: University of North Carolina

Press, 1995); Jean Pfaelzer, *Driven Out: The Forgotten War Against Chinese Americans* (Berkeley: University of California Press, 2007), 198–251.

CHAPTER 5. CONFLICT AND COMMUNITY

1. The historical literature on comparative white supremacies is surprisingly limited. Two comparisons of the United States and South Africa have set the standard. See George M. Fredrickson, *White Supremacy: A Comparative Study in American and South African History* (New York: Oxford University Press, 1981); John W. Cell, *The Highest Stage of White Supremacy: The Origins of Segregation in South Africa and the American South* (London: Cambridge University Press, 1982). Within the context of the United States itself, a small handful of authors have tackled this topic. See especially Gary Y. Okihiro, *Margins and Mainstreams: Asians in American History and Culture* (Seattle: University of Washington Press, 1994); Tomás Almaguer, *Racial Fault Lines: The Historical Origins of White Supremacy in California* (Berkeley: University of California Press, 1994); Claire Jean Kim, "The Racial Triangulation of Asian Americans," *Politics and Society* 37 (1999), 105–38; Najia Aarim-Heriot, *Chinese Immigrants, African Americans, and Racial Anxiety in the United States, 1848–82* (Urbana: University of Illinois Press, 2003); Moon-Ho Jung, *Coolies and Cane: Race, Labor, and Sugar in the Age of Emancipation* (Baltimore: Johns Hopkins University Press, 2006). For a thoughtful and thought-provoking essay on the dynamic nature of white supremacy in the southern context, see the introduction to *Jumpin' Jim Crow: Southern Politics from Civil War to Civil Rights,* ed. Jane Dailey, Glenda Elizabeth Gilmore, and Bryant Simon,(Princeton, N.J.: Princeton University Press, 2000).

2. The phrase "contest of faiths" comes from Susan Yohn's book on the Presbyterian women missionaries working in the Southwest of the United States. Yohn compellingly argues that Presbyterian home missions to Hispanic women constituted an arena of multiple conflicts. While she also examines disputes between missionary women in the field and the male-dominated hierarchy of the home mission board, my appropriation of her terminology applies to her portrayal of contestation between Anglos and Hispanics and between Protestants and Catholics. Susan M. Yohn, *A Contest of Faiths: Missionary Women and Pluralism in the American Southwest* (Ithaca, N.Y.: Cornell University Press, 1995).

3. Wilmoth A. Carter, *Shaw's Universe: A Monument to Educational Innovation* (Rockville, Md.: D. C. National Publishing, 1973), 9.

4. Ibid., 12. Carter's account relies almost exclusively on Henry Martin Tupper's own version of the dispute. See Henry Martin Tupper, "Some Facts Connected with the Lawsuit," January 8, 1877, Henry Martin Tupper Manuscript Collection (hereinafter HMT MSS), box 1, James E. Cheek Learning Resource Center, Special Collections and Archives, Shaw University, Raleigh, North Carolina.

5. *Gideon Perry and Others v. H. M. Tupper,* 70 N.C. 538 (1874). Carter provides descriptions of each of the plaintiffs' transgressions and subsequent exclusions from Second Baptist. Carter, *Shaw's Universe,* 9–10.

6. *Gideon Perry and Others v. H. M. Tupper*, 74 N.C. 722 (1876). This official reporting of the appeal of the original case (70 N.C. 538) contains the report filed by the case's referee and provides an important account of the issues under contention.

7. This account of exclusions is from Carter, *Shaw's Universe*, 9–10.

8. Ibid., 10.

9. *Gideon Perry*, 74 N.C. 722 (1876).

10. Ibid.

11. Carter, *Shaw's Universe*, 11.

12. The referee's report indicates that Capps was a student at Shaw, and Tupper was Shaw's principal. The implication appears to be that Capps acted under Tupper's influence. *Gideon Perry*, 74 N.C. 722 (1876).

13. Carter, *Shaw's Universe*, 11.

14. *Gideon Perry*, 74 N.C. 722 (1876).

15. Tupper, "Some Facts."

16. Ibid.

17. Carter, *Shaw's Universe*, 11.

18. Ibid., 9–10.

19. Ibid., 10–11.

20. *Gideon Perry*, 74 N.C. 722 (1876).

21. Eric Foner, *Reconstruction: America's Unfinished Revolution, 1863–1877* (New York: Harper and Row, 1988), 440–41.

22. Ibid., 503.

23. Tupper, "Some Facts."

24. According to Tupper's account, his life was threatened shortly after Dr. I. Britton Smith, the principal of another black school in Raleigh and also a supporter of Greeley, died of poisoning. Ibid.

25. *Gideon Perry*, 74 N.C. 722 (1876).

26. Glenda Elizabeth Gilmore, *Gender and Jim Crow: Women and the Politics of White Supremacy in North Carolina, 1896–1920* (Chapel Hill: University of North Carolina Press, 1996), 75–77.

27. Evelyn Brooks Higginbotham, *Righteous Discontent: The Women's Movement in the Black Baptist Church, 1880–1920* (Cambridge, Mass.: Harvard University Press, 1993), 196.

28. Blacks were, as Higginbotham explains, "ever-cognizant of the gaze of white America, which in panoptic fashion focused perpetually upon each and every black person and recorded his or her transgressions in an overall accounting of black inferiority." Ibid. See also Gilmore, *Gender and Jim Crow*, 75–77.

29. Chinese Mission School Records, Portland, Oreg., 1873–85, Baptist Church Records, MSS 1560, Oregon Historical Society, Portland. See report for January 1876.

30. Ibid.

31. Ibid.

32. "Baptist Chinese Mission School," *Oregonian* (Portland), November 14, 1876, p. 3, cols. 3–4.

33. *Oregonian*, March 22, 1878, p. 3, col. 1.

34. Ibid.; *Oregonian*, April 20, 1878, p. 3, cols. 1, 3.

35. *Oregonian*, April 20, 1878, p. 3, col. 3.

36. Ibid., col. 1.

37. Ibid.

38. Chinese Mission School Records. See entry for January 23, 1875.

39. *Oregonian*, October 4, 1878, p. 3, col. 2. The event was also reported in the *Baptist Home Mission Monthly*, but the victim's name was spelled "Chen St. Yin." "From the Field," *Baptist Home Mission Monthly* 1:10 (April 1879), 156.

40. Chinese Mission School Records. See entry for January 11, 1879.

41. See, for example, *Oregonian*, October 7, 1878, p. 3, col. 1; Chinese Mission School Records, entry for January 11, 1879.

42. Chinese Mission School Records. See entry for January 11, 1879.

43. For more on the role of cultural brokers, see K. Scott Wong, "Cultural Defenders and Brokers: Chinese Responses to the Anti-Chinese Movement," in *Claiming America: Constructing Chinese American Identities During the Exclusion Era*, ed. K. Scott Wong and Sucheng Chan(Philadelphia: Temple University Press), 3–40.

44. Executive Board of the ABHMS, "Report of the Committee on Occupation of the Southern Fields," *Thirtieth Annual Report of the American Baptist Home Mission Society* (New York, 1862), 50.

45. Tupper, "Some Facts."

46. Ibid.

47. Ibid.

48. Quoted in Sydney Nathans, *The Quest for Progress: The Way We Lived in North Carolina, 1870–1920* (Chapel Hill: University of North Carolina Press, 1983), 76.

49. Ibid.

50. Stephen Kantrowitz, "The Two Faces of Domination in North Carolina, 1800–1898," in *Democracy Betrayed: The Wilmington Race Riot of 1898 and Its Legacy*, ed. David S. Cecelski and Timothy B. Tyson (Chapel Hill: University of North Carolina Press, 1998), 103.

51. Ibid.

52. Raymond Gavins, "The Meaning of Freedom: Black North Carolina in the Nadir, 1880–1900," in *Race, Class, and Politics in Southern History: Essays in Honor of Robert F. Durden*, ed. Jeffrey J. Crow, Paul D. Escott, and Charles L. Flynn, Jr. (Baton Rouge: Louisiana State University Press, 1989), 178. See also Joseph H. Taylor, "The Great Migration from North Carolina in 1879," *North Carolina Historical Review* 31 (1954), 18–33; Frenise A. Logan, *The Negro in North Carolina, 1876–1894* (Chapel Hill: University of North Carolina Press, 1964); Nell Irvin Painter, *Exodusters: Black Migration to Kansas After Reconstruction* (New York: Alfred A. Knopf, 1976), 251–52, 256.

53. Raymond Gavins, "Fear, Hope, and Struggle: Recasting Black North Carolina in the Age of Jim Crow," in Cecelski and Tyson, *Democracy Betrayed*, 189.

54. Ibid., 189–90.

55. Kantrowitz, "The Two Faces," 105.

56. Ibid., 106.

57. Ibid., 107.

58. Timothy B. Tyson and David S. Cecelski, introduction to Cecelski and Tyson, *Democracy Betrayed*, 5.

59. Richard L. Watson, Jr., "Furnifold M. Simmons and the Politics of White Supremacy," in Crow, Escott, and Flynn, *Race, Class and Politics*, 133. For an example of Simmons's postelection campaign for disfranchisement, see F. M. Simmons, typewritten letter, December 18, 1899, in Furnifold M. Simmons Papers, correspondence, Special Collections, Perkins Library, Duke University, Durham, N.C.

60. Shaw would not have another black president until William Stuart Nelson in 1931.

61. See Carter, *Shaw's Universe*, 52–68.

62. Shaw University Annual Report, December 25, 1883, Henry L. Morehouse Files, group 4, box 8, Archival Collection, Board of National Ministries, American Baptist Historical Society, Valley Forge, Pa. Historian James Anderson has noted that the 1880s witnessed the "most significant expansion of industrial education in black normal schools and colleges." *The Education of Blacks in the South, 1860–1935* (Chapel Hill: University of North Carolina Press, 1988), 66.

63. Author's calculation from Shaw University Annual Report, December 25, 1883; Shaw University Annual Report, June 1892, Morehouse Files, group 4, box 8.

64. Gavins, "The Meaning of Freedom," 196–97.

65. Anderson, *The Education of Blacks*, 66–72.

66. Charles Meserve to A. S. Leonard, February 18, 1898, quoted in Carter, *Shaw's Universe*, 56.

67. Anderson, *The Education of Blacks*, 91–94.

68. C. F. Meserve, "By C. F. Meserve," typescript manuscript, Morehouse Files, group 4, box 8, folder 1.

69. C. F. Meserve, "The New Year at Shaw," *Baptist Home Mission Monthly* 21:1 (January 1899), 13.

70. Robert Edward Wynne, in the most comprehensive study of anti-Chinese reaction in the Pacific Northwest, notes that Oregon experienced fewer large-scale incidents of violence than either California or Washington. *Reaction to the Chinese in the Pacific Northwest and British Columbia, 1850–1910* (New York: Arno, 1978), 73.

71. *Spokane Times*, April 24, 1879.

72. Wynne, *Reaction to the Chinese*, 97.

73. Ibid., 98–99.

74. Jules A. Karlin, "The Anti-Chinese Outbreaks in Seattle, 1885—1886," *Pacific Northwest Quarterly* 39 (April 1948), 103–30. For details on the February riot, see "Putting Down a Riot," *The West Shore* 12:3 (March 1886), 76–80.

75. Wynn, *Reaction to the Chinese*, 103.

76. Ibid.

77. Ibid.

78. Andrew Gyory has disputed the extent to which the West Coast agitation against Chinese immigration led to the exclusion act. He writes, "The motive force behind the Chinese Exclusion Act was national politicians who seized and manipulated the issue in an effort to gain votes, while arguing that workers had long demanded Chinese exclusion and would benefit from it." Nonetheless, he does identify the pressure from workers, politicians, and others in California as "important" if not decisive. *Closing the Gate: Race, Politics, and the Chinese Exclusion Act* (Chapel Hill: University of North Carolina Press, 1998), 1.

79. Report of the Committee on Chinese Missions, in Executive Board of the ABHMS, *Fiftieth Annual Report of the American Baptist Home Mission Society* (New York, 1882), 16.

80. See, for example, "The New Year and Home Missions," *Baptist Home Mission Monthly* 7:1 (January 1879), 102.

81. Chinese Mission School Records. See entry for April 2, 1878.

82. Ibid.

83. Chinese Mission School Records. See entry for September 14, 1879.

84. Ibid.

85. *The Oregonian's Handbook of the Pacific Northwest* (Portland, Oreg., 1894), 119. Back's son, commonly referred to as Seid Back, Jr., but actually named Seid Gain, was an American citizen by birth. He would join his father and mother as a congregant at First Baptist. Ibid.

86. First Baptist Church, Portland, Oregon, "Chinese Members," *Manual and Directory of the First Baptist Church, The White Hall Temple, Portland, Oregon* (Portland, Oreg.: F. W. Baltes and Co., Printers, 1906), 74.

87. "Assimilationist leanings" is Evelyn Brooks Higginbotham's term. *Righteous Discontent*, 194–204.

CONCLUSION

1. H. Leon Prather, Sr., "We Have Taken a City: A Centennial Essay," in *Democracy Betrayed: The Wilmington Race Riot of 1898 and Its Legacy*, ed. David S. Cecelski and Timothy B. Tyson (Chapel Hill: University of North Carolina Press, 1998), 35, 38.

2. C. F. Meserve, "The New Year at Shaw," *Baptist Home Mission Monthly* 21:1 (January 1999), 13.

3. Ibid.

4. Joel Williamson, *The Crucible of Race: Black-White Relations in the American South Since Emancipation* (New York: Oxford University Press, 1984), 195–96.

5. George C. Rable, *But There Was No Peace: The Role of Violence in the Politics of Reconstruction* (Athens: University of Georgia Press, 1984), 19.

6. W. Fitzhugh Brundage, *Lynching in the New South: Georgia and Virginia, 1880–1930* (Urbana: University of Illinois Press, 1993).

7. For this broader definition of violence that includes nonphysical injury, see Peter

Iadicola and Anson Shupe, *Violence, Inequality, and Human Freedom* (Lanham, Md.: Rowman and Littlefield, 2003), 23.

8. J. B. Hartwell, San Francisco, California, to the Executive Board of the ABHMS, New York, May 13, 1886. Reproduced in Executive Board of the ABHMS, *Fifty-fourth Annual Report of the American Baptist Home Mission Society* (New York, 1886), 32.

9. Iadicola and Shupe, *Violence*, 23.

10. Sucheng Chan, preface to *Entry Denied: Exclusion and the Chinese Community in America, 1882–1943* (Philadelphia: Temple University Press, 1991), x.

11. Chan has argued that immigration exclusion made the "normal" development of Chinese communities in America impossible. More recently, however, historians Mary Ting Yi Lui and Madeline Hsu have been critical of normative understandings of community espoused by Chan. Lui argues that immigration restriction, as well as already skewed male to female sex ratios, might have limited the opportunities for and the number of Chinese male–Chinese female pairings and, therefore, families. However, in late nineteenth- and early twentieth-century New York City (which did not have antimiscegenation laws), numerous Chinese men found non-Chinese partners. She casts light on the limitations of understanding monoethnic or monoracial pairings as "normal." Hsu takes heteronormativity as her target. While Nayan Shah has examined how missionaries and government officials applied this standard in order to marginalize and control Chinese populations, Hsu applies this critique to historians. Demonstrating the prevalence of homosocial associations for overseas, migrating Chinese, she argues against the idea that the bachelor societies of Chinese in late nineteenth-century America were necessarily abnormal. Lui's and Hsu's arguments are compelling, and I have used Hsu's research into homosocial organizations and community, in particular, to elaborate my argument in Chapter 5. Nevertheless, one need not agree with heteronormative notions of family or community or with the normative value of monoethnic or monoracial marriages or pairings to argue that the sex ratio heavily skewed toward men, combined with the antimiscegenation laws on the Pacific Coast (Oregon passed its first law in 1866 and strengthened it in 1930; California's laws pertaining to "Mongolians" was passed in 1870) and restricted immigration, made it difficult to sustain and reproduce Chinese-based communities. This, in fact, was exactly the point of the restrictions. It is also important to remember that many of the Chinese men in America had spouses and children and other family in China and that tightened standards for leaving and reentering the United States made the maintenance of these familial and community bonds, even in the transnational perspective, much more difficult. Sucheng Chan, *Asian Americans: An Interpretive History* (Boston: Twayne, 1991), 63; Mary Ting Yi Lui, *The Chinatown Trunk Mystery: Murder, Miscegenation, and Other Dangerous Encounters in Turn-of-the-Century New York City* (Princeton, N.J.: Princeton University Press, 2004); Madeline Y. Hsu, "Unwrapping Orientalist Constraints: Restoring Homosocial Normativity to Chinese American History," *Amerasia Journal* 29:2 (2003), 229–53; Nayan Shah, *Contagious Divides: Epidemics and Race in San Francisco's Chinatown* (Berkeley: University of California Press, 2001).

12. *Plessy v. Ferguson*, 163 U.S. 537 (1896) (Harlan, J., dissenting).

13. Harlan's dissenting opinion in the *Plessy* case, for instance, noted that although the Chinese were deemed "a race so different from our own that we do not permit those belonging to it to become citizens of the United States. Persons belonging to it are, with few exceptions, absolutely excluded from our country," they were nevertheless permitted to "ride in the same passenger coach with white citizens of the United States, while citizens of the black race in Louisiana, many of whom, perhaps, risked their lives for the preservation of the Union, who are entitled, by law, to participate in the political control of the State and nation, who are not excluded, by law or by reason of their race, from public stations of any kind, and who have all the legal rights that belong to white citizens, are yet declared to be criminals, liable to imprisonment, if they ride in a public coach occupied by citizens of the white race." Ibid.

14. *Statutes at Large* 16 (1870), 254; E. P. Hutchinson, *Legislative History of American Immigration Policy* (Philadelphia: University of Pennsylvania Press, 1981), 5–6.

15. U.S. Department of Commerce, Bureau of the Census, *Report on the Population of the United States at the Eleventh Census, Part I,* "Table 10: Colored Population Classified as Negroes, Mulattos, Quadroons, Octroons, Chinese, Japanese, and Civilized Indians" (Washington, D.C., 1895), 397.

16. See *U.S. v. Wong Kim Ark,* 169 U.S. 649 (1898).

17. See, for example, editorial, *Baptist Home Mission Monthly* 21:1 (January 1899), 3. Although as noted in Chapter 5, African American evangelical N. F. Roberts assumed the presidency of Shaw after the death of founding missionary Henry Martin Tupper in 1893, he held the post for only five months before being replaced by Meserve. Shaw would not have its first full-time black president until 1931. For more on the Virginia controversy, see William E. Montgomery, *Under Their Own Vine and Fig Tree: The African-American Church in the South, 1865–1900* (Baton Rouge: Louisiana State University Press, 1993), 243–45; Paul Harvey, *Redeeming the South: Religious Cultures and Racial Identities Among Southern Baptists, 1865–1900* (Chapel Hill: University of North Carolina Press, 1997), 70–74.

18. Raymond Gavins, "Fear, Hope, and Struggle: Recasting Black North Carolina in the Age of Jim Crow," in Cecelski and Tyson, *Democracy Betrayed,* 201–2.

19. Harvey, *Redeeming the South,* 233. Significantly, Harvey also indicates that not all black Baptists pointed their finger at white violence as the root cause of lynching. Some, presumably intimidated by the disciplinary violence and influenced by the pull of respectability, argued that blacks must police themselves and must not give white southerners any opportunity to engage in lynching. Ibid., 233–34.

20. Evelyn Brooks Higginbotham, *Righteous Discontent: The Women's Movement in the Black Baptist Church, 1880–1920* (Cambridge, Mass.: Harvard University Press, 1993), 110–11.

21. Quoted in ibid., 111.

22. Quoted in Executive Board of the ABHMS, *Fiftieth Annual Report of the American Baptist Home Mission Society* (New York, 1882), 53–54.

23. "A Chinese View of the Statue of Liberty," *American Missionary* 39:10 (October 1885), 290.

24. "Report of the Committee on Chinese Missions," Executive Board, *Fiftieth Annual Report*, 16.

25. See the following correspondence to Morehouse in New York, all in Henry L. Morehouse Correspondence, 1887–1893, box 3, folder 5, Archival Collection, Board of National Ministries, American Baptist Historical Society, Valley Forge, Pa.: J. O. Peck, corresponding secretary of the Methodist Episcopal Church Mission Rooms, New York, November 5, 1892, typewritten on letterhead; Joshua Kimber, Domestic and Foreign Missionary Society of the Protestant Episcopal Church in the USA, New York, dictated, March 6, 1893, typewritten on letterhead; T. T. Ellinwood, Board of Foreign Missions, Presbyterian Church, USA, New York, November 16, 1892, typewritten on letterhead; Rev. A. F. Beard, corresponding secretary, American Missionary Association, New York; November 9, 1892, typewritten on letterhead. See also correspondence to Morehouse in New York, also all in Morehouse Correspondence: Henry C. Mabie, corresponding secretary, American Baptist Missionary Union, Boston, November 25, 1892, handwritten on letterhead; Arthur E. Main, corresponding secretary, Seventh Day Baptist Missionary Society, Ashaway, R.I., January 4, 1893, handwritten on stationery; Judson Smith, American Board of Commissioners for Foreign Missions, Boston, January 16, 1893, typewritten on letterhead; Josiah Strong, general secretary, Evangelical Alliance for the United States of America, New York, November 5, 1892, typewritten on letterhead; Henry A. Tupper, corresponding secretary, Foreign Mission Board of the Southern Baptist Convention, Richmond, Virginia, November 5, 1892, handwritten on letterhead; minutes of Geary Act Conference, January 26, 1893, marked duplicate copy, signed by secretary Joshua Kimber. See also Executive Board of the ABHMS, *Sixty-first Annual Report of the American Baptist Home Mission Society* (New York, 1893), 76.

26. Edward W. Gilman, corresponding secretary of the American Bible Society, New York, to Morehouse, New York, November 9, 1892, typewritten on letterhead, Morehouse Correspondence.

27. Minutes of Geary Act Conference. See also clipping from the *Sabbath Recorder*, February 2, 1893, in Morehouse Correspondence.

28. H. L. Morehouse, J. Kimber, and F. F. Ellinwood, *Conference on Repeal of the Anti-Chinese Legislation of May 5, 1892, New York, January 26, 1893*, Morehouse Correspondence. The document did, in fact, note that the Geary Act would adversely effect Sino-U.S. relations and mission efforts in China, but those concerns take a decided backseat to the enumeration of hardships the law was causing among Chinese in America.

29. Executive Board of the ABHMS, *Sixty-second Annual Report of the American Baptist Home Mission Society* (New York, 1894), 99–100.

30. For more on the "politics of respectability" and its double-edged consequences, see Higginbotham, *Righteous Discontent*.

31. Editorial, *Baptist Home Mission Monthly* 21:9 (September 1899), 349–50.

32. Historian Edward J. Blum has convincingly argued that northern Protestant evangelical organizations decreased their spending for mission projects in the South by the early 1870s, thus signaling a retreat from the promise of interracial Christianity and democracy

even before the end of Reconstruction. In small part, according to Blum, this financial re-trenchment was the result of the economic crisis of 1873, but, more importantly, it was the result of the desire of northern religious leaders to emphasize reconciliation with the white South over justice and black rights. Edward J. Blum, *Reforging the White Republic: Race, Religion, and American Nationalism, 1865–1898* (Baton Rouge: Louisiana State University Press, 2005), 106–11. My argument follows Blum, but the chronology is a bit altered. While spending and missionary rhetoric certainly indicate an earlier shift away from evangelicals' egalitarian vision of the immediate post-Emancipation and postwar period, the actual mis-sion work conducted by white northerners, many of whom, like Henry Martin Tupper, had roots in abolitionist or antislavery causes, continued throughout the 1870s and 1880s. But the differences between my chronology and Blum's also lie in causation. For Blum, the desire to bind the nation's wounds in the midst of class conflict, financial crisis, and politi-cal deadlock led northern religious leaders to turn toward white nationalism and to betray the interracial possibilities of the postwar period. While not discounting this argument, I maintain that the logic of mission work simultaneously impelled evangelicals toward pros-elytizing projects that encouraged and created the structures for interracial contact and pro-vided the basis for a hierarchical understanding of the (perceived) fundamental differences between blacks and whites. I also argue that the vicious and sustained violence toward black southerners (and white northern missionaries) curtailed mission projects and the possibility that they might become a foundation for black equality in the late nineteenth century.

33. Editorial, *Baptist Home Mission Monthly* 21:9 (September 1899), 349–50.

34. Ibid., *Baptist Home Mission Monthly*, 365.

35. For a fascinating discussion of social movements, religion, and the meaning of hope, defeat, struggle, and suffering, see G. C. Waldrep III, *Southern Workers and the Search for Community: Spartanburg County, South Carolina* (Urbana: University of Illinois Press, 200), 172–81.

INDEX

Colver Institute, 82. *See also* Richmond Institute

community formation. *See* congregation

Conference on Repeal of the Anti-Chinese Legislation, 161

Confucianism, 85, 118, 207 n.40

Congo Free State, 126

congregation, 12, 14, 46, 60, 102–4, 110, 118, 131, 133, 134, 169 n.12, 175 n.32. *See also* fellowship

"coolies," 28, 37, 150

Constitution (U.S.), 44, 156

Conversion: of Africa, 87, 89; of China, 19, 89; and education, 5, 109, 110, 132; and gender, 91, 95–97; and race, 18, 23, 29, 68–69, 83, 91, 95; religious or spiritual, 5, 7, 16, 21, 23, 56, 68, 69, 76, 77, 108–12, 115, 117–18, 141, 142, 162–63; and social transformation, 10, 16, 23, 58, 68, 82, 100, 111, 112, 116, 157, 164–65

Corbett, Henry W., 66, 79–80, 142, 196 n.77

cosmopolitan Christianity, 10, 130, 159, 164, 173 n.24

Crosby, John O., 124–25

Cross, Hardy, 136–37

cubic air ordinance, 41

cultural racism, 9, 12, 172 n.21. *See also* race; racialization

Daniels, Josephus, 147, 154, 163

David, W. J., 126–27

Deady, Matthew, 40–41

Dean, William, 116

democracy: and black leadership, 125; Christian, 162, 219 n.32; and mission ideology, 23; practice, 13; racial limits to, 146, 157, 162, 165

Democratic Party, 2, 139, 146–47, 153, 178 n.27

disorder, 6, 64; and democracy, 23; and immigration, 19; and race, 4, 24, 36–37, 61; religious and moral, 8, 20, 78

Dolph, Joseph N., 79–80, 142

Dong Gong: and Chinese Mission School (Portland), 33, 56, 60, 66, 76–77, 80, 108–9, 132, 141, 206 nn.34–35; and conflicts among Chinese in Portland, 142–43; migration to U.S., 32; and transnational Chinese Christian networks, 118–19, 121–22, 127–28; and work in China, 3

Dred Scott v. Sandford, 40, 61, 183 n.28. *See also* citizenship

Du Bois, W. E. B., 10, 173 n.26

East Portland, Ore., 41

education: African American, 3, 7, 10, 32, 43–44, 50, 59, 63, 110, 148, 185 n.56; African American leadership and, 103, 112–13, 116–17, 123–24; African American women's, 92, 129; Chinese, 7, 56, 110, 119; Chinese leadership and, 103; Chinese women's, 93; and conversion, 5, 29, 132; domestic, 92, 93; industrial, 92, 148, 200 n. 141, 215 n.62; ministerial or theological, 148, 194 n. 45; religious, 11, 22, 47, 82, 119, 203 n.7; secular or classical, 74, 82, 92, 108–9, 148. *See also* Chinese Mission School (Portland, Ore.); Shaw University

Edwards, Laura F., 106, 206 n.28

Ellinwood, F. F., 161

Emancipation, 5, 7, 32, 35, 36, 42, 50, 59, 67, 86, 164; African American leaders, 114–15, 123, 138, 140, 145; African American mobility and, 44; African American neighborhoods during, 48–49; African American poverty and, 73–74, 113; African American religion during, 45–47, 101, 106, 112; African American

Emancipation (continued)
rights and, 43–44, 61, 131, 154, 157;
anti-African American violence during, 158–59, 163; Baptist missions and,
47–48, 89, 127; immigration and, 2, 4,
14, 20, 22, 24, 42, 62, 102, 104, 152,
164. *See also* Emancipation Proclamation;
Civil War
Emancipation Proclamation, 16, 18, 49, 70
Enrollment Act (1863), 16
Episcopal Freedman's Commission, 48
Estey Hall, 81, 123
evangelical ideology. *See* evangelical nationalism; mission ideology
evangelical nationalism, 7, 8, 21–22, 24,
27–28, 64, 78, 108, 130, 152, 157, 160,
162–63; black, 125
Evans, Joel, 136–39
exclusion: African Americans from Oregon, 39; Chinese and immigration, 4,
7, 10–11, 14, 29, 41–42, 60, 89–90,
93–95, 102–4, 121, 144, 155, 157, 161,
175 n.33, 131 n.198, 217 n.11. *See also*
Chinese Exclusion Act; Chinese immigration; Geary Act

Failing, Henry, 66, 78–80, 142, 195 n.69,
196 n.77
Failing, James, 79, 80
Failing, Josiah, 78–79, 142, 195nn. 68, 70,
196 n. 77
Federal Bureau of Freedmen, Refugees, and
Abandoned Lands. *See* Freedmen's Bureau
fellowship: African American, 46, 101,
102–3, 111, 123, 149, 158, 164; Chinese,
3, 10, 56, 58, 102–3, 117–18, 159; cross-
racial, 58, 60, 110. *See also* congregation
Fifteenth Amendment, 44, 130, 156. *See
also* Constitution (U.S.)
First Baptist Church (Portland, Ore.),
78–80, 195 nn.68–69; and the Chinese

Mission School, 32, 33, 41, 56–58, 60,
66, 75–77, 80, 108–11, 115–16, 118,
120–21, 141–42, 151, 206 n.35, 216
n.85. *See also* Chinese Mission School
First Baptist Church (Raleigh, N.C.): and Af-
rican Americans, 45–46, 66, 71, 107, 133,
135, 185 n.47. *See also* First Baptist Church,
Colored (Raleigh, North Carolina); Ameri-
can Baptist Home Mission Society
First Baptist Church, Colored (Raleigh,
N.C.), 107, 111. *See also* American Bap-
tist Home Mission Society (ABHMS)
First Baptist Church (San Francisco), 75–76
First Colored Regiment, 73
Fish, Hamilton C., 25
Flemming, Lula C., 126
Foner, Eric, 46
Foong Pay Fang, 109
Fortress Monroe, S.C., 16
Fourteenth Amendment, 44, 61, 130,
156–57, 211 n.98. *See also* Constitution
(U.S.)
Francis, John, 76, 119
Fredrickson, George M., 37, 182 n.16, 212
n.1
Freedmen's Bureau, 38–39, 47, 48, 72, 73, 145
freedom: African Americans and meanings
of, 7, 19, 28, 32, 34, 39, 43–47, 49, 50,
59, 63, 73, 101, 104, 106, 111, 115,
122, 125, 130–33, 145, 158, 206 n.28;
and Baptist missions, 10, 22, 111, 156;
Chinese and, 37, 55; and immigration, 5,
13, 37; and labor, 37; limits on, 35, 38,
146, 157. *See also* Emancipation
freedpeople: and Africa, 87; conflicts
among, 133; economic conditions of, 25,
74, 194 n.41; marriage among, 105–6,
206 n.28i; missions to, 13, 20, 47–48,
65, 67–68, 70, 72, 97, 99, 104, 107, 185
n.56; religious practices of, 84, 86, 101;
rights and status of, 5, 19, 32, 38, 42–50,
62, 63; violence against, 38

ACKNOWLEDGMENTS

Researching and writing a book may be solitary acts; the fruits of that labor most certainly accrue solely to the author. Yet this book is evidence that the broader process of scholarship is by no means carried out in isolation. Overlapping communities of friends, family, colleagues, and mentors all participated in the making of this book.

My research benefited greatly from the aid of archivists and librarians in various locales whose knowledge of manuscript collections and printed material was remarkable. Shawna Gandy of the Oregon Historical Society, Betty Layton and Deborah Van Broekhoven of the American Baptist Historical Society Archive Center, Bill Sumners at the Southern Baptist Historical Library and Archives, and Carolyn Baker at Shaw University all made it clear why historians' best friends are those women and men dedicated to archival collections and document retention.

I am grateful also to the Social Science Research Council's Religion and Immigration Fellowship; the Duke University Women's Studies Program's Anne Firor Scott Research Award; and the Southern Baptist Historical Library and Archives' Lynn E. May, Jr., Study Grant for research support.

I became a historian only because of the mentoring—the guidance, expertise, and generosity—of certain key faculty at Duke University. Sucheta Mazumdar arrived in Durham when I did, and I could not have been luckier. She fostered my incipient interest in Asian American history and helped me to see the larger picture. Susan Thorne was—and continues to be—an intellectual and ethical inspiration. Her incisive scholarship, keen insight, and generous spirit have provided a wonderful, if daunting, model for me to follow. Lawrence Goodwyn's entreaty to me to "find my voice" is perhaps the single most important piece of advice I received in graduate school. Sydney Nathans gave me the most precious gift any teacher can provide a student—the space to grow and to grow up. And most of all, Nancy Hewitt found a glimmer of merit in my early work and has continued to be a mentor and advocate. I cannot think of a better role model—as a historian, an educator, an advisor, an activist, and a friend.

Other teachers also inspired me to care deeply about the past. Adrienne Phillips taught me in high school that history encompasses the great variety of human experience and that being able to write is a crucial skill. As an undergraduate at Trinity College in Hartford, Connecticut, I learned what it means to be committed to education and to the ethical study of the past from Jack Chatfield, Cheryl Greenberg, and especially Gene Leach.

While at Duke, a host of people reminded me almost daily of why we study the past. We shared—and argued over—ideas. We also shared food and drink, joy and sorrow, and, sometimes above all else, gossip and basketball. Paul Husbands, Paul Ortiz, Sheila Payne, Vince Brown, Ajantha Subramanian, Chuck McKinney, Hasan Jeffries, Ian Lekus, Mary Wingerd, Noeleen McIlvenna, Jessica Harland-Jacobs, Matt Jacobs, D'Arcy Brissman, Jackie Campbell, Andrew Schneider, Kirsten Delegard, and Andrew Sparling made the exciting, intense, sometimes demoralizing time of graduate school worth it all. Many read pieces of what would become this book in various forms, and their insightful comments, gentle prodding, and high standards were and continue to be inspiring. In a myriad of ways, they are as responsible for me being a historian as any faculty member with whom I worked.

My colleagues in Cornell University's Department of History have been a consistent source of intellectual sustenance, camaraderie, and sometimes commiseration. I was fortunate enough to join the department at a time of transition; I have been able to draw on the wisdom and camaraderie of both "veterans" and "newcomers," especially Ed Baptist, Holly Case, Sherm Cochran, Duane Corpus, Ray Craib, María Cristina García, Durba Ghosh, Karen Graubart, Sandra Greene, TJ Hinrichs, Kats Hirano, Peter Holquist, Michael Kammen, Vic Koschmann, Tamara Loos, Larry Moore, Mary Beth Norton, Jon Parmenter, Dick Polenberg, Mary Roldán, Aaron Sachs, Eric Tagliacozzo, Robert Travers, Margaret Washington, and Rachel Weil. And amid the often difficult grind of assistant professordom, a handful of graduate students—Chris Cantwell, Julian Lim, Javier Fernandez, Annamaria Shimibuku, Gregg Lightfoot, Mike DeGive, Jonathan Ying, and Noriaki Hoshino—reminded me when I needed it most of why intellectual curiosity and scholarly engagement must be an avocation, while the undergraduates who endured my courses modeled a kind of inquisitiveness that, above all else, must be valued.

It is the worst kept secret in academe that staff, not faculty, is responsible for much of the work accomplished in any given department. Judy Burkhard did and Karen Chirik, Barb Donnell, Maggie Edwards, and Katie Kristof do an extraordinary amount of work while demonstrating a kind of transcendent humor and grace.

I have also found amazing colleagues in Cornell's American Studies Program. In particular, I have been touched by the encouragement and support of Michael Jones-Correa, Nick Salvatore, and the program's manager, Darla McCoy. And a discussion series on transnational American Studies sponsored by the program and organized by Ron Mize helped provide important intellectual insights as I was reworking my manuscript.

The Asian American Studies Program at Cornell is a special place. Graciously welcoming, intellectually stimulating, democratically administered, and soul sustaining, it is my home away from home. Sunn Shelley Wong and Viranjini Munasinghe have provided vision, guidance, mentorship, and friendship that are both inspiring and touching. The arrival of Thuy Linh Nguyen Tu and Clem Lai only added to this community of scholarship and fellowship. Long car rides seem to be a litmus test for our program, and I cannot think of any other friends and colleagues with whom I would rather spend hours and hours in a car. Stephanie Hsu, Vladimir Micic, and Anita Affeldt have been largely responsible for creating the atmosphere of warmth and caring that distinguishes our program. I count myself lucky that I get to work with a group of colleagues that I can learn from and laugh with.

Many of the aforementioned people, as well as others, read various drafts and iterations of this book, and they bear mentioning again for their labor and critical insight. Paul Ortiz, Paul Husbands, Vince Brown, Ian Lekus, Noeleen McIlvenna, Jody Pavilack, Chuck McKinney, D'Arcy Brissman, Matt Jacobs, and Jessica Harland-Jacobs all read early drafts. I have also inflicted drafts upon various collectives. Holly Case, Jon Parmenter, Ed Baptist, Eric Tagliacozzo, and Suman Seth read more polished chapters; their penetrating questions and incisive suggestions forced me to return to sections I had hoped were finished. A gathering of Ithaca-based American historians which calls the Chapter House bar its headquarters—Jeff Cowie, Aaron Sachs, Adriane Smith, Michael Smith, Jason Sokol, Michael Trotti, and Rob Vanderlan—has challenged me to be a better historian in so many ways. We often disagree over a range of topics, but I can think of no other group of scholars so dedicated to the craft of history.

I presented portions of this book—arguments, themes, ideas—at a number of conferences and workshops, and I benefited greatly from the comments, criticism, and intellectual exchange provided by generous colleagues. In particular, at a 2006 conference/workshop on "Religion and the American West" at Arizona State University, organized by Tisa Wenger, I enjoyed fascinating discussions with a variety of scholars, including Tisa, Laurie Maffly-Kipp, Rudy Busto, James Bennett, and Duncan Williams. That same year, I attended a conference, organized by Kathryn Kish Sklar, Rui Kohiyama, Barbara Reeves-Ellington, and Connie Shemo, at the Rothermere American Institute at Oxford University. At this conference on "Competing Kingdoms: Women, Mission, Nation, and American Empire, 1812–1938," and at the 2005 Berkshire Conference on the History of Women, I was able to try out new ideas and gain invaluable criticism as I developed my arguments on mission work and gender. I am particularly grateful to the organizers of "Competing Kingdoms" and to my Berkshire Conference panel's gracious commentator, Peggy Pascoe, for their intellectual magnanimity. I also benefited greatly from discussions of my work at the meeting of Social Science Research Council international migration and religion and migration fellows at the University of Texas, Arlington, in 2002; a panel on racial violence at the 2003 annual meeting of the American Studies Association; a panel on evangelical religion at the 2003 annual meeting of the Southern Historical Association; and a panel on race and comparison with my Cornell Asian American Studies colleagues Sunn Shelley Wong and Viranjini Munasinghe at the Asian American Studies annual meeting in 2004.

My appreciation for the work done by my editor at the University of Pennsylvania Press, Robert Lockhart, exceeds what I can express in words. Suffice it to say that this book would not exist without his commitment, support, honesty, and patience. Both Judy Yung and an anonymous reader for the Press provided crucial—and generous—comments that surely made this a better book, and Glenda Gilmore, a coeditor of the series on Politics and Culture in Modern America, read an advanced version of the manuscript and offered compelling guidance.

In so many ways, though, my family is my primary community, and so it is that this book is dedicated to it. I learned from my parents, Katherine Shen and John Chang, the power of hope, faith, and love. Love, if not always uncomplicated harmony, is at the core of my relationship with my siblings—Andrew, Leslie, and Lauren.

That Lauren McFeeley has put up with this project—and with me—

perhaps says enough. She is my life's coauthor. Her patience, faith, generosity, and strength have sustained me, and our most important collaborative endeavor—Max and Isabel—is a testament to her compassion and her capacity for hope and love. This book, above all else, is for her and for our children.